Training for a Smart Workforce

In the hyper-competitive context of the new global economy, building a smart workforce is widely regarded as a key strategy for enterprises. However, is this no more than another 'fast capitalist' slogan? What substance can be given to the idea? What are its associated values and practices? This book explores these issues from an international perspective in both a fresh and challenging way.

Key themes include:

- competence and being competent in the world of work
- experience, common sense and expertise in workplace learning
- social practices and literacies in the workplace
- developing smart, self-directed workers
- taking responsibility for learning in the workplace
- empowering workers as learners in the workplace

These essays are written by leading edge workplace analysts and practitioners from Australia, New Zealand, Sweden and the USA. The wide-ranging, multidisciplinary approach will be of interest to all forward-thinking academics, students and leaders in management, organisational development and workplace learning.

Rod Gerber is Dean of the Faculty of Education, Health and Professional Studies at the University of New England, Armidale, Australia.

Colin Lankshear, formerly a Professor of Education, is now a freelance educational researcher, teacher and writer.

Training for a Smart Workforce

Edited by
Rod Gerber and Colin Lankshear

London and New York

First published 2000 by Routledge
11 New Fetter Lane, London EC4P 4EE

Simultaneously published in the USA and Canada
by Routledge
29 West 35th Street, New York, NY 10001

Routledge is an imprint of the Taylor & Francis Group

Typeset in Garamond by BC Typesetting, Bristol
Printed and bound in Great Britain by
Biddles Ltd, Guildford and King's Lynn

British Library Cataloguing in Publication Data
A catalogue record for this book is available from the British Library

Library of Congress Cataloging in Publication Data
Training for a smart workforce/edited by Rod Gerber & Colin Lankshear.
    p.   cm.
  Includes bibliographical references and index.
  1. Employees–Training of.   2. Organizational learning.   I. Gerber, Rodney.
  II. Lankshear, Colin.
  HF5549.5.T7 T6673 2000
  658.3'124–dc21   99-059977

ISBN 0–415–19551–9 (hbk)
ISBN 0–415–19552–7 (pbk)

Contents

PART 2

Critical aspects for workplace education   45

Figures and tables

Figures

Tables

Notes on contributors

Stephen Billett has an extensive experience in vocational education and training, working with government, higher education and industry on a wide range of projects and policy development. His doctoral studies focused on the use and application of activity theory on learning in different workplaces. Stephen has recently completed a Fulbright Scholarship to the United States to investigate vocational and workplace education and research. He has written widely on workplace learning and has a forthcoming publication on this topic.

Rod Gerber has an extensive record in writing for commercial publishers in several fields including workplace and geographical education. He has published for a range of publishing houses and has an international readership in his fields. He has extensive experience in writing, editing and reviewing scholarly works in the area of workplace education and learning. He is invited regularly to make presentations to academic and professional conferences in countries around the world and has a very strong international network of colleagues in the area of workplace education and learning. He has conducted a range of research studies in the area of workplace learning in a variety of industrial and rural settings, including international collaborative studies.

Colin Lankshear, having formerly been a Professor of Education specialising in literacy education, is currently a Heritage Fellow of the Mexican Council for Science and Technology, a freelance educational writer and researcher, and an adjunct professor in the Faculty of Education and Creative Arts, Central Queensland University. His books include: *Literacy, Schooling and Revolution* (Falmer Press, 1989), *Changing Literacies* (Open University Press, 1997), *The New Work Order* (Allen & Unwin and Westview Press, 1996), *Counternarratives* (Routledge, 1996), and *Critical Literacy: Politics, Praxis and the Postmodern* (State University of New York Press, 1993). He has three new books: *Ways of Knowing* (ACER Press, 2000) (with Michael Knobel), *Curriculum in the Postmodern Condition* (Peter Lang, 2000) (with Alicia de Alba, Edgar Gonzalez Gaudiano and Michael Peters), and *Teachers and Technoliteracies* (Primary English Teaching

Association, 1999) (Ilana Snyder). He is joint editor of the New Literacies series for Peter Lang.

Staffan Larsson is Professor of Adult Education at Linkoping University – the only chair in adult education in Sweden. His research has, since 1997, been concerned with a wide variety of aspects of Swedish adult education. He received his PhD in 1983 at the University of Göteborg. Staffan was trained in the group in Göteborg that developed the phenomenographic perspective on the investigation of learning. He published a textbook on qualitative analysis in 1986. Since the middle of the 1980s, he has introduced the ethnographic tradition into Swedish education research. Titles like *Paradoxes of Teaching* (Instructional Science, 1983), *Initial Encounters in Formal Adult Education* (Qualitative Studies in Education, 1993) give a taste of his interests. Another contribution is a book on the Swedish educational reforms together with Stephen Ball, *The Struggle for Democratic Education* (Falmer Press, 1989) and articles on *The Meaning of Lifelong Learning* (Walters, Zed Books, 1997). He has recently analysed 'study circles' from the perspective of different notions of democracy.

Allan Levett is an independent sociologist of Wellington (New Zealand). He has long tracked changes in work and the economy and their implications for education and public policies. As a consultant, Allan has had assignments with several government departments in New Zealand, Australia and Fiji, and with private sector firms in Australasia and Asia. He was a member of the New Zealand Planning Council and was appointed to government committees advising on scientific research and on social science. He has taught sociology at Victoria University of Wellington and management studies at Otago University, and was a Japan Foundation Fellow at the National Institute for Educational Research in Tokyo. Allan has published articles in sociological, education and public policy journals and books in Australia and New Zealand and is co-author, with Colin Lankshear, of *Going for Gold: Priorities for Schooling in the Nineties* (Daphne Brasell Press, 1990).

Peter O'Connor runs an education and training consultancy (Workplace Learning Futures) in Sydney, delivering a diverse range of educational services, research and publications. His background involves work as a steelworker, community worker, union official and in policy areas related to labour market and employment issues, as well as in health and community services and, for the past dozen or so years, exclusively in adult education.

His main areas of interest in education have been in workplace language and literacy issues, research into workplace cultures and communicative practices, and trade union education. Peter currently does work for industries including food processing, rail and bus transport, mining and manufacturing.

Peter was a founding member of the Adult Literacy and Basic Skills Action coalition, and editor of its journal, *Critical Forum*. He has published extensively in the area of adult workplace language and literacy and on vocational education issues generally.

Charles Oaklief has more than 30 years of administrative, instructional, research and professional experience in the field of adult and continuing education in both university and corporate settings. His teaching and research interests are related to workplace learning, training and development, and programme planning and development. He has held honorary and visiting professorships in Germany, Australia and the United Kingdom. Charles has served in many capacities at the state, national and international levels. He is senior consultant to several universities and corporations with an emphasis on restructuring training and development units, learning at a distance and the design of learning systems. He has served in many leadership positions and continues a line of research on adult participation and the transfer of workplace learning.

Jörgen Sandberg is currently Associate Professor in the centre for Management and Organisation at the Stockholm School of Economics. He received his PhD from Göteborg University in Sweden. His research interests focus on competence and learning in organisations, leadership, social constructionism and qualitative methods, including their philosophical assumptions. As well as contributions to several books and articles in international journals such as the *Academy of Management Journal* and *Instructional Science*, he has also published books such as *Human Competence at Work: An Interpretative Approach* (BAS, 1994), *Managing Understanding: A Competence Perspective on Organizations* (Studentlitteratur, 1998) together with Axel Targama, and has co-edited the book *Invisible Management: On the Social Construction of Leadership* (Studentlitteratur, 1999).

1 Introduction

Rod Gerber and Colin Lankshear

Background

What is the meaning and significance of smartness in the context of workplace learning in the present and foreseeable future? What does it mean for a workplace to be smart? What makes for a smart workforce? What are the advantages or benefits of operating smartly? How can qualities and attributes of smartness be promoted and nurtured within workplaces and work-based education and training activities?

These are some of the key questions underpinning this book. In recent years the idea has emerged that smartness has a lot to do with why some work teams, organisations, and other entities perform better than others of seemingly equal capacity. Of course, there is nothing special about this observation so far as it goes. What has begun to change are people's ideas about what this insight entails. What is new is the acknowledgement that differential workplace performance at the leading edge is no accident and that it is not to be explained in terms of technical know-how and skills. Rather, it is suggested, there is a human dimension involved which, until recently, has been downplayed. This parallels the observation that winning sports teams at elite levels generally have similar physical attributes, competencies and technologies available to them as their competitors. What gives them the edge is smartness in the competitive setting. Furthermore, this smartness is not an innate or 'native' possession that comes ready made. Rather, it is argued, smartness is produced and sustained culturally; it is a cultural production on the part of teams, organisations, competitive entities in general. Smartness, as such, is something to be aimed at and promoted within workplace cultures, albeit something which is (too) often overlooked.

In his book on the mental demands of modern life, *In Over our Heads*, Robert Kegan (1994: 5) claims 'it remains for us to look at the curriculum of modern life in relation to the capacities of the adult mind'. Work is one of the major life roles that adults engage in. Whether they work to the capacities of their adult minds is an issue that confronts societies as they move to the next millennium. This issue can be considered from several standpoints, e.g. do they want to work to their capacity? Are they permitted by the nature of their work to do so? How satisfied are they in their work? Does anyone care about each worker as a person? What happens to their bright ideas? Should they be allowed to think for themselves at work and make decisions that could affect other workers? What happens if they make a mistake? Does anyone care if they do their job well? Are they operating as a group or team, or are they operating as a group of individuals?

These and similar questions are increasingly being asked across organisations, large and small, as companies, managing directors, supervisors, colleagues and consultants all realise that the world of work in the next millennium will be based on more than 'the bottom line' alone. Instead, it will be based on a range of human, cognitive, cultural and organisational factors that workers and managers alike will prize in order to obtain a competitive edge. The challenge will be to maximise the capacities of the adult workers to the benefit of both the organisation and their own life-long satisfaction.

Given this, it is important that workplaces be understood as situations where groups of people interact on common purposes in a productive, profitable and satisfying way to achieve an agreed vision. These situations are a part of the *actual worlds* of all workers for a large proportion of their lives. Hence, it is in the interests of organisational leaders to ensure that the experience of work is enjoyable, rewarding and purposeful. In successful organisations, the work done is achieved within clear goals by people who are motivated by themselves, their colleagues and their leaders. They are, in other words, empowered within an empowering organisation. According to Foy (1994: 1)

> When people in an organisation are empowered, you can walk in the door and feel the difference. People look you straight in the eye. They show a proactive, outgoing curiosity. You sense their confidence; it emanates from individuals, but it is supported by teams, by managers they respect, and by the empowering organisation itself.

Of course, a lot of contemporary talk about empowerment and empowering organisations is hollow, if not downright exploitative. As Delgado-Gaitan (1990: 2) notes, empowerment has often 'been used to mean the act of showing people how to work within a system from the perspective of the people in power'. In the somewhat larger sense implied by Foy and like-minded people, an empowering organisation seeks to enhance and deploy its employees' knowledge and experience. Its leaders recognise that all employees have qualities that must be developed in a collegial working environment, which becomes a collegial learning environment. Therefore, organisations and their leaders need to become 'perpetual learners' (Schien 1997: 361). Perpetual learning recognises that organisations and workplaces are characterised by dynamic qualities including ongoing changes. Leaders, therefore, have to continue to ask: 'How is my organisation going to remain viable in an ever-changing world which I cannot always predict?'

It will not be possible for organisational leaders to know in advance all of the aspects and nuances of the changes that will occur. Rather, it is essential that leaders develop a learning culture within their organisations to prepare employees for change. Schien (1997: 363) highlights the idea that this involves an attempt at 'managing the contradictions of stability, learning and change'. He suggests that the pertinent characteristics of such an organisational learning culture include: the relationship between the organisation and its environment or setting; the extent to which the employees are proactive problem-solvers and learners; a pragmatic search for truth; a belief that ultimately human nature is basically good and mutable; a balance between individualism and groupism; a focus on near-future time; a multichannel communication system that allows everyone to connect to everyone else in the organisation; the stimulation of diversity; maintaining a balance between task and relationship orientations in the organisation; and the ability to think systematically, understand causal effects and use complex mental models (Schien 1997: 364–372). Such a culture does not simply emerge, as if by accident or chance. Rather, it is promoted deliberately by leaders who want to develop a more resilient, collectively organised and sharing workforce.

Zand (1997) claims that leaders need to strike a balance between knowledge, trust and power. We would go further and suggest that this balance is necessary for all employees from the managing director to the most junior front line worker. Furthermore, this balance is generated within a defined context, i.e. the workplace environment. Indeed, it is not so much the balance between people's knowledge, learning and power that is important as the relationships that emerge among workers as they interact with each other and management, using their changing knowledge, learning and power. These connections can lead to what Peter Hartz (1996) calls 'the company that breathes': the idea he used (in his book with the same title) to describe the process by which the Volkswagen company rejuvenated its workforce in the face of the challenges of global competition.

What, then, are we to understand by the concept of smartness in relation to workplace learning, education and training? We believe an experiential account of the concept of smartness in workforces should consider the following six elements as important constitutive aspects in terms of specific work contexts.

1. Possessing and utilising expertise

In workforces, positions are classified according to levels of expertise required to perform them effectively. This inference in the job classification statements for these positions is explicit – those classified higher reflect the need to possess higher levels of expertise than those that have a lower classification. Expertise in one's work is an important ingredient in smartness, since it enables workers to focus quickly on the kernel of problems and move to making clear decisions which bypass irrelevant information and achieve solutions smoothly, effectively and efficiently. It may include competence, technique, skills, knowledge and literacy. Expertise is not, however, the sole ingredient of smartness, as the following elements demonstrate.

2. Thinking and being decisive in one's actions

Conscious, intentional decision-making is an important aspect in effective human behaviour. Workers become effective when they reflect on their actions when doing their jobs. Such reflection is important in the development of competence in one's work. Sandberg (1997: 3) concludes that:

> It is not constituted by a list of specific knowledge and skills a person possesses in relation to work. Instead, a person's knowledge and skills are proceeded by and based on their ways of understanding their work.

Strategic thinking in the workplace is characterised by clarity of purpose and intention. Purposeful actions follow if they are implemented. Associated with this purposeful behaviour is the need to use common sense in workers' behaviour and work practices. The presence or absence of common sense in workers' actions is most pronounced in workplaces because work is applied by its nature. Hence, knowing how to do a work task well is very different from being able to do it well. The artistry of doing work well is often bound up with the extent to which workers take or avoid risks, whether or not they are careful from a safety aspect, how often and how well they think before they act, and how frequently they use their own initiative when performing a work task.

Such attributes are often, if not commonly, assumed and undervalued by management.

3. Exhibiting positive values and attitudes

Successful, smart workers are ones who both hold and exude positive values and attitudes related to their work experiences. They enjoy learning and working. They act confidently throughout their working day and are firmly committed to improving the performance and output of their organisation. Confidence is associated here with empowering fellow workers and encouraging the development of self-reliant, independent work teams. Workers who possess these values are most likely to become committed to their workplaces where participation, involvement, a desire for change, an involvement in decision-making, a freedom to change one's work environment and a respect for one's private life away from work lead to a vibrant, positive work situation during good times and bad.

4. *Constructive social practices developed from working in groups or teams*

Team-based learning is often observed in effective workplaces or reported by workers as a key way in which they learn. This helps explain the growing acceptance that developing work competence is a collective rather than an individual thing. Shared understandings of the work are integral to making sense of it collectively. Working in teams is a cultural experience in which workers share cultural symbols and network frequently within and without the group to achieve desirable results and outputs. Through distinctive work practices, work teams develop smarter ways to: perform tasks, interact with each other, know when tasks are being performed well, care for the whole team in the work activity, and celebrate their successes. Consequently, the quality of life of successful work teams will tend to be high, since their performance is recognised within the organisation. Likewise, self-esteem tends to be high and participants value each other's performance in unselfish ways.

5. *Producing an economic benefit for the organisation*

Most companies believe that work-based organisations are smart when they operate profitably. The concept of self-sufficiency has expanded from commercial enterprises to include government departments, universities, and so-called non-profit organisations. It is not enough just to 'do a good job' in organisations today. Economic self-sufficiency is a precondition for many of these organisations to survive in the medium term. Attaining economic goals is prized in most management circles nowadays. However, the economic benefits that accrue from attaining these goals are derived from conscious decisions that relate closely to the nature of the workforce, the work that it does, and the environment in which the work occurs, and the organisational culture that has been developed. They are not economic alone these days, but include intangible social and psychological elements.

6. *Offering leadership in the workforce*

An interesting perspective on the behaviour of workforces is obtained by examining who offers leadership as opposed to who manages and has substantive power. It is expected that the directors and managers of organisations will take the lead in a wide range of management and decision-making issues. However, 'really smart workforces' contain bosses who not only do these things themselves, but who also value the views, ideas and leadership of all employees in their organisation.

Workers believe that they learn by offering leadership in their work. For their part, managers can offer leadership that leads to a smarter workforce by encouraging more contact amongst workers and more flexibility in the workplace, and by breaking the tyranny of hierarchies.

For many workers, offering leadership is not always a spontaneous activity. Many do so informally by offering advice to colleagues on a work issue when asked to do so. Others have 'greatness thrust upon them' by being invited to lead worksite seminars and demonstrations of equipment. Whatever way it occurs, most workers and managers see the offering of leadership as a satisfying and rewarding experience that improves their capacity to be more effective employees.

Such elements, when combined, offer a holistic and relational way of thinking about smartness in workforces. This orientation to the quality of behaviour and action in workplaces contests the positivistic, rationalist vein of the nature of work in organisations by promoting an interactive, participative approach that is strongly human-oriented rather than knowledge- and skills-based. Active, decisive groups of workers who use different 'tools' are the future of organisations rather than technology. How this can be achieved will be presented in the body of this book.

Overview of the book

In order to address the above challenges, this book aims to:

- develop the concept of smartness in workplaces based on experiential, empirical and constructive approaches;
- explain how key concepts such as competence, common sense, self-directedness, multi-skilling, literacy, transfer of learning and expertise, contribute to the smartness of workforces;
- develop the process of empowering workers for leadership in smart workforces; and
- demonstrate pedagogic implications for work-based training and learning.

It pursues these aims through four sections.

Part 1

The first section, by Allan Levett, establishes the larger backdrop for the book by focusing on megatrends underpinning the changing world of work. He examines the emergence of the post-industrial information society, paying particular attention to the transformation of work. This includes changes in occupations and employment patterns, the impact of computer-based technology and knowledge, the emergence of teamwork, and new kinds of choice and varying views of leadership. He considers also the changing nature of attachment that includes more participation in decision-making by workers, less certainty of work and the growing inequality of reward for work. Key implications of these changes for countries, industries and individuals are identified and discussed.

Part 2

The second section addresses some critical dimensions of smartness from the perspective of workplace education. In the first of three chapters in this section, Jorgen Sandberg examines the concept of competence as an important basis for a smart workforce. He analyses the nature of individual competence at work, concluding that competence is constituted in the ways work is experienced or understood. He next analyses the nature of collective competence, emphasising shared understanding, shared symbols and a distinctive cultural perspective. For Sandberg, smarter workforces focus on collective rather than individual approaches to work.

In the chapter after Rod Gerber focuses on three crucial aspects of workplace learning: namely, experience, common sense and expertise. He begins by clarifying the three concepts and showing how each is relevant to workplace learning. He next demonstrates the interrelationships amongst these concepts. Finally, he argues how a socio-cultural approach is appropriate for lifelong and workplace learning.

In the final chapter in this section, Colin Lankshear examines the nature and implications of literacy as social practice for workplaces and the workforce in 'new' times. He presents a range of analytic tools for enhancing the way we think about literacy in workplaces, arguing that if we are to think and act strategically with respect to literacy and smart work, we need to appreciate different constructions of literacy and how they apply to smart workforces.

Part 3

The third section, also of three chapters, focuses on pedagogic implications and actions. The first chapter in this section, by Stephen Billet, seeks to understand what constitutes a smart workforce by searching for dimensions of performance in the workforce. It is not enough to consider dimensions such as technical skill, work practice and organisational structure in the understanding of workforces. What is also needed is the consideration of the ways that people engage in work practices. He proposes that a cognitive perspective be adopted that uses a socio-cultural perspective based on activity theory. This means that work practice can only be understood when embedded in a specific community of work practice. In making the case, a range of nine dimensions of work practice are identified.

Peter O'Connor next develops pedagogic aspects and actions by focusing on who, and how people, should take responsibility for learning in workplaces. He considers the importance of team-based learning that involves a range of strategies including mentoring and guided participation. Here, he builds on the concept of collective competence addressed in Sandberg's chapter and demonstrates how these and other strategies can be used to promote workplace learning.

In the final chapter of this section Rod Gerber and Charles Oaklief focus on the concept of transfer of learning as a means of strengthening workplace training. They demonstrate how the psychological concept of transfer of learning is being used to improve workplace learning and to improve workplace practices and outcomes. Gerber and Oaklief seek a greater commitment from organisations to use transfer of learning sensibly in their work practices.

Part 4

The final section points to some future considerations in workplace learning to ensure that it plays a key role in lifelong learning. Staffan Larsson, largely through a focus on adult education, concentrates on using the concepts of lifelong and life-based learning as bases for workplace learning. He urges organisations not to treat workplace learning in isolation from other types of everyday learning. If such an approach to adult and workplace learning is selected, Larsson identifies four kinds of consequences: new knowledge, different interests, external changes and better self-confidence. He, therefore, promotes the idea of developing 'all-round' people who live in a society that values 'all-roundedness'.

Collectively, these eight chapters offer an interesting way of looking at smartness and offer a holistic perspective for investigating workplace practices and learning. The contributors have looked toward the future in organisational behaviour, culture and leadership to consider how workforces in different situations can be highly effective, and yet still remain integral to progressive practices of human living. Practices and experiences of workers operating in groups underpin the story of smartness. Together with their supervisors or managers, workers are leaders of the 'smartness' perspective in workplace learning. This approach is characterised by initiative being exhibited across the workplace rather than by policy implemented by management. Where such ideas are promoted, and the collective wisdom of all workers in an organisation unleashed in the kind of way described by Dean Semler in *Maverick* (1993), it is no longer possible for employees to lament that their good ideas were not listened to by management 'because no bastard ever asked me' (Flanagan *et al*. 1993). They would be, instead, empowered and empowering workers who understand their work culture thoroughly and draw on it extensively. The twenty-first century is ready for such decisive, thinking, team-oriented workers!

References

Delgado-Gaitan, C. (1990) *Education for Empowerment: The Role of Parents in Children's Education*. London: Falmer Press.

Flanagan, M., McGinn, I. and Thornhill, A. (1993) *Because no Bastard ever Asked Me*. Canberra: Stakeholder.

Foy, N. (1994) *Empowering People at Work*. Aldershot, Hampshire: Gower.

Hartz, P. (1996) *The Company that Breathes*. Berlin: Springer-Verlag.

Kegan, R. (1994) *In Over our Heads: The Mental Demands of Modern Life*. Cambridge, MA: Harvard University Press.

Sandberg, J. (1997) The nature of collective competence and its development. Paper presented at *The 14th Nordic Business Conference on Business Studies*, 14–17 August, Bodo.

Schien, E. (1997) *Organisational Culture and Leadership*, Second edition. San Francisco: Jossey-Bass.

Semler, D. (1993) *Maverick: The Success Story Behind the World's Most Unusual Workplace*. London: Arrow Business Books.

Zand, D. (1997) *The Leadership Triad: Knowledge, Trust and Power*. New York: Oxford University Press.

Part 1

Megatrends: setting the scene in the changing world of work

2 Changes in work and social life at the dawn of the twenty-first century

Allan Levett

Introduction

This chapter is concerned with recent changes in work – a massive worldwide transformation of occupations and the pattern of employment – and their implications for developing a smart workforce as a strategic response. These changes derive from drastic changes in the international economy, prompting different ways of organising workers and facilitated by new technology. They affect almost every aspect of life in the industrialised countries and beyond.

For instance, consider the obvious manifestations at work itself:

- the emergence of flat management structures and stepped-up intensity of work;
- the increased job uncertainty for almost everyone;
- the weaker unions and individualised attachment to work; and
- the fast-growing disparities in income – the rich getting richer, the poor more numerous and the middle group reducing in size.

Across whole economies the patterns of employment have changed within industrialised countries. In particular:

- there have been big increases in professional and technological occupations and smaller increases in low-paid, unskilled work;
- a majority of women are in paid work;
- up to 35 per cent of people in the workforce are now self-employed, or in contract, temporary or part-time work;
- unemployment, especially youth unemployment, is widespread, apparently permanent and affects mainly the least educated.

Most of these trends have appeared, in varying degrees, in all so-called advanced societies during the past 15–25 years. By way of situating this book's concern with developing a smart workforce, this chapter will address three main questions: where, in what ways, and to what extent, has work become more demanding and requiring of a smarter workforce?

The ripple effects of the work-based shock waves on the lives of individuals and societies beyond work and the workforce are equally profound. So far, the most shattering consequences appear to be on families and parenting. All major institutions are affected, including education, government, politics, leisure, values and beliefs, regions and cities. Communities are more diverse and fragmented. These changes suggest that not only work, but also life itself, has become more demanding of skill and knowledge. In other words, the changes in question have upped the ante for smartness beyond the workforce as well as within it.

The ways in which work is changing and the nature of social fragmentation vary considerably across different societies. The actual outcomes are influenced by the particular combination of features prevailing in any society, including the cultures, institutional histories, the ways the country is connected to the international economy and, above all, by local policies.

Although the governments of nation states are in some ways relatively weaker now than they were 25 years ago, they can still play a major role in how well their society fares in the global marketplace, in how their people and institutions cope with the changes, and in minimising the damaging effects. The debate on these matters is only beginning and governments are by no means clear about what they could do. Much depends on how the issues are perceived. Some believe we are simply facing a new kind of economy, internationally interconnected and much more competitive: that it is a continuation of the industrial society, another turn in the ongoing cycles of capitalism. Changes in work are responses to the greater competitiveness. Once 'we' get on top of the situation by becoming successful, the social pressures, the fragmentation and the inequalities will reduce. Success will require better work-related education and the entire workforces of firms to become smarter and more skilful. Others, however, see a break with the past, and believe that a still-capitalist, new kind of post-industrial society is taking shape. This is a society whose features are not yet clear or firmly established, 'post-industrial' being a temporary label indicating mostly where we have come from. Some go further and see the outline of a particular kind of society emerging; they call it an informational society. Both these groups think that a broad adaptability is required: of individuals, families, communities, organisations and governments.

The debate is important to this chapter. To cover it adequately requires a large canvas, since its implications for the meaning and significance of developing a smart workforce as a strategic response to change are wide. If we identify just a new kind of competitive economy, societies will have to be concerned mainly with improving education for work. If, however, we discern a different, more complex society emerging, wide-ranging, interconnected policies are necessary and the role of education will be pervasive and lifelong, and developing a smart workforce will be a more embedded concern.

Interpreting trends in society

When trying to make sense of recent changes in society it is always helpful first to consider the historical patterns. In that way we are likely to see more than one cause and appreciate the complex interplay between causes and consequences. Here we shall be guided by a father–son combination – sociologists with highly developed senses of history. Charles Tilly has devoted an extremely productive career to the study and interpretation of large-scale social change, while Chris Tilly has contributed importantly to our understanding of work.

In a seminal article that charts the rise and form of labour markets, Tilly and Tilly (1994) summarise phases in the interconnected forces that have marked changes in work and society over the centuries. This chapter is mainly concerned with just the most recent phase, to which they allude at the end of the following passage. Of particular significance in their approach, they include the sometimes forgotten political power, referring to it here as 'coercion'.

> Over the long sweep of human history, major changes in the character of work have resulted from the interplay of technology, coercion, capital, existing social relations and culture. (These include) . . . changing productive procedures, changing uses of force, changing deployments of investment, changing connections to surrounding communities, (and) changing beliefs concerning the effects of different ways of organising work. The near monopolisation of coercive means by bourgeois-dominated states, for example, promoted the consolidation and protection of bourgeois property. . .; these changes in property rights advanced the proletarianization of workers and the investment of capitalists in the fixed costs of factories, mills, and large shops. Changes in the organization of capital such as the spread of joint stock companies and the expansion of credit likewise had fundamental, if indirect, effects on the character of work.
>
> Over the last century the largest alterations of work in Western Europe and North America have no doubt resulted from an interaction among the mechanisation of production and distribution, the expansion of communicative and data-storage devices, the creation of large, heavily-capitalised productive organisations, the imposition of centralised work-discipline, the growth of public-sector employment, the shift from raw-material production to manufacturing and services, and the extension of wage-labor – loosely speaking, capitalist industrialization and proletarianization. These changes constituted a huge increase in the proportion of all labor power offered for sale compounded by a large decline in producer control of labor processes.
>
> Only recently have signs of reversal or alteration of these main trends shown up in the West, with possible moves toward fragmentation of

productive organisations through computer technology, franchising, part-time and temporary employment, shifts of large-scale production (e.g. in ships, steel and automobiles) outside the West, plus permanent unemployment, informal-sector employment, and underemployment of large portions of the potential labor-force.

(Tilly and Tilly 1994: 285–286)

There is one important change in the organisation of work in the industrial era, which particularly needs amplification since it forms an important backdrop to the recent changes with which we are primarily concerned. This is the establishment of a 'centralised work discipline'.

Previously, and especially during the nineteenth century, much work was organised by various forms of subcontracting arrangements. Capitalists exercised little direct control over production but, rather, contracted craftsmen or heads of households to produce goods at stipulated prices and of agreed quality, using labour, which the contractors organised. (Interestingly, Tilly and Tilly point out that subcontracting often relies on existing relationships of kin and friendship and ties of ethnicity and gender for recruitment and promotion. It is thus more likely to produce patterns of favouritism and inequality (Tilly and Tilly 1994: 289).

While the bureaucratic form of organisation had appeared earlier in some church and government services, capitalist owners and managers only gradually began to exercise direct control over the labour process, over hiring and firing, remuneration and the routines of production.

The assembly-line system of mass production, sometimes called Fordism, was established in the early years of this century. In the prototype of this system the worker on the factory floor, the blue-collar worker, was seen as a cog in a machine, a replaceable part, and not required to think or show initiative. Various layers of management and other jobs were added to design, plan and supervise the manufacturing process, to procure parts, to market and sell the products, and to finance the entire operation. It was a system of specialisation and compartmentalisation that came to be applied much more widely than manufacturing. So-called white-collar work, especially in large offices, was similarly hierarchical with the lower levels expected to be compliant and largely unthinking.

Numerous writers have commented on the downside of these arrangements, in terms of alienation of the worker (e.g. Blauner 1964) and the degrading and de-skilling of work (e.g. Braverman 1973). Certainly many assembly- and disassembly-line jobs came to require little more than punctuality and tidiness. Nevertheless, so far as the rewards of work and implications for dignity and quality of life are concerned, in countries at the height of industrial capitalism after the Second World War, a greater proportion of workers enjoyed a higher standard of living than ever before, or since.

It should be noted, however, that although centralised control and big business became dominant during the twentieth century, subcontracting continued, associated with the procurement of parts in industry, with franchising and direct sales and with the large informal sector of individual entrepreneurs and semi-legal enterprise. Typically, despite lip-service to entrepreneurs and to private enterprise, contract work was an extension of large-scale enterprise and accorded lower status and pay.

The centralised phase in the arrangements for work differed widely across societies. The level of technology was only one dimension. In Britain a 'propriety capitalism' emerged, where managerial power was centralised in the hands of proprietors while strong craft groups reduced the need for co-ordination; whereas in the United States the ethnic diversity of unskilled workers and greater mechanisation led to a tradition of professional management (Tilly and Tilly 1994: 292).

As the century wore on, workers mobilised in trade unions and professional groups, more strongly in some countries than in others. The part played by the state varied, affecting such areas as the regulations governing the role of capitalists *vis-à-vis* consumers and workers, rates of pay and recruitment procedures, education and research. In Japan the state strengthened capital and in Sweden and France it provided more protection to labour. In all countries, work itself became an arena for contention and a variety of institutional arrangements and cultural beliefs governed the way that these contending forces interacted.

We are, of course, speaking here of paid work and the organisation of work in labour markets under capitalism – which is the main focus of this chapter. However, there is in each society work that is unpaid: work in households, and work carried out voluntarily. In many countries there is a welfare system whereby the state, using taxes, provides pay without requiring work of certain categories of people. In addition, there is an informal economy where work may be undertaken for food, or for other objects or services. These arenas also have become contentious in modern societies.

Industrialism developed in ways with which we are familiar, reaching a 'golden age' in the 1950s and 1960s. Large-scale mass production was carried out by a few dominant centralised firms in each country; much alienating physical work was ameliorated by protection from strong centralised trade unions and a high point of wage payments. There was low unemployment, few women in paid work, and welfare states, all built on the expectation of stable male-led families. Even as this 'golden era' seemed to last forever there were those who sensed something in the wind.

Early visions of a post-industrial society

The first recognition and naming of the trend towards a post-industrial society occurred in the 1950s. It began with the observation of growth in the services workforce and the relative decline in numbers required in agriculture and manufacturing for the same or greater production. In the United States, white-collar workers exceeded blue-collar for the first time in the mid-1950s. In 1960, 8 per cent of the North American workforce was in agriculture, 39 per cent in manufacturing and 53 per cent was classified as services. Nine years later, the proportions for the United States were 5.2 per cent, 33.7 per cent and 61.1 per cent respectively. Similar trends were noted in all industrial countries (Bell 1974: 16–17). Researchers looked for related phenomena to understand and explain what was happening and to anticipate the future.

In his seminal work, *The Coming of Post-Industrial Society: A Venture in Social Forecasting*, Daniel Bell (1974) focused on the growth of science and technology and how inventions were derived. One of Bell's major insights was the importance of *theoretical* knowledge over the earlier trial and error approach. It speeded up innovation in all fields and enabled widespread applications, especially in the ways goods are produced, leading to changes in work. Knowledge-workers would predominate and benefit. Bell argued that knowledge was becoming the major source of structural changes in society, more important than the ownership of capital *per se*, and would lead to changes in the class structure. He said that knowledge, rather than capital, would affect political decision-making and the distribution of wealth and power in both socialist and capitalist societies.

Bell (1974: 14) listed five new dimensions in outlining his vision of a post-industrial society:

1   Economic sector: the change from a goods-producing to a service economy.
2   Occupational distribution: the pre-eminence of the professional and technical class.
3   Axial principle: the centrality of theoretical knowledge as the source of innovation and policy formulation for the society.
4   Future orientation: the control of technology and technological assessment.
5   Decision-making: the creation of a new 'intellectual technology'.

Elsewhere, Alain Touraine had studied work in France and had come to similar conclusions about the key role of 'knowledge and the capacity of society to call forth creativity [was] as important as capital accumulation' (Touraine 1971: 5) – leading to widespread changes in social relationships. Less optimistic than Bell, Touraine was concerned that the consequential concentration of economic power in private corporations would weaken the nation state and produce 'dependent participation' where people took part in society without authority over economic decisions affecting them. He foresaw the decline of political parties and of trade union influence and anticipated the emergence of social movements as a new form of political participation.

During the 1970s and 1980s there was much activity in social forecasting and many attempts were made to understand the changes that were occurring.

The attempts were both research-based and interpretive, optimistic and pessimistic, cultural and technological, highbrow and lowbrow, in many countries and languages and from all parts of the political spectrum. An eclectic list would include Braverman (1974), Naisbett (1984) and Toffler (1971, 1980) in the US; Masuda (1980) in Japan; Forester (1980) in Britain; and Emery and Bocklow (1978) and Jones (1982) in Australia. While these works were important and influential at the time they require no further discussion here because, by the 1990s, the dramatic changes that occurred from the mid-1970s had yielded clearer views of the nature of the transformation of work and society.

It is now possible, from the vantage point of the late 1990s, to see the events of the past 20 years more clearly. They reveal not just an acceleration of earlier trends, but a major transformation of our material culture with ramifications that are widespread, as anticipated to a remarkable extent by Bell and Touraine, among others.

Social transformation

Many commentators agree that three seemingly independent processes that would have profound effects on society, emerged in the 1970s:

- an economic crisis in capitalism;
- the technological revolution; and
- a series of cultural social movements including libertarianism, human and civil rights, feminism and environmentalism.

These processes, interacting worldwide in various ways, were to transform economic and social life, including work, especially in the industrialised countries. Some commentators, for example Castells (1996) who makes the most persuasive case, emphasise the importance of the information technology revolution as the key catalyst for change. We do not doubt its transformative role. Nevertheless, we will argue that, at the end of the twentieth century, the most significant changes in the organisation of work *per se* resulted more from the operations of capitalism. The full effects of information technology are still to have their widest impact.

The case for the predominant influence of capitalist decision-making on work by the late 1990s rests partly on noting which stage sets were already in place, and where they were located, as the drama began in the 1970s.

The trends analysed by Bell, Touraine and others were already changing work in the major capitalist countries: the shift to service occupations and to knowledge-based industries, the increase of women in paid work, and the growth of contingent work. The predominance of service work and the decline in blue-collar work gave the appearance of enlarged middle classes. Certainly the 1950s and 1960s had produced improved standards of living across the board. By 1970, most people in western countries and Japan thought they were middle class (see for example Vogel 1979).

These shifts in occupations and employment formed one kind of backdrop before which the key actors played their parts.

Another feature also in place by the 1970s in the United States and Western Europe – where crucial capitalist decisions were made – was a set of values among middle-class actors. These values had arisen from the libertarian and, to some extent, from the civil rights movements, and favoured individualism and personal freedom of choice. They were accompanied by a resurgence of beliefs in the power of the market and a decline of faith in the development role of government. This feature emerged as a misty vapour in the comfortable 1960s, but by the 1980s it would permeate all the crucial action front stage.

The crisis in capitalism

Capitalism shuddered in the 1970s, not just because of steep rises in the cost of oil as the key producing nations established a common cause. The world had changed and the older forms of mass production were under enormous cost pressure. In addition, inflation, falls in commodity prices and increasing unemployment were no longer amenable to the traditional Keynesian solutions. National governments could not afford the increasingly expensive interventions and were forced to redefine their roles. A shift in power occurred from governments to capitalists. Business, especially big business, was able to change the rules of the game (Bok 1994; Cappelli *et al.* 1997; Castells 1996).

These economic events coincided with the peak of the enormous population growth that brought more players and consumers into the international market place and toughened economic competition.

In 1930, the world population reached 2 billion. It had taken 100 years to double. Then, despite millions of deaths in the Second World War, the population doubled again in just 34 years, to reach 4 billion by 1974. Higher growth rates than ever before occurred in the late 1960s. Nevertheless, a further 2 billion people have been added in the past 15 years. World population is now over 6 billion. However, the growth rate is slowing. The United Nations *low* projection says world population will peak at 7.8 billion in 2050 and then decline (Cohen 1998: 29–30). The size of the population growth inevitably produced a huge increase in world trade, both within and between countries.

Furthermore, in the 40 years since the 1950s, average life expectancy at birth increased by 20 years, to reach 64.4 years in the period 1990–1995. This means not only the survival of more children but a large growth in the numbers of adult consumers. Moreover, the world population is now more concentrated than it was just half a century ago with almost 50 per cent of people now living in cities. In 1950, there was just one world city with more than 10 million people: by 1994 there were 14 such cities (Cohen 1998).

At the same time, after the Second World War, the world's average economic well-being increased. Many of the new consumers had more disposable income, but economic disparities between rich and poor also increased and are still increasing. There are many consequences of this wealth gap. Among them, the more numerous and affluent middle-class consumers in North America, Western Europe, Australasia and Japan, and growing elites elsewhere, exercised their choice for diverse and distinctive products. Another was the capacity of rich countries to have desired goods produced even more cheaply in the poor countries than at home. At the same time the cost of their safety nets for the poor threatened to expand.

Competition, especially on prices, intensified and resulted in great pressure to lower the cost of producing goods and services. Methods of production in what had been outlying places like Japan, Hong Kong, Taiwan, Singapore and northern Italy, showed up inefficiencies in the established mass production organisations in western countries.

Capitalism was restructured during a period of some 15 years – from around 1975 to 1990 – and came to include the following main features:

- globalisation and trade liberalisation;
- shift of power away from the state, which gave support for various changes;
- growth of income inequality;
- weakening of worker unions;
- workplace reforms.

Let us look at these features briefly.

Globalisation took a number of forms. Much production did move offshore to lower costs. The expenses of doing so added to the growing concentration of economic power in a few major conglomerates. The global movement of capital for investment soon came to exceed the value of international trade and funding by any but the larger national governments. Financiers wanted unfettered access to international markets and contributed crucially to an emerging pressure for liberalising international trade and finance. Few governments could deny the demands.

Governments, meanwhile, had less scope for autonomous national monetary policies and were persuaded to support the productivity goals of capitalism – more readily in some countries than in others and often at the expense of the wider public interest and social protection. (See for example Esping-Andersen (1996) and Freeman 1994, where blocs of countries are surveyed, including in Europe, North and South America, and Australasia.) The inability of governments to control inflation added to the impetus for a paradigmatic change in beliefs about the role of government. In many countries business was allowed unparalleled freedom to alter the rules of the game governing capital and labour, a freedom that it had not experienced since early in the century. There was a shift of power towards business and away from elected government and worker organisations (Cappelli *et al*. 1997).

Large increases in inequality began in 1970s' USA and spread worldwide. In the United States the earnings of most workers remained static or declined in real terms, while the fees paid to chief executives, top managers and consultants in technology, medicine and law increased tenfold. The powerful were more able to act in this way partly because investment funds increasingly came from impersonal sources such as insurance and pension schemes, ironically often contributed by workers. The pay of government staff, teachers and professors declined relatively (Bok 1994).

Worker organisations were early casualties as business strove to make labour more amenable. Unions had begun to lose membership in the 1960s as manufacturing and unskilled work declined and white-collar work grew. They were weakened further by legislative changes in the 1980s, which made worker mobilisation more difficult and hastened membership decline. In the early 1950s unions in the United States represented about one-third of all workers and, by the mid-1990s, just one-tenth. A majority of voters in most democracies, afraid of growing unemployment and/or tired of old controls on their freedom of choice, supported governments that made the changes. There is evidence, however, that in those countries where unions remained strong and where education systems were effective for a wide range of workers, the least inequality resulted from economic restructuring (see for example Freeman 1994).

The specific changes to work will be treated in later sections. Meanwhile, we should note that waves of workplace reforms to improve productivity not only drastically changed work but also increased unemployment to levels that, in some countries, had not been experienced since the 1930s. Some employers looked to technology, others to cheaper labour – often females and immigrants. Responses differed between countries: in the USA low rates of unemployment were maintained by the retention of 'dumb jobs'; in Europe and Japan stronger unions and greater use of technology allowed fewer jobs for unskilled workers. The UK and Australasia fell between these situations. The changes exacerbated the decline of whole regions, as manufacturing was relocated and services such as finance, tourism and information processing expanded.

The information technology revolution

Diffusion of microelectronics began in 1971 with the advent of the microprocessor – the so-called 'computer on a chip' – and, crucially, occurred in the freewheeling culture of California. The applications – including microcomputers and appropriate operating systems, digital switching, the use of optical fibres and the gateway technology that would lead to the communication network, the internet – spread around the world with great rapidity in a brief 15–20 years (see for example Castells 1996: Ch 1). Furthermore, micro-electronics were capable of wide-ranging applications that penetrated most domains of human activity. The technology produced an extraordinary reduction of costs that affected virtually every branch of the economy, including banking, the manufacture of washing machines, the measurement of forests, and the re-stocking of supermarkets.

Despite its huge impact, however, the computer has not so far been accompanied by striking economic gains. Productivity growth has been slower in the 1980s and 1990s than in the first three decades after the Second World War. In the United States, average productivity increased 1.1 per cent per year after 1973 as computer use expanded, compared with nearly 3 per cent per year during the period 1948–1973 (Madrick 1998: 29). Information technology could not avert the severe economic recession that emerged in the late 1990s in the so-called miracle economies of East and Southeast Asia, which had gained particular advantage from its applications.

The microprocessor, the 'computer on a chip', gave enormous information processing power that was quickly enhanced, best illustrated by the growth of memory capacity from 1024 bits in 1971 to over 16 million bits in 1993 (Castells 1996: 40). This capacity to collect, store, process and diffuse information at minimum cost greatly reduced the time required to complete tasks such as sorting mail and processing the census, and to tackle other tasks, including banking with a plastic card, which had never been considered before. The early applications included fibre optics, laser transmission, VCR machines and the personal computer, which in turn facilitated medical research in areas such as genetics, the development of industrial robots and the operation of automobiles and everyday washing machines.

Within manufacturing industry, in addition to robots and other machinery that replaced human workers, information technology greatly reduced time/storage and linked up networks of component and material suppliers that allowed 'just in time' production, and permitted closer integration of production with demand, that led to 'just in time' selling. These processes made possible enormous savings in energy and were quickly taken up after the sudden, large increases in the cost of oil in the 1970s – especially by Japanese industry, which was the most dependent on imported oil energy (Vogel 1979).

Around the world, the pressures to restructure work built up at the end of the 1970s and unemployment and inflation were both increasing. The most fundamental changes in work were made in the 1980s just as information communications technology was becoming available, clearly affecting the nature of the changes. Although certain key industries, including automobile manufacturing and finance, were quick to take up electronic technology, the widespread use of computers did not occur until the 1990s (Madrick 1998).

Employers had the choice of adopting the technology, which involved the expense of increasing worker skills and reducing overall costs in the medium term, or carrying on as before and reducing wages. Both options were taken by different employers, adding to the decline in living standards for the low paid and to the growth of inequality.

It is clear that information communications technology facilitated the internationalisation of manufacturing and finance, speeding up world trade; it reduced the amount of available unskilled work and contributed to growing unemployment; assisted in the shift to services; and accentuated the growing diversity of choice for consumers. But capitalists – powerful people – made the key decisions. Technology is always a tool and never an independent cause of human arrangements.

The new technology enables human skills and knowledge to be codified, thus reducing many routine tasks required in manufacturing and in the operation of machines. Increasingly, the technology is being applied to services-based tacit knowledge, useful for design, planning and other creative operations – and it is in these areas that the workforce is now growing. Recent research in the United States, which classified data on jobs according to function rather than industry, shows that office work accounted for 59 per cent of all new jobs between 1979 and 1995, and now comprises 40 per cent of all work. Many of the office workers are people who supply ideas and innovation for the increasingly diverse and complex economy. More than half of such workers have degrees, including:

> managers and executives, communications and financial experts, marketers, business consultants, lawyers, high-level sales people such as real estate and stock brokers, and scientists and engineers who work in management rather than in the classroom or the laboratory . . . In the contemporary era cheap standardised products have been replaced by more customised and sensitive products. . . . Heightened competition has required that firms be much more agile in terms of marketing and positioning their product. . . . Furthermore, as society has gotten richer it has had to allocate a higher proportion of the labor force simply to managing its physical and monetary resources.
>
> (Carnevale 1991: 163)

Although the service industries now employ as many scientists and engineers as manufacturing, Carnevale makes clear that the office economy may require better communication and social skills, and basic reasoning abilities, as much as technological expertise. We see that several types of smartness are required for the new workforce, including technical, conceptual, communication and social skills, a point that will be further elaborated below. We shall see further that many of these workforce skills are also required for living in the post-industrial societies.

Social movements and post-industrial lives

The key social movements that emerged in the affluent industrialised countries in the 1960s, during the golden era when average wages reached their highest levels, had far-reaching effects. The movement that was to become most directly influential on work arrived last and, interestingly, was the least publicised.

All these social movements had the effect of uplifting a category of people, which translated to the level of individuals of that category, enabled them to assert greater rights – eventually for themselves. To that extent, the social movements contributed to greater individualism and diversity (see Castells 1997: chs 2–4).

Initially, each movement was directed towards a great cause with new enlarged world-views that broke up existing coalitions and belief systems. Communities with a common set of values fragmented, diverse groups were created, and the larger society was forced to recognise the rights of each group and thereby to live with greater diversity. Freedom of choice became a credo especially practised by those groups and individuals that could afford to exercise it. As the great collective causes of the 1960s that had bound individuals together initially lost their meaning or receded, beliefs about individualism and individual rights were asserted. Ideas of socialism were replaced by notions of liberalism; the radicals became yuppies.

This point can be briefly elaborated by reference to some of the key social movements.

The civil rights movement in the United States began in the 1950s primarily to address long-term issues of the black minority. Its call for freedom helped stimulate the student protest and anti-war protest in the 1960s, and later an indigenous peoples' movement in many countries that continues to the present day. In many countries the civil rights movement resulted in some increased places for blacks, indigenous peoples and other minorities on educational ladders that would take them higher up the income pyramid. In most countries, however, the large pool of poorly educated people remains at the bottom, suggesting more intractable structural problems than can be solved by social movements.

The student protest movement began among the most privileged young people and called for a political freeing up, including participatory democracy and opposition to big bureaucracy and centralised authority. Many students took part in civil rights activities and then focused their protests against the Vietnam War and compulsory military conscription. This movement also sought to enlarge personal freedom, in particular over the use of drugs other than alcohol and tobacco.

The women's movement reflected the new positions educated women were occupying in the economy. There was a call for equality of treatment, redefinition of gender roles and greater choice to be exercised by women over their own bodies. The movement added to the spirit of liberation and individual freedom that emerged in the 1960s and 1970s and was diffused throughout the advanced economies. However, many of the jobs for women are low-wage, part-time and contingent, which for many women limits the freedom the movement promises.

The affluence enjoyed in the advanced economies that built up from the 1950s helped create sizeable middle classes that increasingly demanded more customisation of the products they purchased. It was a mood that added to the call for increased freedom of choice from other social movements, underpinned by affluence and a technology that provided for more individualism. In changing the nature of products sought by the well-to-do, consumerism undermined the cheap mass production of many goods and added to the competitive pressure on firms to be responsive more quickly to marketplace trends.

Consumerism can also be seen as a further important ingredient in the political climate of the 1980s and contributed to the particular choices made in countries about the ways in which work would be changed. Consumerism would add support to the neo-liberal alternatives that included weakening compulsory trade unionism and favouring economic flexibility over social protection. At the same time consumerism and its precursors paved the way for the diversity of responses that would enable people to better adapt to post-industrial living.

The transformation of work: how jobs change

The changes that have occurred in work in the modern era since the industrial revolution are like the gradual transformation of a drum, bugle and fife band into a large concert orchestra. At the end of the change there are still drummers in percussion, the bugle is a rare instrument in the brass section, and the fife is occasionally heard among the woodwinds. The waxing and waning in popularity of particular instruments marked the development of music. To extend the analogy, there are now several large sections, of complicated instruments, making up the orchestra.

While change has occurred spasmodically throughout the entire period — fast-changing in some decades and countries, slower in others — since the industrial revolution, the pace of change has stepped up in the past 20 years. Continuing the analogy, buglers who could not move to the valve trumpet or French horn are out of a job. All musicians have individual contracts. Some are part-time, and some, in public relations and advertising, work from home. The leader is no longer a man marching in front with a mace. A conductor, occasionally female, with a baton coordinates the music. Backstage, there is a sizeable management and beyond that, complicated ownership and sponsorship.

Let us now consider the major changes and the sequence in which they occurred. Although there is an overall pattern, the influence of different participants and the process of contention differ from country to country, producing the variety of results that we see across many societies. The changes did not just happen. Tilly and Tilly (1994: 305) remind us that

> . . . in the world of labour markets jobs change as a result of incessant, if unequal, bargaining among capitalists, workers, governments, organizations including labour unions and labour supplying households. Over the long run capitalists have the largest influence.

Added to this is the shift in world economic thinking in the past three decades. As the post-industrial changes began to impact, we moved away from an era in which national governments sought to exercise control over their economies, providing some protection for workers and families, to an era in which ideas of deregulation, privatisation and open competition have dominated. The result tilts the bargaining further in favour of capitalists.

Quantitative changes in work

The first major change was the decline of farm, forestry and fishing work, a movement out of the jobs that had involved most of humankind since time immemorial. The change began earlier in some countries and has been completed during the twentieth century in the developed countries, where the primary production workforce is now usually less than 5 per cent of the total. The change in agriculture this century, for example, shows clearly that the source of productivity growth lies in the application of knowledge.

Various technical and organisational inventions resulted in fewer people being required to produce even greater volumes of food and fibre. Tools for working the land and harvesting released brute physical labour, the internal combustion engine replaced animals and blade shearing, and electricity reduced worker numbers in milking and fencing. A range of machines from chainsaw to satellite measuring of forests has drastically reduced numbers in the timber industry. The process of change continues at an even greater rate with the application of biochemical and genetic inventions to the productive capacity of land, plants and animals. Most of the farm workforce has moved indoors and is to be found in processing, transport, storage, packaging, protecting, financing, marketing, research and development, connected to primary production, to manufacturing and to many unrelated jobs.

The second major change was the growth of manufacturing jobs, which by the middle of the twentieth century absorbed a large part of the workforce in industrial countries. Manufacturing numbers peaked and declined in the 1960s and the third major change was under way: the growth of services and, in particular, the growth of information-rich occupations.

These changes, all anticipated by the post-industrial theory of Bell and Touraine, have been documented for the G7 countries: Canada, France, Germany, Italy, the United States, Japan and the United Kingdom. Castells

(1996: Ch. 4) summarises the data and discusses the variability among these states.

Castells observes that, between 1920 and 1970, agriculture declined to less than 5 per cent of the workforce in most G7 countries and manufacturing grew, except in the United Kingdom, which in 1920 already had the largest industrial workforce of 37 per cent in 1920. In Japan, on the other hand, despite significant industry, 40 per cent of the labour force worked in rural areas as late as 1950, and even today, with state subsidies, the rural workforce is nearly 10 per cent.

In the 20 years from 1970–1990 these countries became post-industrial. Manufacturing declined and a majority of the population in all G7 countries came to be employed in services. Interestingly, Japan and Germany, the two most competitive economies at the time, retained the strongest manufacturing employment and had the lowest service-to-industry ratio. Japan, which had the fastest productivity growth of all the countries, seemed also to have the lowest rate of information employment. This fact, however, could reflect the way statistics are collected. Castells notes that in Japan, for example, because of a different management style, much information processing is embedded in material production or goods handling and is not recorded separately as information work.

The growth of service workers highlights the differences among the seven countries. By 1990 the three 'Anglo-Saxon' countries, Canada, the UK and the US, had between 34 per cent and 40 per cent of their workforces in producer and social services combined. Japan had the smallest proportion of 24 per cent and the European countries were between these two extremes. Castells refers to the first three as the 'service economy model' and Japan and Germany as indicating an 'industrial production model', and suggests that the differences arise from each country's position in the global economy.

Similar differences are revealed by the changing occupational structure. All countries recorded increases in the category 'managerial, professional and technological' workers: Canada, the UK and the US to over 30 per cent, France and Germany in the mid-20 per cent and Japan 15 per cent. The reverse is true for craft and operative workers where Japan has the most and the US the least.

Projections in the United States for workforce requirements in the period 1992–2005 indicate a growing polarisation of the occupational structure. Castells re-calculated the data to distinguish four stratified groups. An upper group of managers and professionals will increase by 1.6 per cent to 25.3 per cent of the workforce. A middle group of technicians and craft workers will decrease by 0.3 per cent to 14.3 per cent. The largest single group, 40 per cent of the labour force – comprising people in sales, clerical and operative work – will decline by 2.7 per cent. Meanwhile, the least skilled group of service and agricultural workers is predicted to increase by 1.1 per cent to become 20 per cent of the workforce in 2005.

Castells reports that a projection carried out in Japan in 1987 found similar trends in its employment structure: a slow decline of manufacturing – which still remains larger than elsewhere – growth of some services and a large drop in the agricultural workforce. An increase in professionalisation of middle-level workers along with continued growth of information processing and knowledge generation work is anticipated. However, Japan has leaner management hierarchies, with power in the hands of relatively fewer managers than in the United States.

The post-industrial theory that was developed following Bell and Touraine, anticipated the expansion of information-rich occupations, but, as we shall see, not the growth of the low-end unskilled service work at the expense of the middle jobs, nor, significantly, the growth in income inequality.

Polarisation of income distribution is more marked, not only because of the growing gap in occupations and the growth of unemployment. On the one hand, real wages have fallen for the bulk of middle-income earners. At the same time, whole families, communities and regions have been cut off from paid work – or from the acquisition of the skills that lead to work in modern societies – for a variety of reasons including ethnicity, gender, dysfunctionality or simply unfortunate location.

On the other hand, with reduced constraints, corporate capitalists have paid certain employees and themselves inordinate increases in personal income. Derek Bok (1993: 224), the former Harvard President, documents the huge salary increases – he calls them 'unjustified earnings' – gained by specialist doctors, elite lawyers and leading business executives in the United States.

> From 1970 to 1990, surgeons, radiologists, anesthesiologists and other hospital specialists raised their earnings by 30 to 50 percent, even though the number of doctors increased more than at any other period this century. Real profits per partner in elite law firms rose by 75 percent or more during two decades when the supply of lawyers almost trebled and competition for corporate clients grew more intense than ever before. CEOs of large firms saw their incomes double at a time when the numbers of MBAs jumped threefold and foreign firms challenged American business more successfully than at any other time in our history.
>
> (Bok 1993: 224)

In the United States, 1973–1993 was a period of real per capita GDP growth; the median annual wage fell by $4000 while the earnings of the top 20 per cent grew. By the early 1990s the top 1 per cent of the population owned 40 per cent of all assets. Apparently, the US is the extreme case of income inequality and declining real wages but it represents the flexible labour market that many other countries are aiming at (Castells 1996: 276, see also Freeman 1994, and Katz in Freeman, 1994).

The fastest growing types of work are temporary and part-time. In the United Kingdom in 1993, 38 per cent of the workforce was employed on a contingent or part-time basis, 85 per cent of which was female. Self-employed work has also increased. Between 1982 and 1992, average growth of the contingent workforce in G7 countries – work that has no job security, no career and no benefits – went from 20 per cent to 25 per cent and is projected to reach 35 per cent in 2000.

Castells, in a bleak outlook, suggests the widespread emergence of dual labour markets within countries, once practised only in Japan. His thinking is similar to that of Reich (1993). This dual labour market can be seen as comprising a *core labour force* formed by information managers (Reich's *symbolic analysts)* and a *disposable labour force* that can be automated, hired, fired, part-timed, outsourced, subcontracted, off-shored, etc, depending on market demand and labour costs.

Qualitative changes in work

The changes in the global competitive environment occurring from the 1980s put pressures on all work organisations to become more flexible and to increase their customer focus. The time for conceiving, producing and marketing products dropped dramatically as organizations searched for new ways to compete (Capelli *et al*. 1997: 31). The best firms required highly skilled and committed employees.

What happened within workplaces as these flexible factories and flexible administrative arrangements were being created? What was it like for the workers, especially during the most intensive period of change, the mid-1980s to the mid-1990s? We will consider both good results and bad results.

To paraphrase the song: 'There was a whole lot of changin' goin' on.' In the United States for example, staff in the 500 largest service organizations grew by 2 million people. Meanwhile staff numbers in the 500 largest manufacturing organizations decreased from 14.4 million to 11.4 million. According to Capelli *et al*. (1997: 53), in a book where much good research on the changes is summarised, the downsizing option taken by many US employers often resulted in short-term cost saving at the expense of long-term cost increases. Restructuring, apparently, has so far produced few enduring gains in that country. The gains and the pains are not evenly shared and the current changes are not widely accepted. Thus we can expect further changes in the organisational arrangements in future.

At the same time as global pressures for improved performance built up, in the west there was a growing concentration of ownership among large institutional holders such as pension funds and bank trusts and a smaller proportion of individual investors (Capelli *et al*. 1997: 33–34). Japan's ownership pattern was always more concentrated. New management control and information systems were also made possible by cheap computer power. Restructuring was under way.

Shoshana Zuboff's (1988) finely observed study of eight organisations, a mix of manufacturing plants and services administration, captured the transformation to advanced computer-based technology in the early stages. For the workers it was a shift away from action-centred work where production had depended on what the body could accomplish with strength and skill. The computer environment demanded a new cognitive commitment to the job. Operators were called upon to deal with explicit, systematic abstract knowledge. Furthermore, Zuboff found that the new technology brought people together to solve problems. Effective communication became crucial. According to Zuboff (1988: 201)

> . . . collaboration will depend largely on the grace and enthusiasm that individuals bring to the participative process. Managers who place a premium on control and workers who feel disaffected do not make good colleagues, for the spirit of hypothesis generation and testing is above all a collegial one. The new technology really brings people together . . . it requires teamwork . . . you have to discuss what you see, what you understand, what you know and what should be done.

New ways of exercising authority are required of managers. Full exploitation of the smart machines calls for critical judgement. High technology organisations require a distribution of knowledge and authority that enables a wide range of members to contribute to the activities of the firm. 'Critical judgment means the capacity to ask questions, to say no when things are not right' (Zuboff 1998: 289) and contributing implies both willingness and an understanding of organisational purposes. Anything that impedes this worker input, such as deference or obedience to managerial authority, becomes dysfunctional. The technology requires a range of organisational changes and shifts in attitudes and culture from all participants. Management has to be streamlined as well.

Whatever the pressures, each company always has choices. According to research, sustained improvements from restructuring are most likely under two conditions: (1) where the company makes integrated, systematic changes in both organisational design and human resources practices; and (2) where the company fosters changes at the corporate and business levels, not just the group and individual (Capelli *et al*. 1997: 54). These include the following specific elements:

- flatter hierarchies;
- devolved decision-making;
- teamwork, including good communication and trust;
- increased variety, responsibility and collegiality;

- investment in training and education;
- contracts for employees that include a financial stake in the organisation.

Capelli *et al.* (1997) point out that the conditions listed here are likely to see improved employee attachment and productivity. They also note, however, the downside. The employees bear more of the risk of doing business – risk is moved downwards in the organisation. Work time lengthens as all workers take on larger workloads. These features bring conflict with families and produce increased stress.

There is another face to organisational restructuring. Some firms simply go out of business. Others shed permanent staff, cut wages, hire contractors, increase temporary and part-time workers or reduce work time. As Capelli *et al.* (1997: 61) put it: 'devastated communities and ruined careers abound'. Unemployment has increased everywhere, especially among young people and the less educated; although rates vary among countries. Job insecurity and job loss produces increased anxiety and stress for the worker and family, and reduces morale and commitment. There are reports of increased work accidents, illness, workplace violence and customer attacks (Capelli *et al.* 1997: 57–63, 193–199).

The social and technical context, in different countries and different regions within countries, affects the choices made by organisations when restructuring. Castells (1996) reports on the differential impact of the introduction of robots into the automobile industries in four countries. In the United States and Italy, workers were simply displaced as the main aim was to lower costs. In France, government policy reduced job losses. In Japan, management increased training and emphasised improved team effort. As a result 'employment increased and productivity shot up' (Castells 1996: 249).

The fastest growing categories of work in all the industrialised countries are temporary labour and part-time work but the rates vary across countries. The highest numbers have been in the United Kingdom, the lowest in the United States and Japan, with rates in Europe lying in between.

Some countries with the highest diffusion of electronic technologies have the lowest unemployment (e.g. Austria, Sweden, Germany), while Spain, a technological laggard, records high unemployment. However, the relationship is not clear-cut. Finland is a high technology user and also has high unemployment.

Carnevale (1991) shows in considerable detail that greater technological complexity requires better particular skills among workers. These include higher levels of reading, writing and oral communication than hitherto; broader maths skills; a general adaptability and creativity for problem-solving; and a number of social attributes not previously considered very important: strong motivation to succeed, goal-setting ability and effectiveness in group settings. These skills are the core skills of the smart workforce at work. However, we have seen that not all employers choose to take this option but avoid high technology and, where laws of the country allow it, pay low wages to unskilled workers, thereby adding to the growth of inequality and subsequent human costs in those countries (see Freeman 1994). Smart work-forces do not necessarily mean smart countries!

Attachment to work

Across all jobs in most countries there is a new kind of flexible attachment to work – marked by individual contracts, high turnover and low organisational commitment – replacing the lifelong attachment that had been common at the height of the industrial era. At the same time there is significant long-term unattachment variously supported by state welfare in different countries.

However, new ways grow out of old and the old endures. For example, there are still well-defined civil-service type jobs with career ladders and measured progress in most countries – more likely in utilities and finance institutions than in supermarkets, and more likely in Japan and France rather than in the US and the UK. Furthermore, despite the widespread emergence of nego-tiated, limited-time job contracts for managers in much of Europe and North America, managerial careers are still shaped and planned in established Japanese companies to produce competent general managers oriented to the organisation as a whole. Changes in the former countries grew out of the tradition of functional specialisation such as accounting and engineering, whereas in Japan general management skills were long favoured (see for example Storey *et al.* 1997).

Many firms, however, have gone altogether, or been amalgamated or re-structured or downsized or otherwise substantially changed in ownership, purposes, structure or size. For employees, the lifetime career with one firm has all but disappeared or, as in the case of Japan, is weakening. Employees negotiate shorter-term contracts that are more individualised and more specific as to what is required of both parties. For skilled workers, attachment to the occupation replaces attachment to the firm.

Protection for individual employees, and thus the degree to which workers must negotiate their own wages and conditions, varies widely. During the 1980s union membership declined, and wage-setting and labour relations became more decentralised in all countries: most in the United States and France, least in the rest of Europe, with Japan in between. However, in European countries, except the United Kingdom and Ireland, firms are required by law to have elected worker councils that cover all employees. The councils 'provide representation inside firms regardless of how unions are doing' (Freeman 1994: 18 and Ch 1). In addition, European countries have legislation that ensures certain workplace rights and benefits that are quite lacking in the United States.

Although attachments to their work organisations may be transient for many employees, some are able to exert a good deal more leverage than others. Among the powerful in the 1990s are young people with newly needed skills – e.g. software engineering – (or high-status skills such as an

MBA from Harvard rather than Podunk U) that are in heavy demand until the education systems produce such people in greater abundance. These so-called 'Gold-collar workers' (Munk 1998) derive extra leverage from belonging to a relatively small birth cohort (1965–1979) that followed the baby boom (1946–1964). They are likely to use their scarcity advantage to enhance their reputations and fulfil highly individual personal goals rather than build careers with strong attachment to the work organisation, as was favoured by their parents at the height of industrialism.

For the majority of workers in full-time employment, the upside is more involvement and participation in decision-making and often in ownership of the firm. The downside is a greater share in the market-place risk that was formerly borne by employers alone.

The reduced certainty of employment also has benefits and costs for both workers and employers. Various kinds of restructuring, such as downsizing, outsourcing and the use of contingent workers, produce short-term gains in productivity for the firm, but at the risk of long-term lowering of staff morale and productivity. Growing numbers in the contingent workforce on the one hand are cheaper for organisations that use them, but on the other hand they further lower worker loyalty and attachment to the firm. This flexibility and reduced commitment is often suitable for young people, parents with young children and of course the 'gold-collar workers' who are able to secure considerable advantages for themselves (Munk 1998).

Implications for developing smart workforces and lifestyles in the twenty-first century

Patterns of work changed rapidly in the last two decades of the twentieth century and more change is probably in store. There is an imbalance about the present arrangements and some adverse effects on other institutions of societies. The downside costs cannot be sustained and are already in contention by mobilised interests – variously in different countries. Where they reduce long-term productivity, weak attachments to work will be strengthened. Growing wage inequality is contested by renewed worker organisations. Work stress is resisted. (See for example, National Defense Counsel for Victims of Karoshi 1990.) High rates of unemployment that result in dysfunctional communities and damage to families and parenting, are provoking a redesign of welfare state provisions and education systems (Esping-Anderson, 1996).

Nevertheless, the core pattern has been established and most of its ingredients form the basis of the new work paradigm: flexible organisations maximising information and communication technology and requiring the application of insight and intelligence from staff at many levels; flattened hierarchies; individually negotiated contracts; and work in teams. Across whole economies there are growing proportions of technological and professional workers, and of low-skilled employees. There are fewer in manufacturing and more in services. Most women, including mothers, are in paid work. There is extensive use of contingent workers, and relatively high levels of unemployment. Internationally there are significant agglomerations of firms, easy financial flows and cheap sourcing of supplies across national boundaries. Above all, there is intense global competition.

Our analysis suggests that now there are stronger interconnections between work and the rest of life than during the height of the industrial era. Once the 40-hour-week rule was firmly established for most workers, it was possible to have a separation between work and 'life'. The post-industrial pattern makes this much less likely.

- Employees are asked to bring more of themselves to work: to bring cognitive, social and emotional skills. They have to be smarter with more abstract knowledge, with greater abillity to negotiate and cooperate, and with the capacity to trust.
- Managers and owners have to be smarter along the same dimensions lest, for example, by restructuring in wrong ways, they create more stress and destroy the essential trust that post-industrial organisations require, or they leave shattered lives on the scrap heap.
- Unemployment can no longer be a time of passive resignation or mindless protest. Rather it can, hopefully, be a temporary period, providing opportunity to refresh work skills and prepare for another period of fast-changing work or sharpen other skills to live fully in different ways.
- Work spills over into life in countless ways, changing relationships in parenting, partnering and friendship. Being smart for post-industrial work will not last long if people are not smart for life as well.

Thus, the particular arrangements for work and other affected sectors in any country will depend on a number of factors. Three key factors will be discussed here: policies of national governments; industrial practices of employers and worker organisations; and responses of individuals and families.

Policies for national governments

Governments in all countries have long had policies about work. Consider the control over trading exercised by guilds in medieval towns of Europe, the state examinations governing entrance to the civil service in ancient China, and the policing arrangements affecting commerce and the slave trade in pre-revolutionary North America.

Modern states have a wide array of regulations governing such features as labour-market relations, trading and professional practices, minimum wages, taxation, infrastructural provisions, safety provisions, accountability standards, statistical reporting, and investment in research and development.

Additionally, in most countries, even in relatively poor ones (see for example United Nations Development Programme 1997), there are a variety of government-sponsored programmes – including income transfer, housing subsidies, health facilities and other forms of social insurance – designed to protect individual workers, families and the elderly from significant economic decline or job loss. State-provided education also has significant effects on the nature of the workforce. The particular mix of both work regulations and social protection in any country is the product of historical political contention in that country.

The rise of the global economy in recent times, with its tougher competition, has made national economies vulnerable to international business and limited the capacity of their governments to administer independent financial policies. Furthermore, worldwide competition gave some advantages to countries with cheaper labour costs and prompted the high unemployment rates that appeared in those advanced economies with high wage costs. (Of course, many of the countries with cheaper labour markets but with traditionally high unemployment rates often stayed that way – even where significant numbers of their people got jobs from such 'off-shored' activity.)

In the face of these challenges, governments were persuaded to assist in the flexibility of their economies. It was argued that there is a trade-off between social protection and economic or employment flexibility: the more social protection the less employment flexibility. Changes were introduced into all advanced economies, which were designed to increase flexibility. These included reduction of public sector employment; the weakening of job security provisions and mandatory fringe costs to employers such as accident insurance, sickness absences and parental leave; and the reduction of income support by governments such as pensions for the elderly and benefits for the unemployed and sole parents.

Countries responded very differently to the economic flexibility challenge, in part according to the kind of welfare states that they had in place in the 1970s. There was some reduction of social protection in all countries. The United States and the United Kingdom favoured wage deregulation, reducing income support and diminishing the public sector. Not all of Europe followed the Scandinavian model, which stressed a retraining strategy and welfare state jobs, but many European countries did subsidize older workers to leave the labour market early and developed programmes that gave subsidies for the employment of the long-term unemployed (Freeman 1994, Esping-Andersen 1996). There are plainly no royal roads to success and each country is both limited and advantaged by its prior arrangements as well as its current capacity to choose options.

The alternatives are outlined and both the positive and negative features of each are discussed in Esping-Andersen (1996: Chs 1 and 9). Neither the labour reduction strategy of the European countries, nor the seemingly benign approach of Sweden, are without their downsides. The low-wage system in the United States both implicitly subsidizes low productivity firms and helps to create huge inequalities that lock a growing segment of the population into declining earnings and poverty traps. Esping-Andersen (1996: 28) quotes a suggestion that the huge prison population in the United States is the American equivalent of Europe's long-term unemployed.

It seems that the trade-off between social protection and economic flexibility is not as strong as the proponents thought, at least in terms of flexibility outcomes. Rebecca Blank (1994) examined a series of studies that contrasted specific social protection programmes in Europe and Japan with programmes in the United States. She concluded: '. . . there is little evidence that labour market flexibility is substantially affected by the presence of the social protection programmes, nor is there strong evidence that the speed of labour market adjustment can be increased by limiting these programmes' (Blank 1994: 181).

Nevertheless, governments in all the advanced economies face the key post-industrial problem that arises from the crucial changes in work and society: developing and maintaining appropriate and changing levels of skill and knowledge in their populations. The objectives are to have a workforce that is immune to cheaper competitors and a population that is relatively self-reliant. There is some evidence that high widespread levels of education in a population are associated with more adaptable and successful economies (Sharp 1986: 281), as new ideas and new technologies will diffuse more rapidly. Cohen and Zysman (1987: 7) make a similar point: 'The mix of available skills shapes the evolution of technology. If we want technologies that support a high-wage, high value-added economy we have to ensure the education and skills to make that possible'.

The social and economic costs of failing to provide adequate levels of education are not only felt at the top end by slowness in taking up new technologies. The costs are made most acute by skill deficiencies among the least skilful. Prolonged unemployment and ignorance can lead to intergenerational isolation of families and of whole segments of populations that pose the risks of political extremism, crime and despair. The instability of post-industrial work means that unemployment will occur in the lifetime of many people. Governments need to ensure that unemployment does not become lifelong.

Esping-Andersen (1996: 264) makes the useful suggestion that governments

> . . . rethink the idea of redistribution and rights: accepting inequalities
> for some, here and now, but guaranteeing at the same time that those
> who fare less well 'here and now' will not always do so; that under-
> privilege will not be a permanent fixture of anyone's lifecourse . . . stress-
> ing a social policy more explicitly designed to optimize the self-reliant
> capacities of the citizenry . . . the core of such a model's social citizenship
> guarantees would combine education and proactive income maintenance.

A related area of considerable concern to governments is the fate of children. The post-industrial economy is one where women are needed in the labour force and want to work and have children without being penalised. Increased marital instability has had adverse effects on children's learning and development, with the associated long-term impacts. Governments are required to develop policies that ensure family well-being and adequate parenting for the sake of future generations (Hage and Powers 1992; Esping-Andersen 1996).

During the period of transition to post-industrial economies, governments gave excessive attention to economic issues and, under the emerging conditions, their societies fragmented. It may now be time to rebuild political coalitions in pursuit of greater social integration.

Post-industrial work practices

We have seen that smart work organisations need as much information, insight and intelligence as employees can provide in order to make good decisions. The focus of concern shifts to the workers' minds and personalities. Effective employees require a strategic understanding of the organisation and its purposes. Wise leaders of smart workforces will have the capacity to enunciate strategies and provide clear goals.

Zuboff showed that traditional power structures with hierarchical and occupational boundaries are often antithetical to the easy flow of information in an organisation and to staff members proffering insights. Effective work organisations will develop group problem-solving methods and matrix authority structures (see for example Hage and Powers 1992).

Successful firms must have flexible organisation and this may lead to less job security than hitherto. At the same time, firms need to ensure that employees feel secure enough to share information, skills and feelings with each other. This is seldom accomplished by repeated downsizing as the main means of restructuring. Downsizing can lead to a kind of organisational anorexia whereby, once severely reduced in size, the firm rarely recovers an effective level of trust. Rather, firms need to demonstrate why there must be changes (*Economist* 1994).

Employee organisations have an important role in post-industrial work. Lynch's (1994) comparative study found that the European system of work councils performs useful democratic and economic functions. According to Lynch, the latter

> include better intrafirm communication and the diffusion (across as well as within firms) of advanced practices with regard to training, technology, compensation, and other ingredients in industrial upgrading. Works councils are a means to greater social consensus and a greater capacity to respond to changed economic circumstances in broadly beneficial ways.
>
> (Lynch 1994: 148)

Unions continue to be important in wage-setting, despite the decentralisation of the 1980s, and can provide protection for workers and promote practices that benefit the entire economy in the long run – for example with regard to training and parental leave – although at negotiable costs (Freeman 1994: Chs 1 and 7).

Post-industrial lives

In his brilliant book reviewing the turbulent history of the twentieth century, Eric Hobsbawm (1994) makes an insightful comment about the impact of work changes at the end of the century, particularly the worldwide loss of jobs affecting all classes. 'These were times when people, their old ways of life already undermined and crumbling, were likely to lose their bearings' (Hobsbawm 1994: 416). The question to be addressed is: how may people reconstruct their bearings in the changed world of the twenty-first century? There will be no linear life course and people must expect and anticipate periods of crisis and renewal.

The changes can be regarded positively. Hage and Powers (1992) compare industrial and post-industrial work roles and show how the latter are having a profound impact on the nature of face-to-face social relationships and on the character of the social self at work and in the family. They go on to suggest how the new roles will operate (cf. Hage and Powers 1992: Ch 1).

The old structure was marked by hierarchy, authoritarian decision-making, functional specification, gender-specific division of labour, rules and, for many, the expectation of lifetime employment. In the 'ideal type' post-industrial organisation, roles are defined by goals and people determine how their work will be done. There is an increase in behaviour that is not rule-bound with fewer gender-specific roles. Work roles are frequently redefined via negotiation and even conflict (Milkman 1992). Hiring and promotion are based on the employee's 'feel' for the occupation, creativity, problem-solving, the ability to work in teams and to respond flexibly to new situations (see Hirschorn 1997, Levine 1996). Individuals need to be flexible and responsive, able to negotiate and work-skill smart.

Such changes cannot be limited to workplace roles but will intrude into all areas of life, particularly into family and education. To recognise this we need only to consider the growth of part-time work and paid work from home, and the lengthening of work hours.

Under these conditions the meaning of a 'good' parent is redefined. A parent is no longer a person who fulfils routine obligations. There is greater variety of female, male and parenting roles, an emphasis on team effort, listening and responsiveness, and a willingness to give quality time (cf. Hage and Powers 1992: Ch 7).

Learning becomes more important than teaching or schooling. Institutions that place the process in limiting age brackets, such as our present schools, may increasingly become an impediment to lifelong learning. The teacher role, as well as a facilitator of access to knowledge, is also the stimulator of teamwork and group solving of learning problems (see for example Gardner 1998, Gee *et al.* 1996).

Hage and Powers (1992: 202) argue that the honest expression of emotions and feelings becomes more important in post-industrial relationships. They maintain that:

> Intuition and insight are more likely to emerge when individuals are in contact with their feelings. Emotions are also critical for creativity and problem solving because they allow us to more easily detect the ideas and suggestions of others. If we are in better contact with our feelings, we more readily observe those of others; that is we become better listeners and interpreters of symbolic communication.
>
> (Hage and Power 1992: 202)

At the same time, individuals will be tougher and require strong individual skills and negotiating ability. Post-industrial societies are more individualized and provide less social protection than industrial societies during their golden age after the Second World War.

Conclusion

This chapter has aimed to provide a background to a larger discussion of the meaning, significance and prospects of developing a smart workforce as a strategic economic, educational and training approach to contemporary conditions of work. By way of concluding, let us consider where the ideas advanced here place us in relation to developing smart workers and a smart workforce.

It has been argued that the changes in work during the latter decades of the twentieth century reflect a wide transformation of societies. Not only does work require smarter people to bring insight and intelligence, and to operate cooperatively with greater flexibility and less security; work has changed the way we live and affects all levels of society and all major institutions. We have to live smarter as well as work smarter.

The changes we have surveyed here did not simply happen. There was a long build-up that included changes in the world economy; a shift in attitudes among powerful segments of the populations in the advanced societies; and new technology that facilitated more options and opportunities. Directions were taken that favoured capitalists, and governments assisted in efforts to increase economic flexibility.

Social fragmentation increased in all countries. Individuals and families face more choice and less social protection. There are subtle changes that affect intimate areas of life, including interpersonal relationships, parenting and gender roles, and self-identity. Individuals will contend with more changes, crises and chances of renewal during their lifetime than ever before.

The times we live in call for smart workforces and populations that live smart. We have argued that these can come about as a consequence of smart governments, smart employers and smart workers each playing a part. Similarly, the conditions for living smart will require the same concordance of actors.

It is not simply a matter of cognitive knowledge and technical skills. Social relationship changes demand flexibility and new forms of communication that involve emotional awareness, creative thinking and interpersonal sensitivity.

Post-industrial society poses challenges to educational systems that have not been satisfactorily met in any society so far. The rigid, three-tiered, age-graded pyramid of the industrial era persists everywhere, when flexible learning systems are required at all levels of society. Breaking out of that deeply entrenched mould is an educational and political challenge. It calls for new visions by intellectuals and educationalists, practical programmes by organisational providers and also a major shift in political leadership.

Appropriate, flexible educational programmes are required by employers, the employed and the unemployed throughout their lifetimes. Countries need smart workforces, but these will not be sufficient on their own because work has spilled over into all facets of life. All citizens need lifelong learning in these fast-changing times, in order to acquire and maintain knowledge, understanding and social sensitivity that will be useful both for work and for living.

References

Bell, D. (1974) *The Coming of Post-Industrial Society: A Venture in Social Forecasting*. London: Heinemann.

Best, M.H. (1990) *The New Competition: Institutions of Industrial Restructuring*. Cambridge, MA: Harvard University Press.

Blank, R. (1994) 'Does a large safety net mean less economic flexibility?' in R. Freeman, *Working Under Different Rules*. New York: Russell Sage Foundation.

Blauner, R. (1964) *Alienation and Freedom*. Chicago: University of Chicago Press.

Bok, D. (1994) *The Cost of Talent: How Executives and Professionals are Paid and How it Affects America*. New York: The Free Press.

Cappelli, P., Bassi, L., Katz, H., Knoke, D., Osterman, P. and Useem, M. (1997) *Change at Work*. New York: Oxford University Press.

Carnevale, A. (1991) *America and the New Economy: How New Competitive Standards are Radically Changing American Workplaces*. San Francisco: Jossey-Bass.

Castells, M. (1996) *The Rise of Network Society*. Oxford: Blackwell.

Castells, M. (1997) *The Power of Identity*. Oxford: Blackwell.

Cohen, J.E. (1998) 'How many people can the earth support?' *New York Review of Books* XLV: 15, 8 October.

Cohen, S. and Zysman, J. (1987) *Manufacturing Matters: The Myth of the Post-Industrial Economy*. New York: Basic Books.

Economist (1994) 'When slimming is not enough'. *The Economist,* 3 September, pp. 59–60.

Emery, F. and Bocklow, M. (1978) *The Emergence of New Paradigms of Work*. Canberra: ANU Centre for Continuing Education.

Esping-Andersen, G. (ed) (1996) *Welfare States in Transition: National Adaptations in Global Economies*. London: Sage.

Forester, T. (ed) (1980) *The Micro Electronics Revolution*. London: Oxford University Press.

Freeman, R. (ed) (1994) *Working Under Different Rules*. New York: Russell Sage Foundation.

Gardner, H. (1998) *The Disciplined Mind: What all Students Should Understand*. New York: Simon and Schuster.

Gee, J., Hull, G. and Lankshear, C. (1996) *The New Work Order: Behind the Language of the New Capitalism*. St Leonards, NSW: Allen and Unwin.

Hage, J. and Powers, C. (1992) *Post-Industrial Lives: Roles and Relationships in the 21st Century*. Newbury Park, CA: Sage.

Hirschorn, L. (1997) *Reworking Authority: Leading and Following in the Post-Modern Organization*. Cambridge, MA: MIT Press.

Hobsbawm, E. (1994) *The Age of Extremes: the Short Twentieth Century, 1914–1991*. London: Michael Joseph.

Jones, B. (1982) *Sleepers, Wake! Technology and the Future of Work*. Melbourne: Oxford University Press.

Levine, D.I. (1996) *Reinventing the Workplace: How Business and Employees Can Both Win*. Washington: The Brookings Institution.

Lynch, L.M. (1994) 'Payoffs to Alternative Training Strategies at Work', in R. Freeman, *Working Under Different Rules*. New York: Russell Sage Foundation.

Madrick, J. (1998) 'Computers: waiting for the revolution', *New York Review of Books*, XLV: 5, 26 March.

Masuda, Y. (1980) *The Information Society as Post-Industrial Society*. Tokyo: Institute for the Information Society.

Milkman, R. (1992) 'Labor and management in uncertain times: renegotiating the social contract', in A. Wolfe (ed) *America at Century's End*. Berkeley: University of California Press.

Munk, N. (1998) 'Gold-collar workers', *Time*, 23 March.

Naisbitt, J. (1982) *Megatrends*. London and Sydney: Macdonald.

National Defense Counsel for Victims of Karoshi (1990) *Karoshi*, Mado-Sha, Tokyo.

Reich, R. (1993) *The Work of Nations: Preparing Ourselves for 21st Century Capitalism*. London: Simon and Schuster.

Sharp, M. (ed) (1986) *Europe and the New Technologies*. Ithaca: Cornell University Press.

Storey, J., Edwards, P. and Sisson, K. (1997) *Managers in the Making: Careers, Development, and Control in Corporate Britain and Japan*. New York: Sage.

Tilly, C. and Tilly, C. (1994) 'Capitalist work and labour markets', in N. Swelser and R. Swedberg (eds) *The Handbook of Economic Sociology*. Princeton and New York: Princeton University Press.

Toffler, A. (1971) *Future Shock*. New York: Bantam Books.

Toffler, A. (1980) *The Third Wave*. New York: William Morrow.

Touraine, A. (1971) *The Post-Industrial Society. Tomorrow's Social History: Classes, Conflicts and Culture in the Programmed Society*. New York: Random House.

United Nations Development Programme (1997) *Human Development Report 1997*, New York.

Vogel, E.F. (1979) *Japan as Number One: Lessons for America*. New York: Harper.

Zuboff, S. (1988) *In the Age of the Smart Machine: The Future of Work and Power*. New York: Basic Books.

Part 2

Critical aspects for workplace education

3 Competence – the basis for a smart workforce

Jörgen Sandberg

Today, developing competence has become a crucial issue for establishing a smart workforce that can achieve competitive success (Kanter 1983; Porter 1990). The rapid pace of technological development within areas such as microelectronics and communications has created essentially new conditions for producing goods and services in many industries. The flexibility in production has increased dramatically, while the product life cycles have become shorter. Such rapid technological change creates a requirement for both different competence and for ongoing renewal of the workers' present competence. Furthermore, as Ellström (1992) argued, an often encountered difficulty for workers when new technology is introduced consists not of learning to handle it, but of using its potential to achieve higher productivity.

A further reason for the increasing importance of competence development is the structural change occurring in Western economies as a result of a movement toward more service and knowledge-based industries. Many current studies of economic development in the industrialised world, such as Ekstedt (1988), Eliasson *et al.* (1990) and Neef (1998), conclude that the production of services increases in relation to the production of goods, while both entities become increasingly knowledge-intensive. The appearance of knowledge-intensive companies during the last decade is a central manifestation of a more knowledge-based industry (Sveiby and Riesling 1986; Alvesson 1989; Lindmark 1990; Starbuck 1992). Bäcklund (1994) also demonstrated that the increasing rationalisation of capital, decentralisation, customer orientation and technical renewal that take place in companies today has led to a requirement for continuous development of new and more advanced competence within work that is usually regarded as uncomplicated and simple.

The increasingly important issue of developing competence in order to create a smart workforce leads to a further demand for efficient ways to manage training and development in organisations. However, in order to manage training and development efficiently, managers need to understand *what constitutes human competence at work*. Without such an understanding, the development of competence cannot be managed effectively and, to that extent, a smarter workforce cannot be established in organisations. The aim of this chapter is to explore what constitutes human competence at work:

firstly, in terms of the competence of individuals and, secondly, in terms of collective competence in organisations. Finally, based on the description of what constitutes competence, ways to create a smarter workforce in terms of competence development are discussed.

The nature of individual competence

Hunting for a smarter workforce is not new. Taylor was one of the first to begin a systematic quest for a smarter workforce by addressing the problem of what constitutes competence at work. In his famous book, *The Principles of Scientific Management* (Taylor 1911), he argued as follows:

> The search for better, for more competent men, from the presidents of our great companies down to our household servants, was never more vigorous than it is now. And more than ever before is the demand for competent men in excess of the supply. What we are all looking for, however, is the ready-made, competent man; the man whom someone else has trained. It is only when we fully realise that our duty, as well as our opportunity, lies in systematically co-operating to train and to make this competent man, instead of hunting for a man whom someone else has trained, that we shall be on the road to national efficiency.
>
> (Taylor 1911: 6)

While working as an engineer, Taylor noticed a large difference between the least and most competent workers' ways of accomplishing their work. To help identify what constitutes competence among the most competent workers, he argued for leadership based on scientific principles from the rationalistic tradition. Based on those principles, he elaborated his well-known 'time and motion studies'. Taylor proposed that by using time and motion studies, management should be able to identify what constitutes workers' competence by classifying, tabulating and reducing it to rules, laws and formulas. Using these descriptions of competence as a starting point, Taylor demonstrated that managers could set up systematic training and development activities that would yield improvements in workers' competence and consequently increase their effectiveness in organisations.

Current rationalistic approaches to competence

The dominant approaches used to identify competence within management today do not consist of time and motion studies, but of job analysis (Armstrong 1991; Cascio 1995; Ferris *et al.* 1990; Gael 1988). However, these approaches are essentially based on scientific principles from the rationalistic research tradition. The most central feature of the rationalistic approaches is that they all regard competence as an *attribute-based phenomenon*. More specifically, within the rationalistic approaches, human competence is described as being constituted by a specific set of attributes such as knowledge and skills, which workers use to accomplish their work. Furthermore, attributes are primarily seen as context-independent. That is, a specific attribute such as 'communication skills' is regarded as having a fixed meaning in itself; it is independent of context and can thus be adopted in a range of work activities.

This view of competence originates in a dualist ontology and objectivist epistemology underlying the rationalistic research tradition (Bernstein 1983; Husserl 1970 [1936]; Rorty 1979; Schön 1983; Searle 1992; Shotter 1992; Winograd and Flores 1986). Within the rationalistic approaches, dualist ontology underlies a division of the phenomenon of competence into two separate entities, namely the worker and the work. The objectivist epistemology, in this instance referring to an objective, knowable work beyond the worker, has led to descriptions of work activities that are independent of the workers who accomplish them. From this 'objective' dualist perspective, it follows that advocates of rationalistic approaches identify and describe human competence as consisting of two independent entities: a list of attributes possessed by the worker, and to a separate list of work activities. Three main approaches can be distinguished: worker-oriented, work-oriented and multimethod-oriented (Sandberg 1994; Veres *et al.* 1990).

Within *worker-oriented approaches,* competence is primarily seen as being constituted by attributes possessed by workers, typically represented as knowledge, skills, abilities (KSA) and personal traits required for effective work performance (Veres *et al.* 1990: 87). More recently, the term 'competencies' has been used to stress further the importance of attending to worker attributes that are strictly work-related (Armstrong 1991; Boyatzis 1982; Kolb 1984; McClelland 1973; Morgan 1988; Nordhaug 1993; Spencer and Spencer 1993; Woodruffe 1990). For instance, Boyatzis (1982: 21, emphasis in original) described a job competency as *'an underlying characteristic of a person* in that it may be a motive, trait, skill, aspect of one's self image or social role, or a body of knowledge he or she uses'. Furthermore, Boyatzis argued that 'because job competencies are *underlying characteristics*, they can be said to be generic' (Boyatzis 1982: 21, emphasis in original). The generic or context-independent nature of job competencies means they can appear in many different work activities. In order to capture the relevant attributes, a group of job incumbents and supervisors is often used. The attributes identified are organised into pre-defined categories such as KSA. Finally, the attributes are rated to allow quantitative measurement of the correlation between success in accomplishing the work and possession of the designated attributes.

While advocates of the worker-oriented approaches take the worker as the point of departure, advocates of *the work-oriented approaches* take the *work* as the point of departure when identifying and describing competence. More specifically, they first identify work activities that are central for accomplishing specific work and then transform those activities into personal attributes.

What distinguishes *the multimethod-oriented approaches* from the others is their more comprehensive approach to competence. For example, Veres *et al.* (1990) adopted a multimethod-oriented approach to identifying competence in the work of police lieutenants. Their description consisted of 46 worker attributes expressed in the form of KSA which corresponded to 23 police activities. The work activities and the KSA description were then quantified in percentage terms relating to police work.

Although rationalistic approaches have continued to contribute to our understanding of competence, their view of competence as a set of attributes has been subjected to increasing criticism recently. One form of criticism is that the rationalistic approaches fail to capture what constitutes competence in a satisfying way. For instance, the worker-oriented approaches have been criticised for producing too general and abstract descriptions of competence. For instance, Jacobs (1989) questioned Boyatzis' (1982) generic model of competence in management, which was used as a basis for Competency Based Assessment Centres in the UK and the USA. In a study of more than 500 hundred organisations in the UK that have used Boyatzis' method, Jacobs concluded that different managerial work requires different competencies.

Moreover, following Attewell (1990), Norris (1991) and Sandberg (1991 1994), the rationalistic operationalisations of attributes into quantitative measures often result in abstract and overly narrow and simplified descriptions of competence. Such descriptions may not adequately represent the complexity of competence in work performance. In addition, the use of KSA and other general models of competence within the rationalistic approaches tends to pre-define what constitutes competence. As Sandberg (1994) argued, there is a risk that such pre-definitions of competence may serve to confirm the researcher's own model of competence, rather than to capture the workers' competence. However, a more basic form of criticism comes from a growing body of studies using interpretative approaches to competence. Their main criticism is that advocates of rationalistic approaches overlook the ways people experience or interpret their work. As a consequence, they are not able to capture central features of competence.

Interpretative approaches to competence

The main feature of the interpretative research tradition is its phenomenological base, which states that the person and the world are inextricably related through the persons' lived experience of the world (Berger and Luckman 1966; Husserl 1970 [1900–01]; Schutz 1945 1953). From this standpoint, competence is not seen as consisting of two separate entities. Instead, worker and work form one entity through lived experience of work. Competence is thus seen as being constituted by the meaning the work takes for the worker in his or her experience of it (Dall'Alba and Sandberg 1996; Sandberg 1994). Hence, the shift in the point of departure – from worker and work as two separate entities, to the workers' lived experience of work – gives rise to an alternative way of understanding what constitutes human competence at work. Several approaches to competence have been adopted within the interpretative research tradition. Examples of these studies, which have particular relevance for further clarifying what constitutes competence at work, will be explored below.

In an interpretative study, Dreyfus and Dreyfus (1986) investigated the acquisition of competence among aeroplane pilots, chess players, automobile drivers and adult learners of a second language. A central finding from their study was that attributes used in accomplishing work are primarily not context-free but, rather, are bound to particular type of work situations, regardless of the level of competence acquisition. Results demonstrated that as soon as workers begin getting experience of a particular type of work they begin acquiring knowledge and skills that are not context-free but, on the contrary, are situational or context-dependent. That attributes acquire context-dependency through workers' experience of their work has also been demonstrated in a range of other interpretative studies, for instance in nursing (Benner 1984), and in ethnographic and ethnomethodological studies of competence within sociology (Atkinson 1988; Barley 1996; Fielding 1988a 1988b; Garfinkel 1986; Kusterer 1978; Livingston 1987).

A central feature of the context-dependent nature of competence is its tacit dimension (Polanyi 1967). In Giddens' terms, workers' competence in performing the work activities in which they are involved is 'largely carried out in practical consciousness' – where practical consciousness 'consists of all the things which actors know tacitly about how to "go on" in the contexts of social life without being able to give them direct discursive expression' (Giddens 1984: xxiii). When viewing attributes as context-free, the tacit dimension of competence is overlooked. For instance, drawing on Orr's (1987a 1987b 1990a 1990b) studies and other recent ethnographic studies of workplace practice, Brown and Duguid (1991: 40) conclude 'that the ways people actually work usually differ fundamentally from the ways organisations describe that work in manuals, training programs, organisational charts, and job descriptions'. In similar vein, Fielding (1988a) compared prescriptive definitions of a competent police officer, such as the job analysis of a police lieutenant by Veres *et al.* (1990), described previously, with the competence in policing experienced by the police officers themselves. One central finding was that skills in policing such as 'observation' and 'negotiation' tend to vary in meaning depending upon the ways in which the particular work situation is experienced. Fielding also found that skills in policing are 'differently endorsed and recognised by different officers' (Fielding 1988a: 48).

Within education, Schön (1983) made a similar point in his criticism of universities and other institutions that educate professional workers. He argued that they are mainly based on a rationalistic epistemology which 'fosters selective inattention to practical competence and professional artistry' (Schön 1983: vii). He examined closely what professional workers such as architects, psychotherapists, engineers, planners and managers actually do when they work. Schön discovered that when accomplishing their work, workers do not select a set of appropriate means in relation to an objective and given work, which is separate from their experience. Instead, when workers encounter their work, they frame and set the problem situations of the work through their experience of it. That is, as workers *frame* their work, the attributes used in performing it are not separate from their experience of it. Instead, workers' attributes are *internally* related to work through their ways of framing specific work situations.

To sum up, the findings from the interpretative studies disclose a context-dependent nature of competence. More specifically, the attributes used in particular work acquire their context-dependent nature through the workers' ways of experiencing that work. Although the interpretative approaches further clarify what constitutes competence by articulating the context-dependent nature of attributes, they do not demonstrate how these attributes are integrated in competent work performance. Another concern is that current interpretative approaches do not explicitly capture the variation in competence which may occur within a group of workers. Dreyfus and Dreyfus, and Benner's interpretative approaches capture a variation in competence, in terms of different levels of competence acquisition. However, their approaches do not describe variations in competence that may occur at any one level, for example, among novices, advanced beginners or experts. In other words, they do not sufficiently explain why some perform work more competently than others.

Competence in engine optimisation: an informing case

Building on previous interpretative research on competence, Sandberg (1994) explored how attributes are integrated in work performance, and attempted to capture the possible variation of workers' competence. Phenomenography was adopted as an interpretative approach to competence. A phenomenographic approach to competence was developed and adopted during an empirical study in the department of engine optimisers at the Volvo Car Company in Sweden. The task for the group of approximately 50 engineers (called engine optimisers) working there was to develop engines for new models of cars. Twenty optimisers were selected for the study, which used mainly interview and observation methods. The research interviews were designed to generate rich accounts of the optimisers' understanding of their work.

Three different ways of understanding engine optimisation emerged from the study: namely, engine optimisation as

- Type I, optimising separate qualities;
- Type II, optimising interacting qualities;
- Type III, optimising from the perspective of customers.

Within each understanding, it was also possible to distinguish a number of essential attributes of competence. More specifically, each understanding was characterised by a specific structure of attributes which appear as the optimisers accomplish the optimisation. Results demonstrated that the particular way of conceiving the optimisation work delimits certain attributes as essential and organises them into a distinctive structure of competence in engine optimisation. Moreover, the different ways of understanding give rise not only to a variation in competence, but also to a hierarchy of competence in engine optimisation, established in terms of an increasingly advanced understanding of engine optimisation. The way each understanding constitutes a distinctive competence in engine optimisation, and together form a hierarchy of competence, is elaborated below.

The most characteristic feature of the least advanced understanding, optimising separate qualities, is that the optimisers express, delimit and organise the optimisation work in terms of a number of separate optimising steps, holding the relation between the monitoring parameters and each single quality of the engine in focus. Within each step they test various adjustments of the parameters to optimise a single engine quality, for example, drivability or fuel consumption, according to stipulated requirements. The optimisers take a single quality and optimise it, continuing with each remaining quality until all qualities meet the requirements. Their focus on the relation between monitoring parameters and single engine quality implies that all their key attributes are centred around that relation, forming a distinctive structure of competence in engine optimisation.

In the second understanding, optimising interacting qualities, the optimisation work is expanded so that it includes not only separate steps but also the relation between the qualities of the engine in each step. The parameter-quality relation, which is in focus in the first understanding, forms a background for the relations between the qualities, which is the focus in the second understanding. Delimiting and organising the optimisation work in interacting steps shifts the focus from the relation between monitoring parameters and single engine quality to the relations between the qualities of the engine. These optimisers take all optimising steps into consideration at each single step: if we optimise a specific quality, what will happen to the remaining engine qualities that will subsequently be optimised? Hence, for these optimisers, the primary aim in each step is to optimise a single quality so that it will interact with the remaining qualities ultimately to produce an approved engine. This change in focus implies that the attributes within this understanding appear from the relations between the qualities of the engine, forming a distinctively different structure of competence in engine optimisation.

In the most advanced understanding, optimising from the perspective of customers, the optimisation work is expanded still further so that it consists not only of an interaction between qualities but also of the relation between the optimised engine and customers' requirements. The relation between qualities of the engine, which is in focus in the second understanding, forms a background for the relation between optimised engine and customers' requirements, which is the focus in the third understanding. Wherever these optimisers are optimising the engine, be it in the testing room or on the road, they drive the car as an ordinary customer would. The optimisers relate the single optimisation situation to the approved car and, in so doing, they try to build in customers' requirements at each step of the process. The attributes appearing within this understanding are all centred around the relation between specific qualities of the engine and the customers' requirements, forming a distinctively different structure of competence compared with the other understandings. Hence, the relationship between the increasingly advanced understanding of engine optimisation and hierarchy of competence in engine optimisation means that Type III understanding comprises all three forms of competence, while Type II comprises two forms of competence and Type I comprises one form of competence in engine optimisation.

A new foundation of human competence

Sandberg's study confirms the results from other interpretative studies: namely, that competence is not constituted in terms of a specific set of context-free attributes, such as knowledge and skills related to a separate work. Instead, the ways in which work is experienced or understood constitute competence. The most central findings generated by the phenomenographic approach is that human competence is not primarily constituted by a specific set of attributes. Instead, workers' knowledge, skills and other attributes used in accomplishing the work are preceded by and based upon the workers' understanding of work. At the same time, Sandberg's study also extends the results from other interpretative approaches through its findings that workers' understanding of work has an integrative function in constituting competence. Results demonstrate that the way of understanding a particular work delimit certain attributes (such as knowledge and skills) as essential and organises them into a distinctive form of competence in performing that work. Moreover, a further extension is the demonstration of a possible variation in competence in a particular work related to ways of understanding that work. In addition, the results from Sandberg's study also demonstrate that these different ways of understanding work form a hierarchy of competence at work in terms of increasing advanced forms of understanding that work.

In conclusion, as Sandberg (forthcoming) pointed out, these results provide insights into the central question of why some perform better than others. Within the rationalistic approaches, those who perform better than others are regarded as possessing a superior set of attributes. However, according to Sandberg's (1994, forthcoming) findings, the variation in work performance is not related first and foremost to a specific set of attributes possessed by those who are regarded as most competent. Instead, the reason why some perform better than others relates to a variation in ways of understanding that work.

However, although individuals' competence is central in performing an organisation's task, it is above all in interaction with other individuals that the task can be performed in an acceptable way. In other words, it is the collective competence of an organisation that shapes the extent to which the organisation will achieve effectiveness and be competitive. Hence, in order to develop a smarter workforce, we need not only to understand what constitutes individual competence but also collective competence at work.

The nature of collective competence

Philip Selznik (1957) was among the first to address the question of what constitutes collective competence. He coined the concept 'distinctive competence' which he defined as a company's superiority to its competitors. According to Selznik, a company's distinctive competence is constituted by an aggregated amount of specific activities that the company is able to perform more effectively than its competitors. Selznick's idea about collective competence was further developed by Sjöstrand (1979, 1985). In defining what constitutes collective competence, Sjöstrand (1979) distinguished between 'competence mass' and 'distinctive competence'. The competence mass consists of an organisation's entire resource base, such as personnel, management, support systems, equipment and suppliers. The competence mass of an organisation is seen as a potential ability to perform a certain task. This means that the 'same' competence mass can be organised in different ways and, as a result, create various forms of distinctive competence.

More recently, the question of what constitutes collective competence has mainly been discussed within resource-based theories of competitive advantage in the area of strategic management (Hofer and Schendel 1978; Snow and Hrebiniak 1980; Hitt and Ireland 1985, 1986; Reed and Jason Huang 1992; Prahalad and Hamel 1990; Leonard-Barton 1992; Mahoney and Pandian 1992; Henderson and Cockburn 1994; Collis 1994; Boisot *et al*. 1995; von Krogh and Roos 1996; Stein 1996). These theories have, however, been criticised as blurred. In an overview of the literature, Leonard-Barton (1992) claimed that descriptions 'such as "unique", "distinctive", "difficult to imitate" or "superior to competition" render the term self-explanatory, especially if reference is also made to "resource deployment" or "skills"' (Leonard-Barton 1992: 112). Based on the overview, she pinpoints the following dimensions of what might constitute collective competence:

- Knowledge and skills possessed by the employees. This dimension is characterised by both firm-specific knowledge and skills and general scientific knowledge.

- Knowledge and skills embedded in technical systems. This dimension expresses an accumulation over years of employees' knowledge and skills codified and structured in technological systems.
- Knowledge created and controlled by the formal and informal managerial systems. For instance, knowledge can be created through apprenticeship and a network of partners and it can be controlled through incentive systems and reporting structures.
- The values and norms assigned to the various knowledge and skills of an organisation and its development. For instance, do the value and norms prefer knowledge creation by formal degrees or by experience?

Leonard-Barton (1992: 114) sees these dimensions as 'an interrelated inter-dependent knowledge system'.

A closer look shows that within the rationalistic research tradition, domi-nant theories about collective competence and its development are based on a cognitive perspective (Cook and Yanow 1993; von Krogh and Roos 1996). According to this perspective 'a prerequisite for organisational knowledge to develop in the organisation is the cardinal distinction between the organi-sation and its environment, e.g., "what do we know about our environ-ment?"' (von Krogh and Roos 1996: 166). This 'cardinal distinction' follows from the dualist ontology and objectivist epistemology underlying the rationalistic research tradition described above. As with rationalistic approaches to individual competence, the assumption of a dualist ontology underlies a division of the phenomenon of collective competence into two separate entities, the collective and work. The objectivist epistemology leads in turn to descriptions of work activities that are independent of the collective which accomplishes them. For instance, with reference to Varela (1992), von Krogh and Roos (1996) argue that the rationalistic assumptions underlying the cognitive perspective encourage its advocates to regard the world as 'pre-given, and that the goal of any cognitive system is to create the most accurate representation of this world' (Krogh *et al.* 1996: 162). Moreover, these mental representations are assumed to be stored and retrieved in specific knowledge structures consisting of schemata and scripts of the individuals. Leonard-Barton's (1992) description of collective competence as a knowledge system is a typical example of how advocates of a cognitive perspective describe the constitution of collective competence.

Towards an interpretative perspective on collective competence

Since rationalistic approaches to collective competence treat the collective and work as two separate entities, they are open to criticisms similar to those raised against rationalistic approaches to individual competence. By separat-ing the organisation from its task, advocates of the cognitive perspective are unable to take into account the ways in which the members of the collective experience, and make sense of, their work. By not taking this into account, advocates of the cognitive perspective risk overlooking fundamental aspects of what may constitute collective competence and its development. Hence, as soon as we separate individuals and work, individuals' understandings of their work are nullified. Hence, descriptions of competence arising from rationalistic approaches are incomplete and, consequently, misleading as a basis for managing and organising competence in organisations. Based on the insight provided by the interpretative approaches to individual competence, I will adopt and elaborate an interpretative approach as a way to further our understanding of what constitutes collective competence.

Shared understanding – the basis for collective competence and its development

A basic question concerning the nature of collective competence is what distinguishes it from individual competence. One major distinction is that collective competence cannot be related to a single individual. Instead, it is characterised by an interaction between several persons in performing a specific work. Hutchin's (1993) description of how a group of people navigate a warship demonstrates that collective competence cannot be related to a single individual. Navigating a large vessel in and out of narrow water requires an interaction between several persons more or less simultaneously. Certainly, each person of the navigation team contributes with a specific competence: such as the bearing taker, bearing-time-recorder, the plotter and the keeper of the deck log. Each single person's competence is, however, insufficient in navigating the vessel in an effective way. It is only when those persons interact with one another that a collective competence in navigation is established.

However, in order to interact, the members of a collective must have some form of *shared understanding* of their work. Differently expressed, if the foundation for the individual's competence is his or her specific understanding of the work, then the basis for collective competence must be a group of individuals' shared understanding of their work. For instance, in order to navigate the vessel adequately, the navigation team must have a reasonable shared understanding of navigating vessels. Without a shared understanding of their work, no cooperative interaction will emerge and, by then, no collective competence will appear in the work performance. Cook and Yanow's (1993) description of flute manufacturing illustrates how the collective's shared understanding of the work forms the basis for their competence in performing the work.

Cook and Yanow identify Haynes, Powell and Brannen Brothers as among the most outstanding flutemaking companies in the world. They focus mainly on Powell's way of manufacturing flutes. For Powell it takes about two weeks to complete a flute. Each flutemaker has developed a specific competence in certain aspects of the flute production. When a flutemaker has completed her aspects of work she hands over the flute to the next flutemaker in the manufacturing process. This means that the second flutemaker's work is based on the previous flutemaker's. Each time the second flutemaker experiences something not completely right he takes the flute back to the previous flutemaker in order to get it reworked. That the flute needs to be reworked is often expressed in vague language such as, 'It doesn't feel right' or 'This piece doesn't look quite right' (Cook and Yanow 1993: 380). The first flutemaker investigates then why the flute 'doesn't feel right'. When she thinks she has found the 'error' and corrected it she checks whether the flute still 'doesn't feel right' to the second flutemaker. This interaction continues until both are satisfied with the result of the reworked flute.

Since the flutes are primarily produced by hand by several craftspersons, no Powell flute is exactly the same. Each has its own personality. Despite the difference between each Powell flute, Cook and Yanow remark that:

> a knowledgeable fluteplayer would never fail to recognize a Powell by the way it feels and plays, nor would she confuse a Powell with a Haynes or a Brannen Brothers. Each Powell flute, although unique, shares an unambiguous family resemblance with all other Powells. This family resemblance is the essence of Powell style and quality. And although each Powell has its own personality and aspects of the flute's physical design have been changed from time to time, the Powell style has been maintained. In this sense, a Powell flute made 50 years ago plays and feels the same as one made recently.
>
> (Cook and Yanow 1993: 380–381)

Cook and Yanow's observation that Powell has been manufacturing flutes with a recognisable style and quality for over 50 years indicates that the company's collective competence transcends both the single flutemaker as well as earlier generations of flutemakers. More specifically, Powell's ability to produce a flute with a recognisable style and quality over time is based on an instituted shared understanding of how a Powell should play and feel. This instituted shared understanding, and thus collective competence, can only be acquired fully by being socialised into the collective performance of Powell flutes: that is, to be socialised into Powell's specific way of understanding flute manufacturing. Socialisation, however, involves not only that individuals develop and maintain a specific understanding. Above all, it involves how a collective develops and maintains a specific understanding of their work. According to Cook and Yanow, when a new member is:

> socialised or acculturated into the organisation, learning by the organisation takes place: The organisation learns how to maintain the style and quality of its flutes through the particular skills, character and quirks of the new individual. The organisation engages in a dynamic process of maintaining the norms and practices that assure the constancy of the

product . . . It is an active reaffirmation of maintenance of the know-how that the organisation already possesses.

(Cook and Yanow 1993: 381–382)

If the members' shared understanding of their work is the basis for collective competence, the process that constitutes the shared understanding becomes crucial for how the collective competence is developed and maintained. As the Powell example illustrates, the members of the collective are constantly involved in making sense of their work – what their work is about, and what it means to manufacture Powell flutes. New members are socialised into the collective by being involved in the ongoing meaning-making which gives them a certain understanding of the Powell work and, by then, also a specific orientation and direction in performing the work. In other words, the members' shared understanding of work is cultivated, refined and maintained through their ongoing involvement in collectively making sense of their work.

Collective competence as culture

Adopting a cultural perspective offers a way of further exploring how collective competence is developed and maintained within a collective's 'sense making' of their work. Current research within organisations and management contains a number of different cultural perspectives on organisations (for an overview, see for instance, Alvesson 1993; Alvesson and Berg 1992; Frost *et al.* 1985). The symbolic cultural perspective is closely related to the interpretative approach adopted and developed in this chapter. Alvesson and Björkman (1992) characterise the symbolic cultural perspective as focusing

> on what is common for a certain group: the understanding, those patterns of interpretations and decipherments which help individuals to relate to an intersubjective world, that is, a social reality which to a considerable extent are experienced as similar. Shared symbols are of importance here: material things, patterns of actions, specific events and language use which denote distinctive views and significations and which give guidelines for orientation in life.
>
> (Alvesson and Björkman 1992: 21, translated from Swedish)

When adopting a cultural perspective, collective competence can be regarded as being constituted by a system of shared symbols that denote the central meaning aspects of the collective's work performance. A company's product is an example of a shared symbol which denotes a central meaning aspect of collective competence. For instance, the Powell flutes express a certain meaning to those craftspersons who manufacture them. At a certain step in the manufacturing process the flute denotes that it has reached a certain

Powell style and quality, which makes it possible to pass it on to the next step.

The physical layout of the work design is another example of a central symbol. It expresses a specific work flow in the production which symbolises central meaning aspects of the collective competence in flutemaking. Moreover, symbols such as organisational stories and sagas express criteria, norms and procedures for how to perform the work and, by then, also central meaning aspects of collective competence. For instance, stories can be about 'how-one-does-here' in this particular step in the flute production. The rites and rituals, ceremonies and celebrations which belong to a specific collective also help its members to develop, formulate and maintain a shared understanding of their work.

Seeing shared symbols as constituents for collective competence provides one explanation for why a company such as Powell is able to manufacture flutes with a recognisable style and quality year after year despite the fact that several generations of flutemakers have come and gone. In order for the symbols to be shared they have to be handed over from the more experienced flutemakers to the newcomers. The newcomers are not regarded as fully fledged members of Powell until they have embodied the meaning of the shared symbols that denote Powell's distinctive competence in flute making. The extent to which new and other members act according to the shared symbols of their work is continuously maintained in interaction between the members.

Thus, the symbols can be seen as shaping and maintaining the development of Powell's distinctive collective competence in flute making. More specifically, the symbols that denote the shared understanding of their work are embedded in the daily practice on which they stand. The symbols create a feeling of security and identity in work performance. They tell the flutemakers how to act and who they are: we manufacture flutes in this way and we manufacture Powell flutes. Those symbols become more and more taken for granted the longer time the flutemakers are involved in manufacturing flutes. The flutemakers need almost only to look at a piece of work in order to understand each other. It is only when a new member enters the collective that the other flutemakers have to consciously articulate why a piece of work 'doesn't feel right'.

Formation of collective competence through symbols

As the shared symbols denote a collective's specific understanding of its work, they can be seen as *forming* the collective's distinctive competence. The specific formation of shared symbols functions as a basis and direction for the members in developing and maintaining a distinctive collective competence. IKEA, the Swedish furniture company, can serve to demonstrate further how collective competence is formed through shared symbols. The most basic shared symbols at IKEA are the nine propositions formulated by Ingvar Kamprad (1976), the founder of IKEA, in '*A Furniture Trader's Will*'. For example, 'the assortment – our identity; achieving good results through small means; simplicity is a virtue; to take responsibility – a benefit; most work is undone – wonderful future'.

The will is introduced by a general description of how IKEA understands the furniture business, namely, 'to create a better everyday life for the many people'. IKEA workers see their work as being to develop functional and beautiful furniture that most people can afford to buy. This general description symbolises a certain understanding of the furniture business and also a specific basis for the development and maintenance of a distinctive competence. Furthermore, the distinctive character of IKEA's competence is not only that the workers should be able to develop functional and beautiful furniture but also that most people should be able to afford this furniture. Kamprad's propositions concretise IKEA's distinctive competence formation by symbolising central aspects of IKEA's understanding of the furniture business.

For example, the first proposition, 'the assortment – our identity', is fundamental to IKEA's competence in the furniture business. It symbolises that IKEA should provide a wide assortment of beautiful and functional home furnishings at prices most people can afford. IKEA should strive to provide an assortment that may be used to furnish every space at home, inside as well as out. Moreover, the assortment should have a distinct IKEA profile characterised by simplicity and should be durable and easy to appreciate. Further, the assortment should appeal to every age. Its functionality and technical quality should be of a high standard. The quality should, however, not be an end in itself but be adjusted to customers' needs. The basic intention is to strive for a low price but without reducing the functionality and technical quality of the assortment. This proposition is also sometime labelled 'flat parcels – low price' (Axelsson 1995). Flat parcels have been an IKEA symbol, denoting that IKEA shares the furniture business with the customer. IKEA provides, in flat parcels, prefabricated furniture which customers assemble themselves. Thus, the proposition 'the assortment – our identity' symbolises some of the most basic meaning aspects of IKEA's distinctive competence in the furniture business. It expresses a specific competence in designing functional and beautiful furniture at a low price. Moreover, it expresses a specific competence in how furniture should be designed to be easy to assemble. Further, this first proposition expresses a specific competence in storage and logistics within IKEA.

How these shared symbols generate a distinctive formation as a basis and direction for developing and maintaining IKEA's competence in the furniture business becomes clear when a new furniture store is established outside Sweden. Establishing a completely new furniture store means that a completely new group of people has to develop the distinctive IKEA competence.

Salzer's (1994) study about IKEA's culture demonstrates that the informal network of Swedish managers and decorators is the most important ingredient in establishing a new furniture store. The Swedish managers and decorators build up the new furniture store and train the new personnel. In most cases, a Swedish manager runs the store for up to a year before the business is handed over to a local manager.

IKEA always uses a group of Swedes to establish a new furniture store because they are carriers of IKEA's specific culture – they are able to form IKEA's distinctive competence in the furniture business through a shared set of symbols. Through speech and action this group communicates a set of basic shared symbols that express IKEA's understanding of, and distinctive competence in, the furniture business. The fact that IKEA has been able to establish more than 100 similar stores in more than 20 different countries has largely to do with the formation of IKEA's competence through a clear set of shared symbols.

A collective's shared understanding of work is, then, the most basic feature of collective competence. This shared understanding is constituted through members' ongoing sense making of their work. Through ongoing sense-making of work, a shared understanding is gradually instituted and embodied in the constitution of a distinctive competence in work performance.

Furthermore, as with interpretative studies of individual competence, the interpretative inquiry of what constitutes collective competence provides insights into why some companies perform a particular kind of work – such as transporting or education – better than others. Within rationalistic approaches, companies performing a particular work better than others are seen as possessing a superior set of shared attributes like knowledge and skills in that work. However, according to the interpretative approach developed here, variation in work performance is not first and foremost related to a specific set of shared attributes possessed by those companies seen as superior or most successful. Rather, superior company performance is linked to variations in ways of understanding that work. Powell's success is related to its workers' shared understanding of flute manufacturing, which constitutes a unique and distinctive competence in flute manufacturing. The reason IKEA is so successful in the furniture business is related to its workers' shared understanding of the furniture business.

Creating a smarter workforce through competence development

The interpretative approaches discussed and elaborated upon in this chapter provide an alternative to the rationalistic way of creating a smarter workforce through competence development. Findings from interpretative approaches show that the attributes developed by an individual or a collective are stipulated by their understanding of work. Development of particular knowledge and skills always takes place within a specific understanding of work. Thus, only when individuals and groups of individuals change their present understanding of work to an alternative understanding of work are they able to develop a new form of competence in their work. Hence, from an interpretative perspective, two basic forms of competence development exist: (i) changing the present understanding of work, and (ii) developing and deepening the present way of understanding work.

Seeing competence development as a change in understanding has major implications for how we design and conduct training and development activities for creating a smarter workforce. In particular, it presents a challenge to the development of activities proposed by the dominant rationalistic approaches, which approach competence development as a matter of acquiring the particular set of attributes supposed to constitute a given competence. On that view of competence, the overriding principle for developing competence is *transferring* knowledge and skills considered to be important to those workers who do not possess them. The human resource specialist selects from a list of required attributes those that should be included in a training and development programme. Developing workers' competence focuses on the selected attributes, with the aim of transferring these attributes as efficiently as possible to the workers. Depending upon the features of the attributes, various activities, such as classroom teaching, on-the-job training and job rotation, are used to transfer attributes to workers.

From an interpretative perspective the rationalistic principle of transferring attributes appears problematic. If we take attributes as the point of departure we are unable to encourage development of a particular understanding. Moreover, transferring attributes may actually encourage *less* desirable understandings of work, by simply reinforcing ways of understanding the work in question in terms of attributes. Instead of transferring attributes, findings from interpretative studies suggest changing workers' understanding of work is the basic principle for developing competence in organisations. Identifying the most effective means for accomplishing such changes can only be fully explored empirically. Based on earlier work (Sandberg 1994), I will identify some basic guiding principles that may facilitate the development of competence through changing understanding of work.

Developing individuals' competence

Accepting that the fundamental guiding principle for developing competence is to take workers' understanding of their work as the point of departure does not mean that development activities such as classroom teaching, apprenticeship, on-the-job training and job rotation should be abandoned. Instead, development activities need to be designed and conducted in ways that actively promote changes in workers' understanding of their work. The description of competence in engine optimisation can serve as an example to illustrate competence development as changing the understanding of work. For instance, in enabling optimisers with Type II understanding (optimising interacting qualities) to achieve Type III understanding (optimising from the customers' perspective), the point of departure must be the optimisers' present understanding of optimisation work. Without stimulating reflection on their present ways of understanding the work, there is an increasing risk that these optimisers will not achieve the desired understanding. Taking the desired understanding as the point of departure runs the risk that the only development that occurs among the optimisers may involve transforming attributes of this desired way into the present ways of understanding the optimisation work. The optimisers might then continue to pursue optimisation in much the same way as previously.

Another central guiding principle is to organise particular encounters between the workers and their work as developmental triggers. Setting up encounters between the workers and specific work problems can be seen as directed 'reflective practicum' situations, which Schön (1987) suggested for the school context, and which is being applied here to the workplace. The aim of presenting a challenge is to stimulate reflection among the optimisers about their present ways of understanding optimisation work: why is it not possible to accomplish the encountered optimisation situation in an appropriate way? What is inappropriate in our present competence in accomplishing it? The encounter must also be organised in such a way that when the optimisers begin to realise the limitations of their present understanding the desired understanding is revealed as an alternative way of accomplishing it. However, a shift from one understanding to another is unlikely to take place through a single encounter between optimiser and organised optimisation situation. Even if optimisers change their way of understanding the optimisation situation and begin to understand it according to the desired understanding, they may revert to their former understanding when encountering a new optimisation situation. Therefore, the development of competence is more likely to proceed as a chain of changes in understanding different work situations, rather than a single, major change. In order to reinforce and refine a certain understanding, it is necessary to organise multiple encounters between the workers and the work. Those encounters must highlight the attributes of the newly achieved understanding in different situations.

So far, I have mainly discussed how individuals develop competence by changing their ways of understanding their work. However, as described earlier, individuals' competence at work is not isolated but always embedded in a collective competence. Therefore, further elaboration of how to create a smarter workforce from an interpretative perspective calls for an exploration of the development of collective competence in terms of changing the understanding of work.

Developing collective competence

How a collective develops and maintains a distinctive competence within its present understanding of the work in terms of the development of a shared set of symbols was partly described earlier via the examples of Powell and IKEA. It was argued that both Powell's and IKEA's competence was constituted by a set of shared symbols developed, sustained and changed in communication between the members of Powell and IKEA respectively. Orr's description of service technicians learning at work, reported by Brown and Duguid (1991), can be used to illustrate more specifically how collective competence is developed and sustained through shared symbols in terms of a specific storytelling. On one occasion a service technician received a phone call from a machine operator who complained about a troublesome machine. The technician tried to solve the machine problem both by following formal problem-solving procedures and by using his own tricks of the trade, but without success. He called a specialist but the specialist was not able to repair the troublesome machine.

In an attempt to make sense of the encountered problem the technician and the specialist started to tell stories about the machine error. The stories were made up by investigating the machine through trying to remember earlier occasions where they encountered similar symptoms. Each story generated one possible explanation of the machine error which could be tested at the same time as new insights were produced. In that way the technician and the specialist could generate several new tests and stories. Gradually, their stories made up a more and more coherent explanation of the machine error. After about five hours they had created a story that generated a 'sufficient interplay among memories, tests, the machine's responses, and the ensuing insights to lead to diagnosis and repair' (Brown and Duguid 1991: 44). Through the process of storytelling the service technician and the specialist had created a shared understanding of the previously incomprehensible machine error. They developed both their own competence and the service technicians' collective competence. Moreover, this story became an integrated part of the service technicians' collective competence. A few months later, Orr reported she heard an identical version of this story told in the service technicians' lunch room.

Some situations, however, cannot be dealt with by developing competence within the present understanding of work. Such situations emerge, for instance, when collective competence is questioned because it does not generate the expected result. A crucial condition for a collective to develop a new distinctive competence in such cases is that they change their present shared understanding of their work to a qualitatively different understanding. Edström *et al.*'s (1989) study of SAS and its change from being an airline company to becoming a travel company is one illustrative example of how a new distinctive competence can be developed by changing the employees' understanding of their work.

SAS's understanding of itself as an airline company had developed and been maintained since the company's inception in 1946. A number of central shared symbols had been established which formed a distinctive SAS competence in the airline business. The general focus was highly production-oriented. The technical production of air travel was placed at the centre in SAS. The aircraft, its technical quality and safety were the most central symbols forming SAS's distinctive competence in the airline business. The overarching motto was to improve continuously the production of air travel by maintaining high technical quality and safety. They also invested heavily in new, more technically advanced and safer aircrafts and in advanced equipment for maintenance.

SAS's understanding of itself as a production-oriented airline was successful while the market continued to grow. During the 1970s, however, SAS became less successful as competition among airlines intensified and the market began to reach saturation point. The company entered a downward spiral. Less and less profit was generated and, during the financial year 1979/80, SAS made a loss for the first time in 17 years. More and more people within SAS started to doubt whether it was possible to continue to run the airline business as they had been doing. However, since management to a large extent embodied current SAS understanding of the airline business, they had difficulty in seeing how SAS could run the airline business in a different way. Instead, they tried to stop the accelerating losses by cost rationalisations. What was rationalised most was, however, not the technical production of air travel but the already neglected customer service dimension. Those reductions generated even more dissatisfied customers, a deteriorating internal climate and further financial problems. In the end, the general management of SAS reached a situation which they could not master. Jan Carlzon entered the scene and began the work of changing SAS from an airline company into a travel company.

One central phase in such a change process is to formulate an alternative understanding of the airline business. Since a collective's understanding is materialised in routines and systems it is often taken for granted: 'This is the way we do it here!' Thus, without an alternative understanding it is difficult for those who are acting within a certain understanding to be aware of the way in which they understand their work. One central reason why Jan Carlzon and the other new managers were able to create an alternative understanding of the airline business was that they had both different work experiences and different educational backgrounds than the previous leadership. Jan Carlzon and other new managers had educational backgrounds in business, whereas the previous managers all had technical expertise. Carlzon and many of the other new managers also had work experience from travel agencies and other customer-related companies and, as a consequence, they began understanding the SAS airline business as a travel company.

This new understanding of SAS came to form the basis for developing a qualitatively different distinctive competence in the airline business. Whereas the aircraft were the main focus in the old SAS understanding, the customer became the centre of attention in the new SAS understanding of the airline business. When the customer is placed at the centre, the customer relation is no longer seen as a single relation. Instead, the relations to the customer are seen as a whole chain of relations, such as ticket purchase, check-in, service in the aircraft, punctuality and baggage handling. All these links in the chain influence how customers experienced travel with SAS.

The new leadership tried to make the meaning of SAS as a travel company visible through a set of new symbols. The most basic symbols forming the understanding of SAS as a travel company were summarised by the new leadership in six propositions described by Edström *et al.* (1989): the customer is the basis of SAS business; customer service must be adjusted to different customers and to competitors' behaviour; customers must judge the entire service chain as positive; each customer should be treated individually; network with other airlines to develop attractive travel routes; and create a more flexible organisation that can manage a dynamic and competitive intensive environment.

Through an intensive communication programme of the above system of symbols, most SAS employees became involved in intensive meaning-making of their work and a development of a new distinctive competence in the airline business. The first step in this meaning-making process was to involve top management and, subsequently, middle management and the remaining employees. One way to communicate with all employees was to present the new SAS direction in a pamphlet called *'Carlzon's Little Red'*. This mainly expressed the central theses described above. The new understanding was also gradually materialised and embodied through a number of local change programmes initiated throughout the company. Their purpose was to materialise the new understanding in routines and systems.

To manage the change process, top SAS managers worked hard to develop a more active and dialogue-based leadership among 200 SAS middle managers. For example, one aim for the middle managers was to start up local study circles and engage the employees to reflect actively on what SAS as a travel company would mean for them and their specific work. The study circles generated a number of concrete suggestions as to how the local activities such as routines and systems could be developed. Those suggestions were, to a large extent, also implemented as a way of gradually changing SAS from an airline company to a travel company. In other words, a new distinctive competence in the airline business was developed.

Conclusion

In the introduction to this chapter, the issue of what constitutes competence was identified as the basis for creating a smart workforce. It was argued that understanding what constitutes competence is crucial in order to develop competence effectively and, thus, create a smarter workforce. Ever since

Taylor (1911), rationalistic approaches to competence have been the main route to creating a smarter workforce. Their view of competence as constituted by a specific set of attributes such as knowledge and skills in accomplishing work has been the basis for competence development. More specifically, competence at work has been identified and described in terms of a specific set of attributes. With such descriptions of competence as the basis, advocates of rationalistic approaches regard competence development as transferring important attributes such as knowledge and skills to those persons who do not possess them. Hence, following rationalistic approaches to creating a smarter workforce implies first, identifying the set of specific attributes that constitutes the competence of the smartest workers and second, transferring those attributes to workers who do not possess them.

The interpretative approaches discussed and elaborated provide a challenge to the rationalistic route to a smarter workforce. The main findings from the interpretative approaches demonstrate that competence is not first and foremost constituted by a set of attributes but, rather, by workers' ways of understanding their work. An alternative view of developing competence flows from the view of competence as constituted by ways of understanding work. Instead of transferring attributes, changing the understanding of work is seen as the most fundamental form of competence development. Ways of creating a smarter workforce by developing competence in terms of changing the understanding of work were explored at both individual and collective levels. However, developing competence by changing or influencing the understanding of work has been poorly elaborated in comparison to ways of transferring attributes. Thus, further research is needed that highlights how changes in understanding take place and how such changes can be facilitated to enhance competence at work and, thus, create a smarter workforce.

References

Alvesson, M. (1989) *Ledning av kunskapsföretag* (Managing Knowledge-intensive Firms), Stockholm: Norstedts.

Alvesson, M. (1993) 'Cultural-ideological modes of management control: a theory and a case study of a professional service company'. In S. Deetz (ed), *Communication Yearbook* (16: pp. 3–42), Newbury Park: Sage.

Alvesson, M. and Berg, P. (1992) *Corporate Culture and Organisational Symbolism*. Berlin: Walter de Gruyter.

Alvesson, M. and Björkman, I. (1992) *Organisationsidentitet och organisationsbyggande (Organisational Identity and Building Organisations)*. Lund: Studentlitteratur.

Armstrong, M. (1991) *A Handbook of Personnel Management Practice*. London: Kogan Page.

Atkinson, P. (1988) 'Ethnomethodology: a critical review', *Annual Review of Sociology* 14: 441–465.

Attewell, P. (1990) 'What is skill?' *Work and Occupations* 4: 422–448.

Axelsson, T. (1995) 'The culture of IKEA'. Seminar given at Stockholm School of Economics.

Bäcklund, A-K. (1994) *Just-in-time. Hur industriella rationaliseringsprocesser formar arbetsdelning och kompetens.* (Just-in-time: How Rationalisation Processes Form Division of Work and Competence). Lund: Lund University Press.

Barley, S. (1996) 'Technicians in the workplace: ethnographic evidence for bringing work into organisation studies', *Administrative Science Quarterly* 41: 404–441.

Benner, P. (1984) *From Novice to Expert. Excellence and Power in Clinical Nursing Practice.* San Francisco: Addison-Wesley.

Berger, L. and Luckmann, T. (1966) *The Social Construction of Reality.* Harmondsworth: Penguin.

Bernstein, R. (1983) *Beyond Objectivism and Relativism: Science, Hermeneutics, and Praxis.* Philadelphia: University of Pennsylvania Press.

Boisot, M., Griffiths, D. and Moles, V. (1995) 'The dilemma of competence: Differentiation versus integration in the pursuit of learning'. Paper presented at the *Third International Workshop on Competence-Based Competition*, Ghent.

Boyatzis, R. E. (1982) *The Competent Manager.* New York: Wiley.

Brown, J. S. and Duguid, P. (1991) 'Organisational learning and communities-of-practice: toward a unified view of working, learning and innovation', *Organisational Science* 1: 40–57.

Cascio, W. F. (1995) *Managing Human Resources: Productivity, Quality of Work Life, Profits.* New York: McGraw-Hill.

Collis, D. J. (1994) 'Research note: how valuable are organisational capabilities?' *Strategic Management Journal* 15: 143–152.

Cook, S. and Yanow, D. (1993) 'Culture and organisational learning', *Journal of Management Inquiry* 2: 373–390.

Dall' Alba, G. and Sandberg, J. (1996) 'Educating for competence in professional practice', *Instructional Science* 24: 411–437.

Dreyfus, H. L. and Dreyfus, S. E. (1986) *Mind over Machine. The Power of Human Intuition and Expertise in the Era of the Computer.* New York: Free Press.

Edström, A., Norbäck, L-E. and Rehndal, J. (1989) *Ledarskapets förnyelse (Renewing the Leadership).* Stockholm: Norstedts.

Ekstedt, E. (1988) *Humankapital i brytningstid: Kunskapsuppbyggnad och förnyelse för företag (Human Capital in Transition: Knowledge Development and Renewal of Companies).* Stockholm: Allmänna förlaget.

Eliasson, G., Fölster, S., Lindberg, T., Pousette, T. and Taymaz, E. (1990) *The Knowledge Based Information Economy.* Stockholm: Almqvist and Wiksell International.

Ellström, P-E. (1992) *Kompetens, utbildning och lärande i arbetslivet: Problem, begrepp och teoretiska perspektiv* (Competence, Education and Learning in Working Life: Problems, Concepts and Theoretical Perspectives), Stockholm: Publica.

Ferris, G. R., Rowland, K. M. and Buckley, R. M. (eds) (1990) *Human Resource Management: Perspectives and Issues.* Boston: Allyn and Bacon.

Fielding, N. G. (1988a) 'Competence and culture in the police', *Sociology* 22: 45–64.

Fielding, N. G. (1988b) *Joining Forces. Police Training, Socialization, and Occupational Competence.* London: Routledge.

Frost, P. J. (ed) (1985) *Organisational Culture.* Newbury Park: Sage.

Gael, S. (ed) (1988) *The Job Analysis Handbook for Business, Industry and Government.* Volume I, II. New York: Wiley.

Garfinkel, H. (ed) (1986) *Ethnomethodological Studies of Work*. London: Routledge and Kegan Paul.

Giddens, A. (1984) *The Constitution of Society. Outline a Theory of Structuration*. Cambridge: Polity Press.

Henderson, R. and Cockburn, I. (1994) 'Measuring competence? Exploring the firm effects in pharmaceutical research', *Strategic Management Journal* 15: 63–84.

Hitt, M. A. and Ireland, D. R. (1985) 'Corporate distinctive competence, strategy, industry and performance', *Strategic Management Journal* 6: 273–293.

Hitt, M. A. and Ireland, D. R. (1986) 'Relationships among corporate level distinctive competencies, diversification strategy, corporate structure and performance', *Journal of Management Studies* 23: 400–416.

Hofer, C. W. and Schendel, D. (1978) *Strategy Formulation: Analytical Concepts*. Minnesota: West.

Husserl, E. (1970 [1900–01]) *Logical Investigations*. Volume II (translated by J. N. Findlay). London: Routledge and Kegan Paul.

Husserl, E. (1970 [1936]) *The Crisis of European Sciences and Transcendental Phenomenology* (translated by David Carr). Evanston: Northwestern University Press.

Hutchin, E. (1993) 'Learning to navigate', In S. Chaiklin and J. Lave (eds) *Understanding Practice. Perspectives on Activitity and Context*. London: Cambridge University Press.

Jacobs, R. (1989) 'Evaluating managerial performance: The need for more innovative approaches'. Paper presented at the meeting of the *European Foundation for Management Development on Knowledge as a Corporate Asset: An International Perspective*, Barcelona, Spain.

Kamprad, I. (1976) *A Furniture Trader's Will*. IKEA International A/S.

Kanter, R. M. (1983) *The Change Masters. Corporate Entrepreneurs at Work*, London: Unwin Hyman.

Kusterer, K. C. (1978) *Know-How on the Job: The Important Working Knowledge of 'Unskilled' Workers*. Boulder, CO: Westview.

Leonard-Barton, D. (1992) 'Core capabilities and core rigidities: a paradox in managing new product development', *Strategic Management Journal* 13: 111–125.

Lindmark, L. (ed) (1990) *Kunskap som kritisk resurs*. (Knowledge as a Critical Resources), Handelshögskolan i Umeå: Umeå universitet.

Livingston, E. (1987) *Making Sense of Ethnomethodology*. London: Routledge and Kegan Paul.

Mahoney, J. T. and Pandian, R. J. (1992) 'The resource-based view within the conversation of strategic management', *Strategic Management Journal* 13: 363–380.

Neef, D. (1998) *The Knowledge Economy*. Boston: Butterworth-Heinemann.

Norris, N. (1991) 'The trouble with competence', *Cambridge Journal of Education* 3: 331–341.

Orr, J. (1987a) 'Narratives at work: story telling as cooperative diagnostic activity', *Field Service Manager* June, 47–60.

Orr, J. (1987b) *Talking about Machines: Social Aspects of Expertice*. Report from the Intelligent Systems Laboratory, Xerox Palo Alto Research Center, Palo Alto, CA.

Orr, J. (1990a) 'Talking about machines: an ethnography of a modern job'. PhD Thesis, Cornell University.

Orr, J. (1990b) 'Sharing knowledge, celebrating identity: war stories and community memory in a service culture', in D. S. Middleton and D. Edwards (eds), *Collective Remembering: Memory in Society*. Beverley Hills, CA: Sage.

Polanyi, M. (1967) *The Tacit Dimension*. London: Routledge and Kegan Paul.

Porter, M. E. (1990) *The Competitive Advantage of Nations*. London: Macmillan Press.

Prahalad, C. K. and Hamel, G. (1990) 'The core competence of the corporation', *Harvard Business Review* 3: 79–91.

Reed, R. and Jason Huang, H. (1992) 'Moving targets: reinvesting in distinctive competence'. Paper presented at the *Business Policy and Strategy Division of the Annual Academy of Management Meeting*, Las Vegas, NV.

Rorty, R. (1979) *Philosophy and the Mirror of Nature*. Princeton, NJ: Princeton University Press.

Salzer, M. (1994) *Identity Across Borders. A Study in the 'IKEA-world'*. Linköping Studies in Management and Economics, Dissertations No 27.

Sandberg, J. (1991) *Competence as Intentional Achievement: A Phenomenographic Study*. Paper presented at the Tenth International Human Science Research Association, Göteborg, Sweden.

Sandberg, J. (1994) *Human Competence at Work: An Interpretative Approach*. Göteborg: Bas.

Sandberg, J. (forthcoming) 'Understanding human competence at work: an interpretative perspective', *Academy of Management Journal*.

Schön, D. A. (1983) *The Reflective Practitioner. How Professionals Think in Action*. New York: Basic Books.

Schön, D. A. (1987) *Educating the Reflective Practitioner. Toward a New Design for Teaching and Learning in the Professions*. San Francisco: Jossey-Bass.

Schutz, A. (1945) 'On multiple realities', *Philosophy and Phenomenological Research, A Quarterly Journal* 5: 533–575.

Schutz, A. (1953) 'Common-sense and scientific interpretation of human action', *Philosophy and Phenomenological Research, A Quarterly Journal* 14: 1–37.

Searle, J. (1992) *The Rediscovery of the Mind*. Cambridge, MA: The MIT Press.

Selznick, P. (1957) *Leadership in Administration*. New York: Harper and Row.

Sjöstrand, S. E. (1979) 'Stagnation, kris och kompetens' ('Stagnation, crisis and competence'), in B. Hedberg and S. E. Sjöstrand (eds), *Från företagskriser till industripolitik*, pp. 71–89. Malmö: Liber.

Sjöstrand, S. E. (1985) *Samhällsorganisation (Society's Organisation)*. Lund: Doxa.

Shotter, J. (1992) '"Getting in touch": the meta-methodology of a postmodern science of mental life', in Steinar Kvale (ed), *Psychology and Postmodernism*, pp. 58–73. London: Sage.

Snow, C. C. and Hrebiniak, G. L. (1980) 'Strategy, distinctive competence, and organisational performance', *Administrative Science Quarterly* 25: 317–336.

Spencer, L. M. and Spencer, S. M. (1993) *Competence at Work. Models for Superior performance*. New York: Wiley.

Starbuck, W. (1992) 'Learning by knowledge-intensive firms', *Journal of Management Studies* 6: 537–554.

Stein, J. (1996) *Lärande inom och mellan organisation (Learning Within and Between Organisations)*. Lund: Studentlitteratur.

Sveiby, K-E. and Risling, A. (1986) *Kunskapsföretaget – Seklets viktigaste ledarutmaning?* (The Knowledge Company – The Most Important Management Challenge in this Century?), Malmö: Liber.

Taylor, F. W. (1911) *The Principles of Scientific Management*. New York: Harper.

Varela, F. J. (1992) 'Whence perceptual meaning? A cartography of current ideas', in F. J. Varela and J. P. Dupuy (eds), *Understanding Origins: Contemporary Views on the Origin of Life, Mind and Society*, Dordrecht: Kluwer.

Veres III, J. G., Locklear, T. S. and Sims, R. R. (1990) 'Job analysis in practice: a brief review of the role of job analysis in human resources management', in G. R. Ferris, K. M. Rowland and R. M. Buckley (eds), *Human Resource Management: Perspectives and Issues*, pp. 79–103. Boston: Allyn and Bacon.

von Krogh, G. and Roos, J. (eds) (1996) *Managing Knowledge. Perspectives on Cooperation and Competition*. London: Sage.

Winograd, T. and Flores. F. (1986) *Understanding Computers and Cognition: A New Foundation for Design*. Norwood, NJ: Ablex.

Woodruffe, C. (1990) *Assessment Centers: Identifying and Developing Competence*. London: Institute of Personnel Management.

4 Experience, common sense and expertise in workplace learning

Rod Gerber

Two workplaces

Juanita Capella and Dennis Cairns are two Australian workers who are employed in quite different industries. Juanita is an apprentice papermaker in a large paper manufacturing plant and Dennis is an experienced plant operator for a large cotton farm. Both people are dedicated to their work, but they obviously have differing amounts of experience in their respective work – Juanita, as an apprentice papermaker, is learning her job, whereas Dennis has been in his job for almost 20 years and knows all aspects of his work thoroughly.

Both Juanita and Dennis bring different life experiences to their work. Juanita, a 22-year-old, completed her secondary schooling, did not want to go on to higher education and so searched for a job. She had trouble finding permanent work and settled on a sales assistant position in a large department store. While at school she developed an interest in how motor vehicles worked and she learned at weekends to strip and assemble car engines. She had a talent for things mechanical. She became bored with her sales job, tried to find other work and eventually became unemployed at 20. This enforced 'freedom' gave her more time to work on mechanical items, and so when the chance for an apprenticeship in the papermaking plant emerged, Juanita was ready for a new challenge. She had mechanical skills, a fairly broad view of the world from working, recreating and being unemployed. Most of all, she was eager to learn in a world of mechanical 'toys'. As an apprentice papermaker, Juanita was a member of a self-managed work team. She had to complete some formal training during her apprenticeship. However, she learned most from her work colleagues. She asked numerous questions, tried some approaches based on her intuition, obtained advice from skilled workers and even gave advice to more senior staff. For Juanita, this apprenticeship enabled for her to bloom as a decisive, learning employee.

Dennis found himself at quite a different stage of his working life. He had left school aged 15 years (at that time the minimum school-leaving age). He attended the local vocational training college and gained a machinery certificate, which he used to obtain work as a machine operator on a grain farm. He

There, he worked with two other adults, operating different kinds of machines, tractors, planters and harvesters, during different stages of the grain production cycle. After a few years, this work became monotonous and so Dennis looked around for a different job involving farm machinery. The cotton industry was starting up in his region and several large companies were advertising for experienced machinery operators. Dennis did not know what machines were used on cotton farms, but he convinced the farm manager that he had the skills, the experience, the common sense and the motivation to be successful. He won this job 20 years ago and he is still doing it today, even though he has been promoted to the position of machinery supervisor. He now has a chance to share his expertise, which he has developed using large cotton machines, earthmoving machines, cultivators, harvesters and trucks – with fellow operators. He is respected as one of the smartest operators in the region and his confidence is reflected in the performance of the operators on the large farm.

Learning for life using experience, common sense and expertise in workplace learning

Robert Kegan (1994) in his intriguing publication, *In Over our Heads: The Mental Demands of Modern Life*, paints a complex picture of the mental demands that are made on people in their various life roles. In their public and private lives, people experience mental challenges through such roles as parenting, partnering, working, healing and learning. To be successful in these roles, it is necessary for people to act according to different 'orders of consciousness' or principles of mental organisation. Kegan (1994: 314–315) identifies five such 'orders':

- Single point, impulsive momentary and illogical perceiving.
- Concrete, logical thinking involving organising things from a distinct point of view.
- Cross-categorical thinking and knowing involving self-reflection and abstraction.
- Complex or integrated systemic knowing that involves the development of intra-institutional relationships and multiple role consciousness.
- Trans-systemic knowing that deals with the inter-institution relationships and self-transformation in knowledge creation.

He sees workplaces as complex places that involve complex or integrated systemic knowledge or fourth-order consciousness. The mental demands involved in work are summarised in Figure 4.1. Even though self-employed people are actually the ones who own or invent jobs, each employee is the creator and owner of his/her own work. As self-evaluating and self-correcting workers, people develop their own internal standards – a process of establishing what is valuable – which they use throughout their work activities.

At work

Be the inventor or owner of our work (rather than see it as owned and created by the employer): distinguish our work from our job.

Be self-initiating, self-correcting, self-evaluating (rather than dependent on others to frame the problems, initiate adjustments, or determine whether things are going acceptably well).

Be guided by our own visions at work (rather than be without a vision or captive of the authority's agenda).

Take responsibility for what happens to us at work externally and internally (rather than see our present internal circumstances and future external possibilities as caused by someone else).

Be accomplished masters of our particular work roles, jobs or careers (rather than have an apprenticing or initiating relationship to what we do).

Conceive of the organisation from the 'outside in', as a whole; see our relation to the whole; see the relation of the parts to the whole (rather than see the rest of the organisation and its parts only from the perspective of our own part, from the 'inside out').

Figure 4.1 The mental demands at work for highly conscious people
(*Source:* Kegan 1994: 302)

Workers develop their own vision of the job to be done by developing a capacity to organise their knowing in a way that produces value. They act consciously to take responsibility for what happens to them (and maybe other colleagues) and so change the way that people interact in the workplace. These workers become masters in their minds of their work roles. This may be associated with their being appointed to positions of recognised expertise or they may be linked to extensive experience in a particular job. Finally, their workers are able to see the organisation as a whole to obtain the big picture from 'outside in'. They know the smart workers and those who know how the organisation works strategically and how its parts are interrelated.

These mental demands occur in a world that is experiencing continuous change. Gee *et al.* (1996: xii) declare that 'change is a leading motif of our times'. It is fuelled by increased competition and technology – competition for markets and technology to mass-produce 'customised' product. If, as Zuboff (1988) suggests, we do live in 'the age of the smart machine' then it is very important that we realise that the smart machine offers people greater access to information of all kinds that is relevant to doing the work better. As a result, organisations or workplaces become informated places where a major challenge is to manage the decision-making processes and to improve their efficient use. As Byham (1992) declares, this is the chance for organisation leaders to 'Zapp!' their employees to achieve 'extraordinary feats of improvement and bottom line success'. This process of empowerment of people in workforces requires people to have:

- direction as expressed in key result areas, goals and measurements;
- knowledge involving skills, training, information and goals;
- resources such as tools, materials, facilities and finance;
- support including approval, coaching, feedback and encouragement (Byham 1992: 137).

However, such empowerment does not occur in isolation. It occurs in different workplace situations, each of which contains its own organisational culture. Such a culture has been summarised by Schien (1997: 8–10) as containing: observed behavioural regularities when people interact, e.g. language, customs, traditions and rituals; group norms, e.g. 'a fair day's work for a fair day's pay'; exposed values, e.g. the highest quality client service; a formal philosophy that guides a group's actions towards different stakeholders, e.g. employees or customers; the rules by which the members in the organisation function with each other; the climate in which the work occurs in the organisation; the special embedded skills that are passed from one generation of workers to the next generation, e.g. special ways to perform a task; habits of thinking or linguistic paradigms that are shared with or are taught to new members of the organisation in the socialisation process; shared meanings or understandings that are created as group members interact; and integrating symbols that demonstrate the group members' emotional and aesthetic responses. It involves 'a striving toward patterning and integration' (Schien 1997: 11).

This organisational culture is grounded in the following assumptions:

- Since culture is a set of shared assumptions, it is best developed in a group or team-based situation.
- Since only those people in the culture can understand it, it is more important to create a vehicle for members' understanding than to try to elaborate their understanding.
- Not all parts of an organisational culture are relevant to any given issue that is faced by the organisation, therefore it is not practical to study the entire culture.
- Organisation members need the help of outsiders to help sort their assumptions into achieving or constraining ones.
- Changes in organisational practices are best achieved by building on existing assumptions. They will merely involve the whole organisational culture (Schien 1997: 148–149).

Members of workplace organisations use these assumptions in their collective experience and practice of their culture. As Sandberg (1997: 5) notes, the nature of this collective experience is a process of constantly making sense

Table 4.1 Different types of workplace learning (Granath *et al*. 1996: 2)

Type of learning	Single loop learning	Double loop learning	Triple loop learning
Passive/ correcting	Idiosyncratic adaptation	Adaptation to environment	Problem-solving
Active/ generative	Generative idiosyncratic adaptation – new routines	Generative adaptation to the environment – new norms	Generative problem solving – new values

of one's work, knowing what one's work is about and what it means to produce a product. Therefore, 'the members' shared understanding of work is cultivated, refined and maintained through their ongoing involvement in collectively making sense of their work' (Sandberg 1997: 5).

The collective aspect to workplace behaviours that is involved in the development of an organisational culture also relates to the nature of the learning that occurs. While some workplace managers believe that workers learn individually or in teams, Granath *et al*. (1996: 2) state that this may be true, but ultimately the promotion of organisational learning is what should be the goal in different organisations. They explain the attainment of such learning in terms of a learning hierarchy that defines different forms of learning at individual, team and organisational levels (see Table 4.1).

These forms may be characterised as follows.

1   Idiosyncratic adaptation or the correction of action in relation to fixed plans, standards, norms, values and instructions. Here, negative feedback allows for incremental steps in learning that lead to minor changes. It leads to a mechanical and self-correcting system that searches for increased efficiency.
2   Adaptation to environment represents the results of confrontation between existing ideas, rules and plans for actions and observations in the environment. Here, 'old' knowledge is abandoned and 'new' knowledge is accepted to perform new patterns of action and behaviour. The aim is for increased effectiveness as a reaction to a given work environment.
3   Learning through problem-solving which focuses on the process of learning how to adapt, i.e. improving effectiveness and efficiency under new circumstances.

These three forms of learning can be transformed into generative forms when the learning shapes the work environment and affects it, i.e. it focuses on generating new knowledge as an active process, thus developing new routines, norms or values depending on which form of learning is being considered.

Since the main prerequisite for learning is the ability to change, and since most organisations are based on infrastructures and values that naturally resist change, Granath *et al.* (1996: 3) therefore state that:

> To achieve competitive learning we must transfer individual learning both into team learning and into organisational learning, as well as to spread learning between all levels in a continuous process and in co-operation with chosen strategy.

This is difficult to achieve at each level because people have to try new experiences against existing beliefs and mental models at each level. For example, at the organisational level, different organisational experiences have to be tried against the beliefs and mental models of the organisation. However, the types of key elements that are required for change to occur in an organisation include: shared vision, systems thinking, feedback systems, strategies of adaptation, internal and external networks, access to information and knowledge, technical content and environmental implications (Mattsson 1995). Therefore, Granath *et al.* (1996: 4) concluded that individual and team learning may lead to organisational learning in the process outlined in Figure 4.2 only when these elements are understood and used deliberately.

Another way to think about enhancing organisational learning is to think of the workplace employed in the organisation as a source of competitive advantage. Hartz (1996: 45) has demonstrated this point in relation to workers in the Volkswagen company where the code M4 was applied to the overall employee profile to describe the ideal workforce. M4 can be decoded as the following attributes of the workforce.

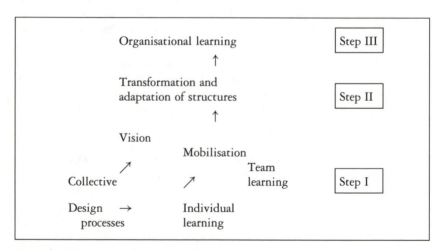

Figure 4.2 The process of organisational learning

- Multi-skilled, i.e. willingness and ability to operate in one's own area; autonomous thinking, acting, questioning: analyses and evaluates; willingness to learn; acquires additional subsidiary skills; applies knowledge/experience to projects; and is environmentally responsible.
- Creative, i.e. thinks entrepreneurially in developing new ideas, identifying new opportunities and acts on these; operates on the principle that change brings opportunities; autonomously rethinks and improves processes, focuses on objectives and sets quality standards.
- Mobile, i.e. supports activities in other locations; is prepared to gain international and inter-cultural experience; and is prepared to go where the tasks are.
- People-orientated, i.e. adopts a constructive approach to solving conflict, demonstrates an ability to think cohesively; applies new values in practice; works well with others in teams; creates a climate of trust and appreciation; identifies with the company; and possesses social skills.

It is based on teamwork and the encouragement to develop new ideas for improving the organisation. These are examples in the promotion of the development of self-directed teams who achieve their own goals (which are consistent with those of the overall organisation) and can achieve their full potential as a work unit through joint success. This involves a transformational process from functional organisation to value-added processes and a change in organisational management through changing paradigms and behavioural patterns. Changes in paradigms may include: from detailed knowledge to contextual knowledge; machines to humans; inertia to innovation; structure to flow; and perfection to time. Resulting relevant behavioural patterns include: a positive attitude; team-orientated behaviours; coherent communications; comprehensible information; holistic decision-making; fulfillable commitments and tangible 'involvement' (Hartz 1996: 186).

If it is to be successful, the organisation should develop a learning culture. Schien (1997: 363–366) sees the development of such a culture as the basis for 'managing the contradictions of stability, learning and change'. The nature of such a culture may be summarised as follows: the organisation dominates in the organisation–environment relationship; human activity is productive; a pragmatic approach to reality and truth is evident; people are basically good and immutable; human relationships are a blend of group and individual activities that are sometimes authoritative and sometimes collegial; planning is futuristic on a medium time scale; there is a high level of intercommunication amongst workers; a high degree of subcultural diversity; task- and relationship-orientated behaviour; and systematic thinking.

The development of a learning culture within an organisation does not happen by accident. It is facilitated by insightful and visionary leaders. This leadership has been termed by Napolitano and Henderson (1998:

111–145) as 'Shaping the Enterprise', which involves both creating a culture and anticipating the future. Creating a culture involves exploring the skills and attributes related to developing core values, taking a systems approach and building a sense of community. The development of core values involves facilitating 'consensus around a set of shared beliefs about what the organisation or work unit stands for; works to ensure that these beliefs are reflected in the systems, structures, choices and decisions of the organisation as a means of shaping its organisational culture' (Napolitano and Henderson 1998: 114). Taking a systems approach involves recognising the interdependency of parts within the system; considering the impact of decisions in the short, medium and long term; and using the tools of systems' thinking to identify opportunities for organisational change. Building a sense of community occurs when a leader 'seeks to forge connections and strengthen personal and professional bonds among staff; stimulates the kind of *esprit de corps* that promotes collective learning, self-organisation, and synergistic outcomes' (Napolitano and Henderson 1998: 123).

Anticipating the future, according to Napolitano and Henderson, involves organisational leaders: staying current with emerging trends; inspiring the pursuit of a shared vision; thinking strategically, employing dynamic planning, and enlarging the capacity for change in the organisation. The pursuit of a shared vision 'involves others in creating a bold and compelling picture of the desired future; engages everyone in imagining and seeking to realise what could be' (Napolitano and Henderson 1998: 137). Dynamic planning points to the charting of a flexible course to move an organisation to achieve its vision, and identifying milestones along the way to measure progress and incorporate new learning. Enlarging the capacity for change involves working 'to shape an adaptive organisation that responds to emerging imperatives; challenges the status quo and encourages others to do the same; champions new initiatives; allows for the discovery of order out of chaos' (Napolitano and Henderson 1998: 145). This form of leadership can be seen to be a basis for developing an empowering organisation.

The concept of an empowering organisation was developed by Foy (1994) to determine how people in an organisation are empowered through a focus on: performance, real teams, visible leadership and good communication. As Foy (1994: 3) declares:

> The empowering organisation actually wants to tap people's knowledge and experience. Therefore, as a wise investment, it must develop people. That means it must develop their teams, too. Development for the managers, like development for individuals, comes from many opportunities to tackle new challenges, learning to co-operate with others; the development of the organisation, in turn, stems from the development of the individuals, teams and managers.

It achieves performance, communication and development through the concept of leadership, which Bennis describes in terms of the leader's actions to: motivate people to achieve; license them to tell the truth and fuse concept and details (cited by Foy 1994: 38). These actions may be conceived as elements in a model which Adair (1983) described as: building the team; achieving the task; and developing the individuals. It consists of a process of empowering through networks which may be formal or informal depending on the people in the organisation. Foy (1994: 118–122) suggests the following rules to increase the quality of informal information in an organisation.

- The effectiveness of a network is inversely proportional to its formality.
- A network needs a focus, i.e. a topic not a goal.
- A network needs a spider, i.e. a secretary, at the centre of the web to enhance its development.
- A network needs a phone number, not a headquarters building.
- A network needs first names.
- A network needs groups rather than committees.

If networking is to be effective, these rules need to be used in an organisation both formally and informally. People in the organisation need to feel confident and competent to generate and to participate in networking experience to make their actions more effective. Part of the decision about whether to network or not will depend on people's attitude to work. Using the American context as a basis, Pollan and Levine (1997: 23) identified six overlapping trends in attitudes to work. These are:

- The Protestant Ethic of working for the glory of God.
- The Craft Ethic, in which people work to the best of their abilities for themselves.
- The Entrepreneurial Ethic in which a person with the right attitude could make it on his/her own through various risk-taking ventures.
- The Career Ethic, in which people seek jobs in large organisations and move up the bureaucratic ladder to positions of greater responsibility and higher status.
- The Self-fulfilment Ethic, in which people search for personal growth through challenges that allow for self-expression.
- The Mercantile Ethic, in which people focus on their work as a job such that people separate themselves from their employer mentally, and their paid work is a income-generating device that allows them to pursue their personal goals.

Pollan and Levine (1997: 24) suggest that people will achieve satisfaction when they practise bifocal vision, i.e. they focus simultaneously on their own and their organisation's goals. Another way to look at how we should be planning our approach to workplace learning is to consider Peters' (1997) *Circle of Innovation* – a hands-on guide to being more effective and better than one's competitors. The main ideas that drive Peters' approach to innovation in the workplace include: physical distance is no longer a barrier to competition; organisations should be destroyed rather than changed; learning to forget old behaviours is a highly strategic action; every worker should maximise his/her organisation as a better place; value is maximised in professional services; all members contribute to adding value in an organisation; a focus on a systems approach; the importance of creating a brand name for a product or a service; commitment to renewal programmes by all members; value gender-based perspectives; value the importance of the concept of design; and adopt a revolutionary zeal for transformational leadership. Peters states that these ideas lead to members in an organisation working to improve themselves and their organisation so keenly that they become obsessive about it and they change as people, from holding an individualised perspective to holding a collective, collegial perspective that is devoid of conservatism.

Therefore, learning for life is a highly valuable approach that is built around changes. Such change needs to be grounded in an understanding of the role and purpose of education and training. Mansfield and Mitchell (1996: 3) identify these purposes of education as follows.

- The preparation of people for independent economic activity, i.e. a means to an end.
- The empowerment of people to become active citizens in a democratic society, i.e. to have access, choice and equality of opportunity.
- Enabling every person to develop their natural talents and capabilities to the fullest extent, i.e. individual progression, improvement and self-fulfilment.

They agree that workplace organisations have moved away from a view of work that 'isolates it from the totality of human action and experience and restricts the description of skills to the manual reflexes which are the base minimum required to meet immediate needs. The nature of work and the nature of competence are part of the very fabric of our democracy' (Mansfield and Mitchell 1996: 5). To achieve the above three purposes: an educational policy related to the needs of the economy is needed; the roles and responsibilities of all people who have a stake in education and training in an organisation need to be articulated; and strategies need to be put in place to implement empowering education and training experiences. This is the challenge of developing a competent, active workforce.

Such an organisational learning is based, according to Cook and Yarrow (1993: 379), on the ability of groups of people to act collectively. This occurs over time in the course of different workplace behaviours and practices in which members of the group generate a set of intersubjective meanings that are expressed as objects, language and actions. As new members join this group, they acquire an understanding of values, beliefs and feelings which have developed in the organisational group. These are acquired through everyday workplace practices using the objects, language and actions. Therefore, the shared meanings are being continuously maintained and modified.

Experiential learning, common sense and expertise in the smart workforce

Many people believe that they work to live while others believe that they live to work. We have been encouraged by Pollan and Levine (1997: 23) to think of a Mercantile Ethic in which we earn a salary from working to pursue personal goals. All of these orientations involve people in conscious decision-making, deliberately making choices and changing through their lives. They are, in fact, engaged in lifelong learning. As Larsson (1996: 9) states, this learning has to do with 'changing the patterns that adults are caught in'. He suggests that these changes may include: learning new knowledge and developing new skills; developing new interests; learning a new kind of working life that is more challenging and provides access to more of one's talents as a geographical educator; enhancing one's self-confidence; and acquiring knowledge that is not available in one's everyday world (Larsson 1996: 10–11).

Various approaches have been taken to adult learning, including those in workforces. Foley (1995: xiv) stated a taxonomy of four forms of adult learning:

- Formal education that is organised by professional educators and trainers, where there is a defined curriculum, and which often leads to a qualification.
- Non-formal education in which some sort of systematic instruction is provided on an infrequent basis.
- Informal education in which people learn from their experiences.
- Incidental learning that occurs as the result of everyday learning in situations unrelated to a person's professional or work activities.

Knowles (1990: 57–62) explained that the focus on adult learners as self-directed operators was based on the assumptions that adults need to know why they need to learn something before undertaking to learn it; have a self-concept of being responsible for their own decisions, for their own lives; come to an educational activity with a greater volume, and a different quality, of experience, than do younger people; become ready to learn those things they need to know and are able to do so in order to cope effectively with their real-life situations; are life-centred in their orientation to learning;

and are mainly motivated by internal pressures such as increased job satis-faction, self-esteem and quality of life. These assumptions do not dictate the form of the learning that is done by adults but they certainly do offer a basis for their learning behaviours. Larsson (1996: 16) establishes that these forms of adult learning should be judged according to their capacity to change the conditions for learning in everyday contexts including in work-places.

He states that:

> A good adult education, must not only have the qualities of challenging everyday interpretations, be relevant and have a genuine meaning for the students – it must be aware that all these interpretations that are com-municated in the educational discourse must be subordinated to the judgement of specific cases in everyday life.
>
> (Larsson 1996: 16)

Such everyday learning occurs throughout people's lives as they become more conscious of the content of their life worlds, interpret it, i.e. develop personal knowledge, and learn through changing their interpretations of this content. The 'situatedness' of such learning is critical to the meanings that people place on events and actions, e.g. learning to act as a team on an assembly line can be quite different for some people than learning to be a part of a football team.

The importance of experience, common sense and expertise in learning in one's work can be demonstrated as being valuable in smart workforces who seek lasting lifelong learning and success in their work activities.

Experience in workplace learning

All members of a workforce can be thinking, reflective and active participants in the success of the enterprise. They can be even more if they possess con-siderable experience in the current workplace culture. The example of Ken, the long-serving assembly line operator in a washing machine manufacturing company who solved the problem of the defective tubs through personal observation and comment, and saved the company's profit margin (Flanagan *et al.* 1993: 109–113), serves to demonstrate how any worker's practical skills, everyday knowledge and interpersonal skills can be vital to the success of the company. Ken's personal experience on the assembly line proved to be more powerful than any formal training that he might have had. For once, Ken had been encouraged to think for himself and he was listened to. Flanagan *et al.* (1993: 111) suggests that, as the result of this type of experience, the Ken of the workforce 'will most likely become a much more productive and committed employee. Ken might even come to love his work. . . . Just think of the power that a few hundred highly motivated "Kens" can apply to the productivity of your plant'.

Another aspect of this type of work experience is the extent to which risks are involved. Elsewhere, e.g. Gerber *et al.* (1995), it has been shown through workers talking about their learning that one very frequent type of learning consisted of making mistakes, reflecting on each mistake, working out how to correct the mistake (either by oneself or with the assistance of other workers) and committing oneself never to make the mistake again (and doing so consistently). Workers declared that they would learn much less in this approach if they suspected that they would always be penalised for making a mistake in their workplace behaviours.

The workers that have been discussed in this section have engaged in experience-based learning. Boud *et al.* (1993) summarised the assumptions underpinning this type of learning as:

- experience is the foundation of , and the stimulus for, learning;
- learners actively construct their own experience;
- learning is a holistic process;
- learning is socially and culturally constructed;
- learning is influenced by the socio-emotional context in which it occurs.

Andresen *et al.* (1995: 208–9) identified six defining features of experience-based learning: the involvement of the whole person; the use of relevant prior experiences; continued reflection on prior experiences to transfer them to deeper understanding; the structure of the experience; the extent of facilitation of the learner's engagement in the experience; and the extent to which the outcomes of learning from the experience are assessed. On an earlier occasion, Boud and Walker (1990: 61–80) developed a model of experiential learning that focused on: the preparation for experiential events; reflection during the experience; and reflection after the events. Whatever context these models are situated in, they usually consist of experiences, reflective processes and outcomes. Educators and trainers in these smart workforces do plan for this form of learning to continue throughout people's lives, including their working lives, in a purposeful manner.

Experience-based learning therefore involves adopting a holistic approach to changing as people, which involves the obvious notion of having experiences in, say, the workforce to improve the outcomes of workplace behaviour in an ethical manner. It is a concept that is being taken further in a more generic sense by Marton and Booth (1997: 33–55) who prefer to see the experience of learning as involving a way of going about learning (learning's *how* aspect) and an object of learning (learning's *what* aspect). Therefore, to experience something in a certain way, they suggest that we:

> . . . have to discern that something from its environment. But on the other hand, in order to discern it from its environment we have to see it as some particular thing, or in other words assign it a meaning. Structure presupposes meaning, and at the same time meaning presupposes

structure. The two aspects, meaning and structure, are dialectically intertwined and occur simultaneously when we experience something.

(Marton and Booth 1997: 87)

Therefore, they would say that an experience has a structural aspect and a
referential (or meaning) aspect. In the case of learning in workplaces, we
should be able to think in terms of what is being learned in different work
situations and how it is being learned. The trick is to realise that the 'how'
and the 'what' aspects of workplace learning are truly intertwined and so
the outcomes of the learning experience are not isolated from the process of
the experience.

The importance of learning is that it involves changing the person–world
relationship (Marton and Booth 1997: 139). By learning something new,
people change some aspect of their world. 'Learning is mostly a matter of
reconstituting the already constituted world' (Marton and Booth 1997:
139). Therefore, in a workplace situation, the smarter employee will realise
that during his/her working day in a work team, the learning that occurs
in working better together or doing a task better really involves conscious
changes and improvements in work practices in a particular situation,
which involves groups of employees deliberately changing themselves
through conscious interactions.

Through these experiences, workers confirm that they do learn in different
ways. Based on several research studies (e.g. Gerber *et al*. 1995 and Gerber
1997), at least 11 ways by which people learn in their work have been
discerned.

1   Making mistakes, correcting them and learning not to make the same
    mistake again.
2   Learning through self-education on and off the job.
3   Learning through practising one's personal values.
4   Applying theory and practising skills.
5   Learning through problem-solving.
6   Learning through interacting with others.
7   Learning through offering leadership to others.
8   Learning through open lateral planning.
9   Learning by being an advocate for colleagues.
10 Learning through formal training.
11 Learning through quality assurance.

While this list does not present an order of importance in the ways that people
learn in their work, it does highlight the diversity of valued approaches to
learning by workers. In addition, it focuses on the proactive roles that
many workers adopt in their experience of workplace learning. They
demonstrate that learning in workplaces is often an experience that involves

colleagues, it is a shared experience that involves changes occurring in different ways depending on the types of worker interactions. It also emphasises the modest importance of formal training in workplace learning.

What these ways of experiencing learning do is promote a practice-based learning model for workplaces, a model that is grounded in the concept of learning communities (Marsick and Watkins 1993). The workplace can be the site for the development of continuing learning by groups or teams of workers. Here, self-directed, collegial and autonomous actions promote the development of empowering learning groups who act collectively to improve their work performance by increased learning.

The power of common sense in workplace learning

How many times have the actions of workers in doing their jobs been noticed by their colleagues as illustrations of the use of common sense? Comments like: 'That was a good illustration of using common sense to solve a production problem' or 'You fixed the problem so easily. If only I had thought to use common sense I could have done it just as well', certainly illustrate the point being made here. However, they are countered by many workers who subscribe to the belief that 'common sense is not very common in workplaces these days'. There is certainly a belief amongst workers that some of their colleagues have the capacity to be highly effective through making simply reasoned decisions that yield smart, effective results. But, what do they mean when they make these observations? What is common sense in workplace learning?

Forguson (1989: 157) offers a start to understand the concept of common sense by stating that: 'the common-sense view of the world is a shared network of beliefs about the world and our solution to it, which is expressed in virtually all of our thought and behaviour'. This involves the use of the following cognitive abilities: the ability to engage in meta-representation; making the appearance–reality distinction; recognising representational diversity and representational change. These are basic abilities that workers should use as a matter of course in their work. They should be able to make judgements about how things vary, change and differ in appearance whilst doing work tasks. The basic reasoning that is utilised in such thought processes is often acquired through normal living rather than through specialised training on the job.

Lonergan (1980: 111) states that:

> Common sense, then, consists of a basic nucleus of insights that enables a person to deal successfully with personal and material situations of the sort that arise in his ordinary living, according to the standards of the culture and the class to which he belongs.

Stewart (1996: 14) suggests that the 'nucleus of insights' referred to by Lonergan consists of a grouping of the ways of understanding that people hold to do certain courses of action, e.g. ways to operate a computer or ways to perform tasks of electronic communication. People operate, here, in a world of immediacy by referring to both the practical and the concrete aspects involved in these actions. These are associated closely with situations that have arisen in the workers' ordinary lives. Lonergan (1957: 173) affirms that intelligence is not the province of scientists and scholars alone:

> . . . one meets intelligence in every walk of life. There are intelligent farmers and craftsmen, intelligent employers and workers, intelligent technicians and mechanics, intelligent doctors and lawyers, intelligent politicians and diplomats . . .

Therefore, people of common sense have insights into problems, weigh up different courses of action, form sensible judgements and make responsible decisions. Because the world of common sense sometimes lacks order and discipline, often people have to learn for themselves using a hit-and-miss process. 'Insights are acquired not in the precise, ordered, rigorous way of scientific inquiry that leads to general or "universal" knowledge' (Stewart 1996: 16).

When common sense is used in workplace learning, people are not attempting to make universally accepted pronouncements. They are not attempting to produce statements on workplace behaviours that are true for all workplaces. They are not attempting to theorise either. Rather, they use ordinary language, not technical language, to meet the problem at hand, e.g. deciding how to fix a non-functioning part of an assembly line. The goal of the use of common sense is a practical result, i.e. learning how to fix the assembly line. Such knowledge allows workers to adjust to varying kinds of work and to come to terms with these challenges both at work and in their wider lives. What makes it common is that its practical results are appreciated by a group of workers in a particular work situation. It is situated in its nature in that the common sense knowledge for a group of miners will be very different from that of a group of surgeons in a hospital or from that of a group of insurance brokers. As Stewart (1996: 17) notes: 'Commonsense provides us with its fund of facts, its information, its certainties'. These forms of information and opinion will vary, therefore, with the type of work. They represent smart, practical ways to get the work done.

Even though the term *common sense* is used infrequently in workplace and management literature, perhaps because it is assumed to occur naturally, important variants of it may be found in the cognition for everyday learning movement and in the capacity of people to act mindfully. Rogoff (1990) demonstrated how children and adults make sensible practical decisions based on their experiences, intuition and their shared understanding of the nature of the challenge. Older, more experienced, people demonstrate how to perform a task to less experienced people through a process of guided participation, i.e. they demonstrate how to do a task and the learner practises it under their watchful eye until she or he can do it proficiently. In workplaces, the guided participation may occur through a deliberate demonstration in a work team or it may occur when one member of a work team observes the actions of one or more colleagues. Either way, the learning worker has to work out effective practical strategies to learn the relevant skill or behaviour.

Additionally, it may be argued that using common sense in one's work is an example of acting mindfully. The concept of *mindfulness* has been defined by Langer (1989) as including: the ability to create new categories of knowledge based on the nature of the situation and the context; openness to new information; and awareness of more than one perspective. Acting mindfully in a practical sense is characteristic of a smart worker who is alert to new ways of doing things in the workplace, who considers different ways to perform certain tasks and so develops for him or herself different understandings or knowledge which may be shared with other members of the work team.

In summary form then, workers who exhibit common sense in their jobs make fewer errors in their decisions; can think through issues rationally and logically; rarely panic in testing workplace situations; are even-handed in judgements of people and their behaviours; can make decisions easily and fluently; act in a confident manner; are respected by their colleagues; and are excellent mentors in a training situation. They use their intuitive powers frequently and effectively.

But how do these behaviours of workers differ from those of workers or managers whom we call experts?

The importance of expertise in workplace learning

Douglas (1994; 36) believes that highly effective people use their mind as an experienced manager to: plan, find and organise others to help them, motivate themselves and others who will be helping, and measure and adjust the activities of themselves and any helpers to ensure that their plans are realised. The people in workplaces who can perform these tasks highly effectively are recognised as experts. They are people who possess special knowledge, and who can perform their work in distinctive ways. In other words, these workers possess advantages over their colleagues that are both recognised and encouraged.

The focus above on common-sense knowledge provides an interesting basis for considering the type of knowledge that experts use in their activities. They possess practical common-sense knowledge like other smart workers, but they also possess excellent theoretical knowledge. Theoretical knowledge is a key construct that Lonergan (1957: 294–295) argues is based on knowing for the sake of knowing. Stewart (1996: 19) summarises this understanding as follows:

> . . . the thrust of intelligence is directed towards knowing things in rela-
> tion to other things and in their mutual interactions. It is knowing rather
> for the sake of knowing. Its chief concern is not with practical results but
> with knowing truth. Whereas commonsense is generally satisfied with
> knowing things as described, the world of theoretical meaning finds
> satisfaction only in knowing things as explained.

Theoretical knowledge constitutes knowledge that is essential for a worker or
manager to explain accurately, clearly and precisely using specialist technical
terminology to other employees. It is the specialised language that health professionals use when describing in detail a particular procedure to colleagues.
It is the special language that an engineer uses to describe the construction of
different types of bridges. It could even be the specialised language used to
describe computing software that many workers use on their workstations.
Whatever it is, this technical, theoretical knowledge may be seen to be
knowledge for the sake of knowledge. However, in the smart workforce it
is specialised technical knowledge that is also shared amongst co-workers
to explain precise workplace actions and functions; like common-sense
knowledge, theoretical knowledge is understood and used by expert workers
and understood by others who prefer to use common-sense descriptors. For
example, many experienced nurses will learn theoretical knowledge through
their regular interaction with medical surgeons even though their jobs do
not demand that this happens. They do so in order to be more effective
nurses.

  Some workers are identified by their positions or by their colleagues as
experts because they possess what Johnson (1983: 78–79) terms 'expertise'.
It consists of the following attributes:

- knowing what must be learned;
- being able to do things that most people cannot, and being proficient at
  generalising information;
- operating smoothly, fluently and efficiently in one's activities;
- knowing numerous tricks, caveats and short cuts for tackling and
  resolving problems;
- quickly dismissing irrelevant information to focus quickly on the kernel
  of the problem;
- recognising problems as instances of familiar types of problems; and
- being able to transfer performance across specific tasks.

The workers/managers who fit into the category of expert, practise these seven
attributes on a regular basis in their work and to the satisfaction of their co-
workers. Sometimes, they volunteer their expertise to assist a work situation.
On other occasions, they are called upon by other members of a work team to
demonstrate their expertise through overcoming a workplace difficulty, e.g.

a mechanical breakdown. In either situation, these workers/managers act professionally for their goal is to improve the performance of their work group or organisation.

Another variation of this understanding of expertise has been offered by Benner (1984) in her adaptation of the Dreyfus model of skill acquisition to the nursing field. Her highest level of performance (of five levels) was the *expert* level, where nurses no longer relied on analytic principles, e.g. rules, procedures and maxims, to link their understanding of a situation to an appropriate action. With their intuitive grasp of the workplace situation, these expert nurses are able to focus precisely on the nature of the problem in minimum time. Such people often possess more knowledge than is necessary to solve a particular problem. They often think beyond the specific problem to related workplace issues.

Possessing expertise should not be underrated by those workers who are tagged as 'smart'. The decisiveness with which these workers or managers operate is quite attractive to other members of their organisation. Through formal and informal interactions with acknowledged expert workers, the whole workforce can improve its performance. These interactions may involve explicit communication or learning through observation and self-practice. Sometimes, the expert worker will mentor a less experienced co-worker. It all depends on the work situation in which these interactions occur.

Being good as an expert worker also has something to do with being a very good verbal and non-verbal communicator. Skills in verbal communication are necessary when a worker is explaining a procedure or a technique. Alternatively, skills in non-verbal communication are necessary when phys- ical demonstrations of these procedures and techniques take place at work.

Models for promoting experience, common sense and expertise in smart workforces

If the advice from research that has been discussed earlier in this chapter about how people learn in their work is taken seriously, then models for promoting experiential learning, common sense and expertise should place the worker in control rather than the manager. This is a direct call for organisational leaders to facilitate workplace learning through conducive learning environments, and cohesive and interactive work teams who are willing to take risks in their learning and have an expressed willingness to 'Lead the journey in organisational improvement' (Belasco and Stayer 1993).

Various models for workplace learning have been proposed in this chapter. The model of experiential learning developed by Boud and colleagues (Boud and Walker 1990) with its focus on preparation for experiencing a workplace event, reflection during the experience and reflections after the event, gives a good general impression of learning through experience on the job. This is the type of learning that Dennis Cairns, mentioned in the introduction to this chapter, exercised. Juanita Capella, also mentioned in the introduction, similarly engaged in reflective experiential learning, but she differed from Dennis in the extent to which she reflected on her workplace experiences. She was more prone to learn by making mistakes, correcting them and not making the same mistake again. Juanita enjoyed the experience of learning much more than the reflection on experience.

A variation of experiential learning in workplaces has been termed *self-directed learning*. From roots such as Knowles (1978) and Argyris and Schon (1974), the term 'self-directed learning' has been differentiated from life-long learning to emphasise what often happens with learning in workplaces. Piskurich (1993: 4), for example, defines it as 'a training design in which trainees master packages of predetermined material, at their own pace, without the aid of an instructor'. As such, self-directed learning deals mainly with organised or packaged learning in workplaces. Unlike the broader experiential learning, self-directed learning focuses on one aspect of the learning that an employee does on the job – the organised learning. There are, however, many learning activities in workers' lives that may be self-directed, but which do not fit Piskurich's definition. For example, during their work, Juanita or Dennis may choose to check out an alternative way to do an operation. They are not using any predetermined material, but they are acting in a self-directed manner. There will also be occasions when Juanita and Dennis will choose to take a prepared learning package into their workplace to use its contents as a diagnostic tool in their work. They are placing a lateral perspective on the learning package and extending its use beyond its intended purpose.

Whether the learning that goes on in workplaces is experiential or self-directed, it is certainly *situated learning*. This focus is important for it forces people who are interested in workplace management and learning to think of individual workers learning and acting in a socially organised group. This focus embodies an epistemological challenge to traditional ways of knowing in places such as workplaces. Knowledge learned in this way is 'not just *used* in the course of cognitive activity but also [is] jointly *constituted*' (Resnick *et al*. 1997: 5). Knowledge, therefore, exists in a workplace as long as the group that is constructing it is present and interacting. This is because the knowledge is constituted from the interacting contributions of all workers who are operating in a particular work activity.

One particular type of situated learning was proposed by Rogoff (1990) in which she developed the approach of *guided participation*. Such an approach could be an excellent basis for extending the idea of smart workforce learning. It may be, as Rogoff declares, the basis for developing people's 'apprenticeship in thinking' (1990: 8). The simplest way to demonstrate how guided participation can operate in work situations is to focus on the five components in the process of guided participation. These are as follows.

1 **Building bridges from workers' current understanding and skills to reach new understanding and skills**

In this holistic approach to learning, trainers, supervisors, colleagues and managers build bridges that help workers understand how to act in new situations, interpret behaviour and events, and classify objects and events. This may involve workers watching how a particular task or procedure is done; then trying to do the task with varying degrees of success; watching a further demonstration; and practising how to do the task consistently. This results in the development of a mutual understanding between the worker and the demonstrator. Learning occurs through observation and doing.

2 **Choosing and structuring of learning situations and activities**

Workplaces are cultural institutions that are organised differently according to different organisational visions and policies. The rules and inter-relations between workers and trainers, coaches or mentors, will vary according to the extent to which these people select and structure the workplace learning activities. Careful negotiations between these two groups of people can lead to productive learning activities between all participants if they choose to be involved in the decision-making activity.

3 **Structuring responsibility in joint problem-solving**

One form of social interaction between workplace educators and workers as learners is the way that the educators structure workers' involvement in learning situations through joint participation. These workplace trainers, mentors, coaches and other leaders engage in a process of organising or 'scaffolding' the workers' performance in learning through actions such as motivating workers to want to investigate a problem; simplifying the task into manageable components; continued encouragement of the workers' focus on the goal of the activity; monitoring discrepancies between the workers' outcomes and the real solution; minimising risks and frustrations in problem-solving; and discussing an optimum solution with workers in a debriefing session.

4 **Transfer of responsibility for managing activities**

When workplace educators and leaders become aware that their workers are sufficiently familiar with different workplace activities they should decide to give the workers the responsibility for managing these activities. These educators and leaders must become sensitive to the development of competence by workers in regard to specific activities. They possess a tacit understanding when the workers are ready and able to take responsibility for certain learning tasks.

5   Shared thinking and problem-solving

This approach to workplace learning culminates in a mutual, intentional engagement between educators or trainers and the workers. By working together on problem-solving tasks, trainers and workers share actively in the thinking, learning and problem-solving tasks that abound in workplaces. Guided participation epitomises the nature of this collaboration and the development of shared understandings through problem-solving experiences.

The overall approach recognises that workers may act creatively to make changes in their understanding and that their trainers or leaders or mentors are sensitive to these changes and allow them to occur. Part of this approach involves the recognition that there is not one single correct way to solve a problem.

There is no doubt that Juanita and Dennis would benefit from the use of some of these learning models in their workplace education. Each model or approach has merit in workplace education. Personal choice may dictate when they are utilised to improve workplace learning. However, woven within them are varying requirements for the use of experience, common sense and expertise. It is not, therefore, desirable to single out experience, common sense or expertise as the dominating element in the workplace learning activities or events. In a relational way, all three play different roles in making the workplace learning experience as rewarding as possible and the improvement of the organisation's culture and performance fully owned by the whole workforce.

References

Adair, J. (1983) *Effective Leadership.* Aldershot, Hampshire: Gower.

Andresen, L., Boud, D. and Cohen, R. (1995) 'Experience-based learning', in G. Foley (ed) *Understanding Adult Education and Training* (pp. 207–220), Sydney: Allen & Unwin.

Argyris, C. and Schon, D. (1974) *Theory in Practice: Increasing Professional Effectiveness.* San Francisco: Jossey-Bass.

Belasco, J. and Stayer, R. (1993) *Flight of the Buffalo.* New York: Warner Books.

Benner, P. (1984) *From Naive to Expert: Excellence and Power in Clinical Nursing Practice*, San Francisco: Addison-Wesley.

Boud, D. and Walker, D. (1990) 'Making the most of experience', *Studies in Continuing Education* 12(2): pp. 61–80.

Boud, D., Cohen, R. and Walker, D. (1993) 'Understanding learning from experience', in D. Boud, R. Cohen and D. Walker (eds) *Using Experience for Learning.* Milton Keynes: SHRE and Open University Press.

Byham, W. (1992) *Zapp!! The Lightning of Empowerment.* London: Century Business.

Cook, S. and Yarrow, D. (1993) 'Culture and organisational learning', *Journal of Management Inquiry* 2(4): 373–390.

Douglas, G. (1994) *The Revolution of Minds.* Eastern Heights, Australia: AIPS.

Flanagan, M., McGinn, I. and Thornhill, A. (1993) *Because no Bastard ever Asked Me.* Canberra: Stakeholder.

Foy, N. (1994) *Empowering People at Work.* Aldershot, Hampshire: Gower.

Foley, G. (1995) *Understanding Adult Education and Training.* Sydney: Allen and Unwin.

Forguson, L. (1989) *Common Sense.* London: Routledge.

Gee, J., Hull, G. and Lankshear, C. (1996) *The New Work Order. Behind the Language of the New Capitalism*, Sydney and Boulder, CO: Allen & Unwin and Wellview Press.

Gerber, R. (1997) Understanding how geographical educators learn in their work: An important basis for their professional development. Paper presented to *Geographical Association Conference*, London, April.

Gerber, R., Lankshear, C., Larsson, S. and Svensson, L. (1995) 'Self-directed learning in a work context.', *Education and Training* 37(8): 26–32.

Granath, J., Lindahl, G. and Rehal, S. (1996) 'From empowerment to enablement: An evolution of new dimensions in participatory design', *Logistic and Arbeit.*

Hartz, P. (1996) *The Company that Breathes.* Berlin: Springer-Verlag.

Johnson, P. (1983) 'What kind of an expert should a system be?', *Journal of Medicine and Philosophy* 8: 77–97.

Kegan, R. (1994) *In Over Our Heads: The Mental Demands of Modern Life.* Cambridge, MA: Harvard University Press.

Knowles, M. (1978) *The Adult Learner: A Neglected Species.* Houston, TX: Gulf Publishing.

Knowles, M. (1990) *The Adult Learner: A Neglected Species*, 4th edn, Houston, TX: Gulf Publishing.

Langer, E. (1989) *Mindfulness.* Reading, MA: Addison-Wesley.

Larsson, S. (1996) 'On the meaning of life-long learning'. Mimeo.

Lonergan, B. (1957) *Insight: A study of Human Understanding.* New York: Philosophical Library.

Lonergan, B. (1980) *Understanding and Being: An Introduction and Companion to Insight.* New York: Edwin Mellow Press.

Mansfield, B. and Mitchell, L. (1996) *Towards a Competent Workforce.* Aldershot, Hampshire: Gower.

Marsick, V. and Watkins, K. (1993) *Sculpting the Learning Organisation.* San Francisco: Jossey-Bass.

Marton, F. and Booth, S. (1997) *Learning and Awareness.* Mahwah, NJ: Lawrence Erebaum.

Mattsson, P. (1995) *Generative Learning: A Pedagogical Milieu Study of Knowledge Intensive Manufacturing Industry 1991–1993.* Stockholm: Industrilitteratur.

Napolitano, C. and Henderson, L. (1998) *The Leadership Odyssey.* San Francisco: Jossey-Bass.

Peters, T. (1997) *The Circle of Innovation.* London: Hodder & Stoughton.

Piskurich, G. (1993) *Self-directed Learning.* San Francisco: Jossey-Bass.

Pollan, S. and Levine, M. (1997) *Die Broke.* New York: Harper Business.

Resnick, L., Pontecorvo, C. and Saljo, R. (1997) 'Discourse, tools and reasoning', in L. Resnick, R. Saljo, C. Pontecorvo and B. Burge (eds), *Discourse, Tools and Reasoning: Essays on Situated Cognition.* Berlin: Springer-Verlag, pp. 1–22.

Rogoff, B. (1990) *Apprenticeship in Thinking.* New York: Oxford University Press.

Sandberg, J. (1997) 'The nature of collective competence and its development'. Paper to the *14th Nordic Business Conference on Business Studies*, Bodo, Norway, August.

Schien, E. (1997) *Organisation Culture and Leadership* 2nd edn, San Francisco: Jossey-Bass.

Stewart, W. (1996) *Introduction to Lonergan's Insight*. Lewiston, MA. The Edwin Mellen Press.

Zuboff, S. (1988) *In the Age of the Smart Machine: The Future of Work and Power.* New York: Basic Books.

5 Getting smart around literacy: current social practice, workplaces and the workforce

Colin Lankshear

Telling tales

Case 1

Catherine Kell (1996) relates the literacy practices of an 'illiterate' South African community leader, Winnie Tsotso. Tsotso is a middle-aged woman living in a squatter community. As a child she was needed to care for her grandmother and, consequently, never attended school. Her first language is Xhosa. She is fluent in Afrikaans and English, and also speaks Sotho, Zulu and Tswana.

Tsotso is a local branch organiser for the ANC, a long-standing member of the squatters' Civic Association, and serves on the local health, pre-school and Catholic Welfare and Development committees. She also runs a soup kitchen for pensioners – purchasing, preparing and serving the food. She is a qualified first-aid worker, and more besides. In a 'technical' sense she is illiterate and sees herself as such, yet by means of social procedures she has developed with others, she easily manages the print requirements of her various roles.

Kell describes Tsotso's role within the welfare and politically focused work she does as that of an authority and leader. While she cannot decipher much in the way of print, let alone *write* texts, she *mediates* the literacy components of diverse work practices effortlessly. She does this by calling on well-developed networks of support, as well as on what she has learned informally by participating in these routines over many years. When she attends zone level meetings she brings the typed agendas home with her and has her daughters read them. She remembers the items and business associated with them and raises them at the branch meetings for local action. Similarly, when the delivery man brings vegetables and other supplies for her soup kitchen, Tsotso gives him her invoice book to enter what she has bought and the costs – to be checked later by her daughter. 'As I left, Portia [daughter] entered the room, picked up the book without a word passing between the two of them, and ran through the page very quickly' (Kell 1996: 240).

On the well-intentioned advice of supportive ANC officials, cognisant of the intensifying role of print within the changing ANC *modus operandi*, following the party's coming to power as the South African government, Tsotso began attending a beginners' literacy class at the local night school. Kell contrasts her struggles, night after night, to write out her name and sound out syllables, with her fluent competence and efficacy in diverse print-mediated practices within her working life as a community leader. The literacy curriculum of the night class bore little relationship to Tsotso's work, and within a few months she was rarely attending.

Case 2

In his book *Out of Control*, Kevin Kelly (1994) paints a workplace scenario of the near future. He invites us to imagine an office of the future located within a hypothetical Silicon Valley *automobile* manufacturer he calls 'Upstart Car Inc'. The company intends to compete with the industry leaders in Japan.

Here is Upstart's blueprint. A dozen people share a room in a sleek office building in Palo Alto, California. Some finance people, four engineers, a CEO, a coordinator, a lawyer and a marketing person. Across town in a former warehouse, crews assemble 120 mpg, non-polluting cars made from polychain composite materials, ceramic engines and electronic every-thing else. The 'high tech' plastics come from a young company with which Upstart has formed a joint venture. The engines are purchased in Singapore; other automobile parts arrive each day in barcoded profusion from Mexico, Utah and Detroit. The shipping companies deal with the temporary storage of parts; only what is needed that day appears at the plant. Cars – each one customer-tailored – are ordered by a network of customers and shipped the moment they are completed. Moulds for the car's body are rapidly shaped by computer-guided lasers, and fed designs generated by customer response and targeted marketing. A flexible line of robots assemble the cars.

Robot repair and improvement is outsourced to a robot company. Acme Plant Maintenance Service keeps the factory sheds going. Phone reception is hired out to a small outfit physically located in San Mateo. The clerical work is handled by a national agency that services all the other groups in the company: similarly with computer hardware. The marketing and legal people each oversee (of course) the marketing and legal services which Upstart also hires out. Bookkeeping is almost entirely computerised, but an outside accounting firm, operating from remote terminals, deals with any accounting requests. In total, about 100 workers are paid directly by Upstart, and they are organised into small groups with varying benefit plans and pay schedules. As Upstart's cars soar in popularity, the company grows by helping its suppliers grow, negotiating alliances, and sometimes investing in their growth (Kelly 1994: 247–248).

Snags

The apparently unproblematic, straightforward notions of 'literacy', 'workplace', and 'workforce' are anything but (O'Connor 1994). Is Winnie Tsotso literate? I would say 'yes'. Others would disagree. Is Winnie Tsotso a smart worker? What is the workplace, under conditions like those of Upstart Cars Inc? Indeed, *where* is the workplace? And where and what is the *workforce*? If Upstart Cars Inc has a smart workforce, what is that workforce in relation to Upstart Cars Inc? It is certainly not Upstart Cars' workforce in any proprietary sense. Elements of that workforce 'belong' to other companies, are 'free agents' and so on. We are speaking here, in many ways, of a 'radically decentred workforce'. Which raises questions about where responsibilities for training that workforce lie, and how Upstart Cars came to get a smart workforce. To what extent does the smart workforce associated with Upstart Cars Inc reflect a smart hiring and contracting approach, as opposed to anything having to do with putting in place *training* in order to get it — at least on the part of Upstart? What can we say about literacy in relation to the workers associated with Upstart's operation?

Introduction

This chapter will present a range of analytic 'tools' for helping us think about literacy in relation to what might be called 'smart work' and educating a 'smart workforce' under contemporary conditions. In doing so it will aim to address both conventional (print-based) and technological (digital) practices of literacy, and speak to different kinds of workplace arrangements.

The following section addresses elements of current thinking about 'literacy' arising from work that 'problematises' traditional notions of literacy — particularly *educational* constructions. The key idea advanced is of literacy as 'three-dimensional socio-cultural practice' — i.e. spanning the conventional print-based literacies as well as the so-called 'technological literacies' associated with 'digital–electronic apparatus' (Ulmer 1989).

Secondly, 'smart work' must be understood within the context of what is often called 'the new capitalism' and the unfolding global informational economy (Carnoy *et al*. 1993; Castells 1996; Gee *et al*. 1996). The constructs and trends associated with changing work in recent times yield a clutch of analytic tools for thinking about smart work and its links to literacy. These tools include distinctions between 'analytic–symbolic', 'routine production' and 'in-person service' work (Reich 1992), and features associated with leading-edge work.

Thirdly, a taxonomy is provided of five predominant constructions of literacy within current education policies and reform agendas (Lankshear 1998). The taxonomy prompts questions about the possible relationships between these views of literacy and the ideal of smart work.

Fourthly, quite different constructions of a smart workforce are possible. Some theorists seem to confine smart work to a narrow range of symbolic-theoretical work (often referred to as 'knowledge work'). For others, however, work of all kinds might attain the status of being smart: the acid test being the capacity of how the work is undertaken to enhance efficiency or productivity per unit of input; to achieve multiplier effects and/or eliminate errors; to generalise applications creatively, and otherwise 'add value'. From this perspective, talk of smart work may extend to such things as making incremental innovations within basic routines. Exploring such distinctions helps sharpen the issues and interfaces involved in relating literacy to developing a smart workforce.

Finally, with these analytic tools in place, some brief examples will be provided of how they may be applied to thinking and acting strategically with respect to literacy and smart work.

Literacy

Traditional and socio-cultural views of literacy

Literacy is still widely understood, in the 'traditional' manner, as the ability to read and write (Gee 1996: 49), in the sense of decoding (deciphering) and encoding (inscribing) texts – typically of the print variety. Until recently, educators have tended to see literacy 'as a largely *psychological* ability – something to do with our heads' (Gee *et al.* 1996: 1). From this perspective, being literate has meant having the 'internal' cognitive capacities and 'skills' involved in 'being able to "crack the code"' (especially, alphabetic print) and 'get meaning out of texts' as a result. These days, of course, texts are seen to include digital as well as conventional print texts.

This view of literacy also contains an 'external' technological aspect. Literate people can use the 'tool' or technology of print and other means of 'codification' to access or convey meanings. The idea here is that the literate person draws on his or her cognitive capacities in applying the technologies of literacy to all manner of activities and within many different areas of life: from writing notes to one's children to writing novels for publication; from reading for leisure to reading instructions at work; from the most simple to the most complex and sophisticated levels of text production, whatever kind of texts they may be. In this sense of literacy, Winnie Tsotso would not be judged literate – which is why she was encouraged to go to literacy classes. Of course, the tool/technology side of literacy is highly visible at present in notions of 'technological literacy', as involving mastery of computer applications.

The traditional cognition and technology view of literacy as reading and writing has been challenged increasingly since the 1970s by a 'socio-cultural' view of literacy as embedded social practice. The underlying idea here is that we simply cannot describe and understand what happens in actual literacy

practices if we see literacy (as reading and writing) in cognitive and technological terms alone. This is because reading and writing are always a matter
of reading or writing *something in particular*, and doing so *with understanding*
(Gee *et al*. 1996: 1–4). In this sense, I personally can 'read' (decode) a page
of an advanced chemistry text, but I cannot *read it* in any meaningful sense
of 'reading' – because I do not 'know' chemistry. The point is that 'getting
to know' in the required sense involves much more than just cognition and
technology – it can only be achieved via participation in relevant social
practices.

Different kinds of text require 'somewhat different background knowledge
and somewhat different skills' if they are to be *read* (or written) meaningfully
(Gee *et al*. 1996: 2). Moreover, particular texts can be read in very different
ways, depending upon people's varying experiences of practices in which
these texts occur. For example, a fundamentalist Christian will read biblical
texts in radically different ways from, say, a liberation theologian. They read
out of different practices; they read differently; they are differently literate.
This difference is about much more than simply cognition and technology.
In addition, there are differences in enculturation and socialisation: different
people become familiar with, and participate in, *social practice* within which
texts play integral roles.

Indeed, there are *many* literacies, and even very high levels of 'skill' in
encoding and decoding, in grammatical precision, accuracy with spelling,
and so on, are no guarantee of successful performance of a given (contextu-
alised practice of) literacy. The fact that a person can encode and decode
prose does not mean that they will actually get their message across, sell a
vision, persuade us or entertain us. Often they do not. From another angle,
the literacy of a priest or a lawyer will be very different at points that
matter from the literacy of a graffiti artist, a bill poster, a team leader on
the factory floor, a producer of video game software, etc.

Any useful notion of literacy, therefore, must make sense of reading, writing and meaning-making as integral elements of social practices. Such an
account is provided by James Gee (1991: 8), who defines literacy as 'control
of secondary language uses' or, to put it another way, as control of language
uses in secondary Discourses (with a big 'D'). In his subsequent work, Gee
distinguishes between Discourse and discourse, as observed hereafter (cf.
Gee 1996). This definition of literacy involves a distinction between 'primary'
and 'secondary' Discourses, and a helpful account of the relationship between
Discourse and language.

According to Gee, Discourses are socially recognised ways of using language (reading, writing, speaking, listening), gestures and other semiotics
(images, sounds, graphics, signs, codes), *as well as* ways of thinking, believing,
feeling, valuing, acting/doing and interacting in relation to people and
things, such that we can be identified and recognised as being a member of
a socially meaningful group, or as playing a socially meaningful role (cf.
Gee 1991, 1996). To be in, or part of, a Discourse means that others can

recognise us as being a 'this' or a 'that' (a pupil, mother, priest, footballer, mechanic), or a particular 'version' of a this or that (a reluctant pupil, a doting mother, a radical priest, a 'bush' mechanic) by virtue of how we are using language, believing, feeling, acting, dressing, doing, and so on. Language is a dimension of Discourse, but only one dimension, and Gee uses discourse (with a small 'd') to mark this relationship – discourse being the 'language bits' in Discourse (Gee 1993, 1996).

If we think in terms of workplace Discourses, we might contrast worker Discourses on the factory floor with executive Discourses in the boardroom. People are different and behave differently in the one as opposed to the other, along all the sorts of dimensions we have just identified. To talk in the boardroom in the way someone does on the floor might be very inappropriate. Likewise in terms of dress and gesturing. Beliefs and values may vary dramatically across the two scenes. So might goals and purposes. In addition, identities are likely to differ greatly.

With respect to the distinction between 'primary' and 'secondary' Discourses, our primary Discourse is acquired and operated within immediate face-to-face contexts involving intimates/our kinship group. 'Primary' is defined here in relation to kin, our initial community of interactants. Within our primary socialisation we become *enculturated* into the ways of our particular primary group. We learn to do and be in a particular way, and these ways vary greatly from social group to social group along lines of ethnicity, religion, social class and the like. The important point is that learning to talk – our primary language use – is acquired within the Discourse of our primary socialisation, but that within this primary Discourse, we acquire so much more than our first language alone. We come to use our acquired 'language, behaviour, values and beliefs to give . . . a shape to our experience': to make our world meaningful in a certain way, and to make ourselves identifiable in a certain way – which differs from the ways 'Others' do it (Gee 1996: 7).

We move into the realm of secondary Discourses when we enter the world of secondary institutions (school, church, workplace, club, bureaucratic departments, etc), beyond our face-to-face social group. Just as different primary institutions (tribes, families, clans; nuclear families, extended families; working-class families, middle-class families) have their distinctive ways of talking, believing, interacting, valuing, and the like, which add up to different ways of being, different ways of 'doing life', different ways of relating, making sense of the world and organising our experience; so do secondary institutions. Just as our primary groups involve us in particular Discourses and ways of being, so do secondary institutions. These secondary Discourses may differ quite a lot from our primary Discourses, and there may be tension between them. How well we do in certain secondary Discourses is a function of how well they 'fit' with our primary Discourse. While we have just one primary Discourse (by definition) we will encounter many secondary Discourses in our lives – because we live our lives in and through many secondary institutions. In fact, we often encounter a range of secondary Discourses within a single secondary institutional setting. These secondary Discourses always involve language, but they involve all the other dimensions of Discourses as well.

As noted, Gee defines 'literacy' in terms of *secondary* Discourses. To be literate is to have control of language uses in secondary Discourses (or, secondary language uses). Since there are many secondary Discourses and, hence, many secondary language uses, there are many literacies, and people such as the readers of this book engage in numerous literacies. According to this definition, being able to speak effectively and appropriately to different people in different capacities in different contexts, as well as to complete a range of written communications and, possibly, to convey information using graphs, tables, diagrams, and other things besides, will represent some of the dimensions of literacy in workplace settings. The exact range and proportions, as well as the content and 'style' of these language uses may vary considerably from role to role, location to location, Discourse to Discourse (production team Discourse, company executive Discourse, trade union Discourse, employer Discourse) within the workplace. A given person might range over several workplace Discourses (such as a team member who is also a union representative and a shareholder in the company, or a member of the board of directors).

This account has interesting and important implications for cases like that of Winnie Tsotso. Clearly, she *had* mastered a number of secondary Discourses, *including their language uses*. In fact, she had mastered these in ways that mere facility with encoding and decoding print – in cognitive and technological terms alone – could not ensure. She *was* literate in terms of these secondary discursive language uses. The point was that these Discourses were in the process of being *displaced* in ways that would change what would officially be recognised as control of their secondary language uses. Whether the new Discourses and literacies that displaced them would produce 'better', 'higher-quality' outcomes more 'efficiently' is an empirical question. Whether Winnie's learning to 'read and write' would fit her any better for performing those Discourses and literacies is likewise an empirical question. What is clear from this perspective on literacy is that there is no easy relationship between possessing cognitive capacities with technologies of 'codification' and having mastery of secondary Discourses. To the extent that smart work, smart workplaces and smart workforces have to do with mastery of relevant secondary Discourses and their embedded language uses, we may need to renegotiate our (traditional) understandings of literacy considerably.

Dimensions of effective literacy: operational, cultural and critical

These ideas can be pushed further by reference to three integral dimensions of effective literacy. From a socio-cultural perspective, literacy must be seen in

'3D', as having three interlocking dimensions – the operational, the cultural, and the critical – which bring together language, meaning and context (Green 1988: 160–163). An integrated view of literacy in practice and in pedagogy addresses all three dimensions simultaneously; none has any necessary priority over the others.

The *operational* dimension refers to the 'means' of literacy, in the sense that it is in and through the medium of language that the literacy event happens. It involves competency with regard to the language system. To refer to the operational dimension of literacy is to point to the manner in which individuals use language in literacy tasks, in order to operate effectively in specific contexts. The emphasis is on handling the written (text, image, other semiotics) language system adequately. From this perspective, literacy is a question of individuals being able to handle the language bits of Discourses in a range of contexts, in appropriate and adequate ways (see Green 1988; Lankshear *et al.* 1997: vol. 1). Entering data into a spreadsheet, for example, requires knowing how to operate spreadsheet software, having first mastered how to operate the computer to the point of opening the spreadsheet program.

The *cultural* dimension involves what may be called the meaning aspect of literacy. It is never simply a case of being literate 'in and of itself', but of being literate with regard to something: some aspect of knowledge or experience. The cultural aspect of literacy is a matter of understanding texts in relation to contexts – to appreciate their meaning; the meaning they need to make in order to be appropriate; and what it is about given contexts of practice that makes for appropriateness or inappropriateness of particular ways of producing and accessing texts. To take the case of spreadsheets, these are not all the same. Moreover, people do not simply *produce* spreadsheets by going into some software program and 'filling in the spaces'. Spreadsheets have to be *compiled* – which means knowing their purpose and constructing their categories, axes and matrices accordingly. To know the purpose of a particular spreadsheet requires understanding relevant parts of the *culture* of the immediate work context; to know why one is doing what one is doing now, how to do it, and why what one is doing is appropriate. Whereas the operational dimension of being literate is a matter of mastering certain techniques for handling language (e.g. printing, keying, accessing files, etc), the cultural dimension is about achieving an understanding of 'language use' in relation to the Discourse as a whole.

The *critical* dimension is also integral to effective literacy, and has particular relevance for 'smart' workplaces. Very often there are better – more efficient, more accurate – ways of doing things textually than currently operate. Workers in smart workplaces do not simply employ technological literacy to *follow* procedures. They can add value by *improving* procedures. A 'smart' worker might hit on a better way to compile a spreadsheet for a particular function, and should certainly always be on the lookout for better ways. The critical dimension of literacy presupposes competence in the operational and cultural aspects, on the basis of which workers keep an eye out for 'spaces' where they can stand back and evaluate the efficiency or 'optimality' of what they are doing and how they are doing it, and develop and recommend improvements and changes accordingly. One cannot be critical without having operational and cultural knowledge. At the same time, one cannot operate with maximum efficiency or meet the cultural goals of the enterprise without attending to the critical. Critical literacy insights, then, might lead to revisions in the operational and/or cultural dimensions, after which the process enters a new 'round' in its ongoing dynamic – with new operational elements occurring within a somewhat changed cultural setting, providing new stimuli for further critical scrutiny and development, and so on.

Technological literacies in workplaces

With the exponential growth of the 'digital–electronic apparatus' (Ulmer 1989) during the past two decades, the idea has taken hold among literacy educators that in addition to being 'literate' in terms of conventional print media and texts, learners must now acquire *some new kind of literacy* associated with the burgeoning use of computer-mediated communications technologies in everyday life. The new literacy is commonly referred to as 'technological literacy'. Of course, any notion that literacy has become *technological* with the emergence of the 'digital–electronic apparatus' involves a kind of conceptual and historical blindness. Understood as some form or other of *written* language, literacy is always-already 'technologised'. That is, literacy always comes with some technology or other 'built in'. Literacy comes into being only and always in the form of, and through the medium of, available technologies of information and communication (Lankshear *et al.* 1997: vol. 1: 20). The spate of contemporary talk about *technological literacies* seems to reflect the tendency for those technologies integral to conventional (print) literacy to have become 'invisible' because they have always 'been there' and, consequently, become 'naturalized'. The emergence of a new literacy medium suddenly makes its associated literacy, or literacies, appear to be 'technological'. Recognising this historical blindness for what it is, we may understand conceptions of 'technological literacy' to be variations around the theme of practices in which texts are digitized electronically, with particular emphasis on computer-mediated textual practices.

Drawing on what has already been said about 'literacy', three main points stand out with respect to 'technological literacy' in workplaces. First, the idea subsumes a whole range of contributing practices, relevant to the mastery of secondary Discourses, which involve the use of new technologies. These may include such things as: being able to access knowledge about the technology (tool) from a manual or from experts; being able to use technologies to carry out and enhance one's performance of literacy tasks (text production and dissemination); knowing useful things about the technology and being

Table 5.1 Some typical elements of technological literacies in workplaces

Generic practices (D/ discourses)	Contextual elements (cultural and dimension)	Activities/tasks (cultural and operational)	Techniques/procedures (operational)	Evaluation (critical)
Computer-Mediated Workplace Networking	Purpose of the network	E-mailing	Create folders, build mailboxes, compile address lists, store messages	Enhanced access to others?
		Videoconferencing	Adjust video image	A clear agenda/ programme?
	Range of people to be accommodated	Set up a LAN or WAN	Set computer ports	Stability of the network maximised?
		Establish lists on server	Set up majordomo list	Discussions worthwhile?
		Maintain security	Set up fire walls	Have we been hacked?
	Kind of information to be communicated	Searching online databases	Identify key words	Is the information reliable and of good quality?
	Available resources	Compare costs and benefits across different options	Analyse catalogues and compare boxes and prices	Are we getting value for money?
	Technical options	Compare costs and benefits across different options	Analyse catalogues and compare boxes and prices	Are we getting value for money?

competent around it; and understanding one's text production, data entry, symbolic representations and so on, as ways of getting the job done (effective memos, revving up/inspiring the troops, keeping accurate and up-to-date information moving across subsystems, producing an effective marketing device or new opportunities for outsourcing etc).

Secondly, technological literacies will be many and varied. For example, producing a computer-assisted design is radically different from producing a word-processed letter to creditors or debtors, or compiling a spreadsheet or database. In this regard we may ponder how much of such varying 'technological literacies' is *technological:* that is, how much of the difference is accounted for by the particular technologies in question and our facility with them?

Thirdly, there is much more to technological literacy than just 'working a computer'. A technologically literate person has mastery of computer-assisted (or enhanced) language uses within some workplace Discourse, which means having considerable cultural awareness or knowledge, as well as appropriate kinds of critical capacity. This idea can be illustrated by reference to computer-mediated workplace networking as a secondary discursive practice. Table 5.1 captures some typical components of this literacy in ways that encapsulate literacy as three-dimensional sociocultural practice.

It is important to recognise that the growing shift from print to digital electronics means we have to go beyond notions of literacy based on the idea of *text*, and also to recognise that different species of software will be important media of literacy within workplace settings.

The model of the text as the printed page is too narrow for dealing with digital texts. Digital texts include web pages created in hypertext, as well as artefacts produced using virtual reality mark-up language. These know no margins, they are not linear and they do not stand still. They incorporate sound, animations and so on. Digital texts are not 'enclosed' in the manner of conventional print texts. They may be sequenced entirely differently, and they do not *exist* in the fixed and finite form that operates with conventional print texts (see Lankshear *et al.* 1996, and Peters and Lankshear 1996 for more detailed discussion).

Moreover, ideas of literacy based on the literary model of text marginalises *information* in ways that are inappropriate in the information age. Artefacts produced using databases and spreadsheets, as well as diverse texts incorporating sound, video clips and other animation, models, and all manner of graphics and images, which fall loosely under the rubric of 'information', have become ubiquitous. Literacy needs to be understood in ways that integrate text *and* information and do not subordinate information to 'usage' and 'understanding' (Green 1997; Lankshear *et al.* 1997: vol. 1: 33–35).

Finally, in the electronic age, our understanding of literacy must accommodate at least the following dimensions of technological literacy, and in terms of both 'stand-alone' and 'networked' forms of computing:

- *text*-based (or -oriented) computing/software – e.g. word processing, desktop publishing;
- *information*-based (or -oriented) computing/software – e.g. database, spreadsheet;
- *programming*-based (or -oriented) computing/software – e.g. LOGO, PERL, BASIC, C++;
- *games*-based (or -oriented) computing/software – e.g. Tomb Raider, Dungeon Master, Diablo, Super Mario Brothers, Streetfighter.

The new capitalism and smart work

Whatever (else) is meant by 'a smart workforce', it means a collectivity of workers (employees, executives, free agents) who are able to perform in ways that keep an enterprise *viable* (competitive, efficient, successful) under conditions of the new capitalism. These are conditions broadly framed by increased global hypercompetition, massive technological changes, global economic integration and penetration, and changes in consumers and consumption priorities and patterns.

Analysts of work in the global informational economy identify key features associated with success and viability under current and foreseeable conditions. Four key features recur across influential accounts.

1   The bases of productivity in the new capitalism depend increasingly on applying science and technology in processes of production, distribution, consumption and change. Productivity is no longer mainly a matter of just injecting more labour and/or capital into production processes. Rather, productivity edge is generated by 'new inputs' consisting of 'the deeper penetration of science, technology, labour skills, and management know-how' (Castells 1993: 15–16). This produces uneven skills and knowledge requirements across the workforce. For example, as computer programs take over much of the work of drafting and design in engineering and architecture, low-level 'professional' workers know less, with their expertise more and more an artefact of their manipulation of the machine. Those who design and program the technology know more and have more flexibility and power in their work.

2   The second feature is that the new capitalism is characterised by 'an ever-growing role' being played within the organisation of work and the enhancement of productivity by 'the manipulation of symbols' (Castells 1993: 17). We find a pronounced trend away from material production and toward information processing activities. Not only is a greater and greater proportion of developed countries' GNP accounted for by trade in 'data, words, oral and visual representations' (Reich 1992: 177), but a greater and greater proportion of the workforce is employed in such activities, either as 'foot soldiers of the information economy . . . stationed

in "back offices" at computer terminals linked to worldwide information banks' (Reich 1992: 175), or as 'symbolic analysts' involved in higher-order problem solving (cf. Reich 1992: 175). According to Castells, the quality of the information and the efficiency in acquiring and processing it 'now constitute the strategic factor in both competitiveness and productivity for firms, regions, and countries' (Castells 1993: 17–18). From the *consumer* end of the equation we can see that our contemporary world is very much a *semiotic* world, a world of signs and symbols, a world where 'design' and 'life*style*' often count more than the materiality of products or the concrete social practices of people and institutions. Catering for design and style are very much matters of manipulating symbols. Hence, symbol manipulation ranges from information and data entry and transferral, all the way to aspects of innovation in design and clever 'takes' on marketing and advertising.

3   Leading-edge work organises production and other economic processes in new ways. Goods production has shifted from standardised mass production to *flexible specialisation* and increased *innovation* and *adaptability*, calling for corresponding characteristics in individual workers as well as across different sectors/units within the enterprise. The turn to high-quality flexible production necessitates changes in the *social relationships* of work. The 'vertically integrated large-scale organisations' of older days have given way to 'vertical disintegration and horizontal networks between economic units' (Castells 1993: 18). This is partly a matter of flatter hierarchies, increased devolution of responsibility to individual employees, the creation of quality circles, multi-skilled work teams with interchangeable tasks, and enlarged scope for workers to participate in decision-making. In addition, horizontal relationships of cooperation, consultation and coordination, in the interests of flexibility, decentralisation and adaptability in production, often extend beyond the confines of a specific business or firm to include other 'partners' within an integrated productive enterprise: such as collaborative arrangements between manufacturers and suppliers that help keep overheads and stock inventories down, allowing competitive pricing which can undercut opponents. This is the idea of enterprises as 'distributed systems'. In summary, hierarchy is lowered among employees; borders are eased between businesses (e.g. producers and suppliers) and business units. Decentralisation, networking, flexibility, cooperation, collaboration, customisation and 'close to the customer', as well as a small, flexible and local organisation – these are major motifs in descriptions of leading-edge work.

4   Work is increasingly 'outsourced', in many cases over large distances. For many workers, their competition is no longer just another local worker looking for a job but, rather, entire labour markets abroad. What holds for individual workers holds equally for enterprises. In many cases, for local workers and enterprises to survive it is a matter of offsetting

'cheapness' of labour costs elsewhere with 'smartness' of work/operation here. Once again, Kelly's Upstart Cars scenario serves as an illustrative example here.

Within this context, more and more production is being accounted for by three main types of work. Reich (1992) refers to these as 'symbolic analytic services', 'routine production work', and 'in-person service work'. Between them they will eventually account for almost all the paid work performed in modern economies.

Besides the repetitive blue-collar activities of traditional mass production, routine production services include basic data entry tasks as well as many supervisory jobs performed by low- and middle-level managers: 'foremen, line managers, clerical supervisors, section chiefs – who run repetitive checks on subordinates' work and [enforce] standard operating procedures' (Reich 1992: 174). In-person service work is also largely made up of repetitive tasks, albeit 'in direct contact with the ultimate beneficiaries of [the] work': e.g. the work of retail salespersons, hospitality workers, janitors, cashiers, drivers, secretaries, flight attendants, security guards (Reich 1992: 176). Symbolic–analytic work involves services that are delivered in the forms of data, words, and oral and visual representations. It comprises diverse problem-identifying, problem-solving, and strategic brokering activities (Reich 1992: 177). According to Reich, symbolic analysts deal with problems by manipulating symbols: simplifying reality 'into abstract images' and other symbolic forms. These forms can then be 'rearranged, juggled, experimented with, communicated to other specialists, and then, eventually, transformed back into reality' (Reich 1992). These workers draw on a combination of experience and their facility with analytic tools, which range from philosophical or legal arguments, to scientific principles, to algorithms, to gimmicks, to psychology-based ideas about how to amuse, and so on (Reich 1992: 178). As such, symbolic–analytic services span the work of research scientists, all manner of engineers (from civil to sound), management consultants, investment bankers, systems analysts, authors, editors, art directors, video and film producers, musicians, and so on.

Besides these categories of work – whose descriptions may seem a little too rigid and static for our tastes – there are also the various forms of administrative, coordinating, 'skilled trade', professional–managerial, educational and training work (among others).

Constructions of literacy

Five main constructions of literacy are apparent in current literacy policies and official educational agendas, which I call 'lingering basics', 'new basics', 'elite literacies', 'foreign language literacy' and 'technological–information literacy' respectively.

Lingering basics

The notion of basic literacy as a mastery of fundamentals of encoding and decoding print texts continues to 'linger' from the 1960s and 1970s. This notion is framed in terms of mastering the building blocks of code-breaking: knowing the alphabet, how to put the script together to make words, how to add words to read and write sentences, etc. At the level of child education, this is typically seen as 'foundational' literacy, enabling progress to further literacies and 'knowledge' – generalisable techniques and concepts presumed to be building blocks for subsequent education. In the case of adult literacy learners, the idea is often defined largely in terms of a body of *content* intended to meet demands for 'functionality', rather than as a foundational basis for further ends: that is, in terms of baseline functional competencies or 'life skills' that all adults should have, emphasising the ability 'to perform specific literacy-related tasks in the context of work, family and other "real-life" situations' (US Office of Technology Assessment 1989: 32).

New basics

A central motif in current thinking about education and training is that the 'old – or lingering – basics' are no longer sufficient for effective participation in modern societies. The qualitative shifts in social practices variously associated with the transition from an agri-industrial economy to a post-industrial information/services economy; from 'Fordism' to 'post-Fordism'; from more personal face-to-face communities to impersonal metropolitan and, even, virtual communities; from a paternal (welfare) state to a more devolved state requiring greater self-sufficiency, and so on; all these shifts are seen to call for qualitatively more sophisticated ('smart'), abstract, symbolic-logical capacities than were needed in the past. In new times, it is argued, the old 'base' needs to be raised. As '*new* basics', literacy is seen as a combination of 'critical thinking' – a generic grab bag for higher-order skills of comprehension, problem-solving and analysis – and reading, writing, speaking and listening.

'Elite' literacies

Ideals of education for excellence have generated talk of higher-order literacies, understood as high-level mastery of subject discipline literacies, such that being literate means here being able to manipulate symbols, theories and theoretical knowledge, information, etc, in the manner of scientists, mathematicians, various sorts of designers and engineers, advertisers, writers and composers, and so on. Such '*elite*' literacies can be understood in terms of mastering the 'languages' and 'literatures' (Hirst 1974) of academic disciplines. The *language* of an academic discipline refers to the 'logic' or process of inquiry within that field. A discipline's *literature* comprises the 'content' of work in the field – the accumulated attainments of people working in that subject area.

Command of the language and literature of a field of inquiry permits critique, innovation, variation, diversification, refinement, and so on, to occur. This may range from producing entirely new approaches to managing organisations, or new kinds of computer hardware and software (from mainframe to PC; DOS to Windows, the addition of sound and video), to producing new reporting processes for literacy attainment and new ways of conceiving literacy; from variations within architectural and engineering design, to variations on mass-produced commodities which provide a semblance of individuality or novelty.

This is very much the literacy of what Robert Reich (1992) calls 'symbolic analysis', and Peter Drucker (1993) calls 'knowledge work'. This is now widely seen as the real 'value-adding' work within modern economies. The scientist, historian, architect, software designer, composer, management theorist and electronic engineer, all manipulate, modify, refine, combine, and in other ways employ symbols contained in, or derived from, the language and literature of their disciplines to produce new knowledge, innovative designs, new applications of theory, and so on. These can be drawn on to 'add maximum value' to raw materials and labour in the process of producing goods and services.

Foreign language literacy

Recent educational policy directions have given renewed attention to enhancing second language proficiency. Two main factors have generated the emergence of second language literacy education as a new (and pressing) capitalist instrumentality. Firstly, trading partners have changed greatly for Anglophone countries, and many of our new partners have not been exposed to decades (or centuries) of colonial or neo-colonial English language hegemony. Secondly, trade competition has become intense. Many countries now produce commodities previously produced by relatively few. Within this context of intensified competition, the capacity to market, sell, inform and provide after-sales support in the customer's language becomes a crucial element of competitive edge.

Technological-information literacy: literacy for the knowledge economy

Current talk of literacy abounds with ideas of harnessing new information and communications technologies to literacy practices. Often, however, these amount to little more than adding a new technology dimension to familiar constructions of literacy (think: word processing as opposed to writing or typing texts). In 1996, President Clinton's announcement of America's 'technology literacy challenge' brought talk of 'technological literacy' to the highest level of official policy prominence. Within the Clinton agenda, technological literacy is defined loosely in terms of 'communication, math, science, and critical thinking skills essential to prepare [students] for the Information Age' (Winters 1996). Communication skills include the ability to learn through use of computers and the 'information superhighway', and to handle modern computers efficiently. Of course, framed in this way' 'technological literacy' appears to be little more than 'the new basics' harnessed to information and communications technologies. Notwithstanding such limitations, however, these ideas enjoy strong currency in work-oriented education and training agendas.

A further 'technological' construction of literacy is emerging in the form of 'information literacy'. It is argued that the knowledge economy demands a competency that 'links information management skills, systems thinking and learning skills and information technology competency at various levels of sophistication' (Tinkler *et al*. 1996: 73–74). Information literacy is understood as

> a literacy that combines information collection and analysis and management skills and systems thinking and meta-cognition skills with the ability to use information technology to express and enhance those skills. In a society of information 'glut' the ability to detect 'signal' from 'noise' will become increasingly valued. Students will require the development of information literacy to be effective citizens and workers in a knowledge economy, while teachers/learning facilitators will require this literacy to be able to develop it in their students and to carry out their professional responsibilities as knowledge workers.
>
> (Tinkler *et al*. 1996: 73–74)

Such accounts – which are becoming increasingly common – attempt to frame a distinctive conception of text–information handling practices integral to post-typographic conditions, and to come to terms with the escalating trend toward electronic networking using technologies combining text, image, voice, simulations and virtual reality with interactivity.

Alternative constructions of a smart workforce

At the level of a 'unit of analysis', the very notion of a smart *workforce* is vexed in ways that have deep implications for educational and training strategies. When we think of the workforce at a *national* level, we are thinking of 'our' workers being smart in relation to those who reside in other countries within a global labour market. This might entail developing workers whose efficiency/productivity/value-adding capacities offset their higher wages (and higher costs of living) against the advantages that accrue to enterprises from recruiting workers in other (low-wage, low-cost) countries (Reich

1992: 301–302). At this level, the education and training issue calls for national strategies, beginning at school. At the opposite extreme, however, we might think of a smart workforce in terms of a *single enterprise*. At this level, there may be very little for the enterprise to worry about at the level of training and education if, for example, they can recruit 'smart' workers in accordance with a 'smart' corporate strategy. Any matters of maintaining and enhancing smartness could be dealt with by means of short-term contracts, rolling recruitment and highly focused and specialised training as required (e.g. revamping the company's electronic network, acquainting relevant employees with new software, brushing up an executive's foreign language ability). This shifts the weight of analysis on to what counts as 'smart work' for the particular enterprise, and on matching labour recruits to the enterprise's production.

Similar issues, however, arise with talk of smart work. If 'smart work' is identified with 'value adding' work, and this in turn is identified mainly with 'symbolic–analytic' work, the literacy implications for smart work might focus mainly on developing 'elite literacies', 'foreign language literacy' and, perhaps, the higher reaches of 'new basics' (e.g. higher-order problem-solving strategies). At the level of developing a smart workforce on a *national* scale, this might be interpreted as trying to turn as many as possible of a country's learners into 'symbolic analysts' (Reich 1992), or 'knowledge workers' (Drucker 1993). Conversely, if smart work is defined in terms of efficiencies and productivity considerations across the entire gamut of work in an enterprise, the literacy implications of smart work will extend all the way to shoring up worker 'functionality' with concern for 'lingering basics'. Here, the crucial issue might be how to ensure that the operational, cultural, and critical dimensions of literacy are properly addressed, whichever literacy constructions are at stake in the cases of particular workers. More radically still, it might mean that our literacy and education work in training and development is better conceived if we *ignore* the categories and constructions of literacies as they come to us in 'policy-speak' and education and training agendas; and focus, instead, on understanding what it means for workers, at whatever levels and in whatever areas of an enterprise, to master the language uses of the Discourses in which they are involved, with appropriate attention to each of the 'operational', 'cultural' and 'critical' dimensions – and to provide training as necessary.

Finally, for present purposes, we may note that different kinds of enterprises may distribute the expertise of their smart workers in very different ways, in accordance with differing purposes and conceptions of core business, and with significant implications for literacy. A comparison of two small Australian enterprises involved in providing 'digital' services for clients provides illustrative examples here.

'Edge Tech' provides computer-based marking products, particularly web pages. It is a very successful small enterprise owned and managed by Angus, a highly creative, innovative, tough-minded entrepreneur. In recent years, Edge Tech has pioneered numerous developments in commercial use of the internet, and has won prestigious awards for its work. Its major and subsidiary websites carry massive traffic and have attracted worldwide attention. Besides Angus, Edge Tech employs two young people adept at web page technology and production. Conceptual leadership, however, is invested solely in Angus, who does all the entrepreneurial work, drumming up clients and 'selling' them the company's services. He has established rigorous and logical specifications for web pages: e.g. they must download quickly, hence there are standards that must be followed in terms of graphics. Besides these standards, the conceptual parameters of web page design are further framed and circumscribed by Angus and the clients, negotiating together. Edge Tech's 'smart parts' (web workers) are typically presented with specifications for the pages, within which they have some scope for manoeuvre. They develop drafts which are then presented to Angus and the client for comment and decision. While the employees engage in forms of symbolic analytic activity – symbol manipulation and symbolic representation – this is very tightly circumscribed and admixed with considerable 'routine production' and not a little in-person service work (cups of tea, working the phone). When the web workers find the work unchallenging – something which they admitted to freely – they leave, but are easily replaced.

'Wedge Tech' provides a range of services, including CD-ROMs produced for clients to use in training programmes, and offering training for clients in the use of new communications and information technologies. At the same time, Wedge Tech is itself a training organisation. It takes in young people and uses product development for clients as a training context. Its aims to develop and turnover talented people (smart workers) – not by burning them out, but by developing young people to the point where they can 'go out and do likewise, even setting up in competition'. The thinking is 'if Jack is still here in two years we haven't done our job'. Wedge Tech must, nonetheless, remain viable. The products it delivers must be of high quality to keep the company solvent. Nevertheless, Wedge Tech's rationale requires that all of its 'smart parts' (workers) are given full opportunities to develop the full range of expertise commanded by its leaders. They have to learn how to interact with and respond to multiple environments (clients, jobs, sectors of practice) by mastering aspects of design, becoming able to communicate knowledge and skills efficiently in training provision contexts, and learning how to spot (and create) markets, clients and trends, to negotiate tasks and products, to develop effective networks, to keep abreast of innovations in the field (software, tastes and fashions, design, etc).

In the terms employed earlier, Wedge Tech's approach involves all employees learning how to control an entire range of secondary Discourses and their language uses: that is, it emphasises becoming operationally, culturally and critically competent in multiple and diverse Discourses. Edge Tech's approach, in contrast, requires a much narrower range of distributed 'smart' expertise. Indeed, the employees are given almost negligible scope for 'critical' practice in their work. They are kept away from the Discourses associated with the entrepreneurial/market-creation side of the business. They need an altogether narrower range of *literacies* at their command.

Applications and implications

There is no simple relationship between literacy and developing a smart workforce. There cannot be, since neither construct is itself simple. Indeed, literacy and smart work(force) are both deeply contested concepts. People frame them in very different ways because they prioritise different values, purposes, and ways of approaching the world (see O'Connor 1994 for a range of relevant perspectives).

My aim in this chapter has been to contribute to our options for understanding literacy in relation to work in new times. From one standpoint, a problem exists around talk about literacy and smart work insofar as both concepts are readily co-optable for ideological work. At a very obvious level, claims about 'inadequate levels of adult literacy' have been invoked *ad nauseam* to explain away difficulties confronting enterprises as economies and work undergo massive reconfiguration on a global scale. Attention gets deflected away from structural and historical processes, and decisions effectively taken on the basis of serving powerful interests, and gets focused instead on individuals who often occupy the most vulnerable cultural, linguistic, gender, ethnic and social-class positions within the society. Similarly, the notion of 'smart work' is readily turned to justifying – or, at least, 'explaining' – the growing gap and polarisation between well-paid workers and low-paid workers, and between more and attractive conditions of work (Gee *et al.* 1996: 44–48). It is very important to avoid getting trapped in unduly narrow views of available options and dehistoricised accounts of contemporary change.

We *do have* options available for thinking about smart work and smart workplaces. We most emphatically have options available for thinking about literacy. We also have options available for thinking about matters of allocation and distribution. And we have options available for thinking about progress. More importantly, these options for thinking provide us with options for acting. The more easily we dismiss the idea that people like Winnie Tsotso are literate, the more readily we dismiss the notion that people like Winnie Tsotso engage in smart work, the more readily and easily we submit to rhetorics that equate 'progress' with 'greater technological sophistication'; that displace existing and functioning practices ('ways of getting things done') with new practices that are seen to be 'better' because they are more 'technological' (e.g. more 'digitally saturated') or more 'literate' (e.g. employ inscribed texts more intensely, as opposed to recognising alternative ways of controlling language uses in secondary Discourses).

Likewise, there is all the difference in the world between identifying smart work with the work of a critical symbolic, analysis, which simply focuses on finding more efficient modes of symbolic manipulation to achieve taken-as-given ends, and identifying smart work with practices that call for workers to engage all three dimensions of literacy as they go about their training and their work. These are differences that speak to dignity as well as to value-adding efficiency. And we are rapidly approaching a point where half of such equations may get written out of the picture altogether. During his tenure as Secretary for Labor to President Clinton, Robert Reich suggested that the futures of the best-off and worst-off individuals and groups within 'advanced' economies will continue to polarise — such that without active policies of intervention and regulation, by the year 2020 'the top fifth of American earners will account for more than 60 percent of all the income earned by Americans; the bottom fifth two percent' (Reich 1992: 302). There is, however, as Reich observes, a still deeper dimension to the issue, which goes to the very heart of how we think and talk about literacy and smart work. In Reich's words,

> the problem facing political economies like America is that America's problem is that while some Americans are adding substantial value, most are not. In consequence, the gap between those few in the first group and everyone else is widening. To improve the economic position of the bottom four-fifths will require that the fortunate fifth share its wealth and invest in the wealth-creating capacities of other Americans. Yet as the top becomes ever more tightly linked to the global economy, it has less stake in the performance and potential of its less fortunate compatriots. Thus our emerging dilemma, and that of other nations as well.
>
> (Reich 1992: 301)

As we have seen, issues of distribution are also at stake when we consider the different options taken in cases represented by Edge Tech and Wedge Tech. These options involve trade-offs of various kinds: e.g. maximising efficiency and income versus 'democratising' the distribution of expertise, work and training. Can we entertain multiple constructions of 'smart workforces' that keep alternative options in the picture? More to the point, *will* we?

Conclusion

Finally, considering literacy in relation to developing a smart workforce may call for addressing wider issues, some of which may prove very difficult to face — not least because they go to the heart of some very contradictory tendencies within the new capitalism and work in recent times. A graphic illustration of what is at stake is provided by the work of Glynda Hull and her colleagues in a Silicon Valley computer assembly plant — a context that gets as close to popular conceptions of the literacy–smart work interface as we can get — and will serve to conclude this chapter.

The study investigated a workplace innovation where non-English-speaking background (NESB) migrant workers underwent English literacy instruction and team-based training to prepare them to operate as efficient 'self-directed work teams' (Gee *et al.* 1996: Chs 4 and 5). Their work involved fixing components to computer circuit boards. In the course of their training they learned to maintain fastidious records, use popular conceptual tools like Pareto charts and fishbone diagrams, and run their own team meetings to enhance productivity and quality by reflecting upon and discussing processes and events in their work. Careful observation and analysis showed the work teams engaging frequently in *explaining* – describing work situations and processes in ways that identified problems – and *complaining* – commenting on situations and processes to show how they were problematic and/or to assign blame. Rarely, however, did they *take responsibility* in the sense of making significant decisions and acting on them individually or collectively. The teams identified and discussed problems, but then dropped them. The researchers explained this in terms of a deep contradiction whereby management and company culture seemingly seek to 'empower' workers whilst nonetheless continuing to control them tightly.

A typical example involved manufacturing process instructions (MPIs) produced, often under pressure of time, by the engineers. These often contained errors that impacted on productivity. Despite their 'self-directedness', the workers were obliged to follow the MPIs and in no way change or correct them. In the incident in question, the team examined an MPI and found a mistake. The author had mistakenly written a '1' in the column listing the number of components, when it should have been '11'. This had major implications for calculating productivity, since it takes 11 times longer to load 11 components than one. The 'standard time' allocated for assembling the board was way out of line – as would be the team's productivity if they assembled the board correctly so that it would work, which is what they did: leaving the MPI untouched, and losing earning as a result of their compliant decision. Other teams responded differently, refusing to make the changes they knew were needed, even when engineers gave verbal approval to depart from the MPI. This resulted in faulty product produced to specification.

> 'Don't go by verbal, go by written', Mr Marcos warned his group again and again, having been burnt once too often.
>
> (Gee *et al.* 1996: 123)

With respect to literacy and smart work as much as with any facet of work in recent times, we do well to approach 'the bottom line' carefully and in well-informed ways.

References

Carnoy, M., Castells, M., Cohen, S. and Cardoso, F. M. (1993) *The New Global Economy in the Information Age: Reflections on our Changing World*. University Park, PA: Pennsylvania State University Press.

Castells, M. (1993) 'The informational economy and the new international division of labor', in M. Carnoy, M. Castells, S. Cohen and F. M. Cardoso, *The New Global Economy in the Information Age: Reflections on our Changing World*. University Park, PA: Pennsylvania State University Press, 15–43.

Castells, M. (1996) *The Rise of the Network Society*. Cambridge, MA: Blackwell.

Drucker, P. F. (1993) *Post-capitalist Society*. New York: Harper.

Gee, J. P. (1991) 'What is literacy?', in C. Mitchell and K. Weiler (eds) *Rewriting Literacy: Culture and the Discourse of the Other*. New York: Bergin & Garvey, 1–11.

Gee, J. P. (1993) 'Literacies: tuning in to forms of life', *Education Australia* 19: 13–14.

Gee, J. P. (1996) *Social Linguistics and Literacies: Ideology in Discourses*. 2nd edn. London: Taylor & Francis.

Gee, J. P., Hull, G. and Lankshear, C. (1996) *The New Work Order: Behind the Language of the New Capitalism*. Sydney, and Boulder, CO: Allen & Unwin, and Westview Press.

Green, B. (1988) 'Subject-specific literacy and school learning: A focus on writing', *Australian Journal of Education* 32(2): 156–179.

Green, B. (1997) 'Literacy, information and the learning society'. Keynote address at the *Joint Conference of the Australian Association for the Teaching of English, the Australian Literacy Educators' Association, and the Australian School Library Association*. Darwin: Darwin High School, 8–11 July 1997.

Hirst, P. (1974) *Knowledge and the Curriculum*. London: Routledge & Kegan Paul.

Kell, C. (1996) 'Literacy practices in an informal setting in the Cape Peninsula', in M. Prinsloo and M. Breier (eds) *The Social Uses of Literacy: Theory and Practice in Contemporary South Africa*. Amsterdam: John Benjamins.

Kelly, K. (1993) *Out of Control: The new Biology of Machines, Social Systems, and the Economic World*. Reading, MA.: Addison-Wesley.

Lankshear, C. (1998) 'Meanings of literacy in educational reform proposals', *Educational Theory* 48(3): 351–372.

Lankshear, C., Peters, M. and Knobel, M. (1996) 'Critical pedagogy and cyberspace', in H. Giroux, C. Lankshear, P. McLaren and M. Peters, *Counternarratives: Cultural Studies and Critical Pedagogies in Postmodern Spaces*. New York: Routledge, 149–188.

Lankshear, C., Bigum, C., Durrant, C., Green, B., Honan, E., Morgan, W., Murray, J., Snyder, I. and Wild, M. (1997) *Digital Rhetorics: Literacies and Technologies in Education – Current Practices and Future Directions*, 3 vols. Project Report. Children's Literacy National Projects. Brisbane: QUT/DEETYA.

O'Connor, P. (ed) (1994) *Thinking Work: Theoretical Perspectives on Workers' Literacies*. Sydney: ALBSAC.

Peters, M. and Lankshear, C. (1996) 'Critical literacy and digital texts', *Educational Theory* 46(1): 51–70.

Reich, R. (1992) *The Work of Nations*. New York: Vintage Books.

Tinkler, D., Lepani, B. and Mitchell, J. (1996) *Education and Technology Convergence*. Commissioned Report no. 43. Canberra: Australian Government Publishing Service.

Ulmer, G. (1989) *Teletheory: Grammatology in the Age of Video*. New York: Routledge.

US Office of Technology Assessment (1989) *Adult Literacy and New Technologies: Tools for a Lifetime*. Washington DC: US Government Printing Office.

Winters, K. (1996) 'America's technology literacy challenge' (Washington DC: US Department of Education, Office of the Under Secretary, <k.winters@inet.ed. gov> posted on <acw-l@unicorn.acs.ttu.edu> 17 February 1996); President Clinton's State of the Union address, 1996.

Part 3

Pedagogic implications and actions

6 Performance at work: identifying smart work practice

Stephen Billett

A compelling reason to understand the requirements of contemporary work practice is to determine how best to develop the skills required for that work practice. To paraphrase Glaser (1990), unless we understand clearly what is required for performance it is difficult to organise instruction to secure that performance. Moreover, it seems at this time that there is a growing gap between the requirements of emerging and contemporary work practice and the ability of educational institutions and educational provisions able to meet these requirements (Raizen 1994, Stasz 1997). Therefore, in order to understand the kinds of measures to be adopted in educational provisions for both preparing and enhancing further the ability to perform in the workplace, it is necessary to understand more fully those requirements. Taking up this theme, this chapter proposes a basis for understanding what constitutes work practice. This is achieved through identifying dimensions of activity and engagement that are likely to determine performance in the workplace. It is proposed that smartness is defined in different ways in particular workplaces. Therefore, dimensions of work practice need to be identified that can be used to describe and define the requirements for performance in particular workplace or enterprise requirements. These dimensions of work practice go beyond identifying 'technical skills' and work organisation to include the ways individuals need to engage in work practice that variously may need to be flexible, adaptable or, conversely, highly consistent given the particular requirement of the work practice.

Introduction: a scenario

The plant that performs secondary processing on minerals mined nearby is visible from the highway, both day and night. During the day, the tower-like structures that house the shaft kilns and the loading ramps set it apart from the other buildings on the site and those nearby. At night, festoons of lights illuminate the plant making it highly visible. The plant's kilns and furnaces operate 24 hours a day, every day of the year. Such a large and imposing set of buildings might be thought to require far more workers than are actually employed there. In total, the plant comprises an administration block, and the fusion, calcination and laboratory areas, and the control room work areas. Each of these areas has small teams of employees working in shifts, largely without any formal supervision. These employees enjoy wide discretion with their work tasks within their teams. They discuss, make and enact decisions about their work tasks. There are few work demarcations. Employees with recognised trade skills engage in activities outside their trade area, even undertaking tasks that in other workplaces would be restricted to a trades assistant. Equally, employees without trade recognition will sometimes undertake tasks that, in other workplaces, could only be undertaken by tradeworkers. Decisions are made and understandings developed about when it is necessary for particular tasks to be undertaken and by whom. The workers decide when to have meal breaks and whether all or part of the shift takes breaks at one time. Over meal breaks, the discussion is often work-related, shift tasks are often discussed and decisions made. All employees have access to communication equipment that permits communication with other workers or to monitoring activities occurring elsewhere in the plant. Morale is generally high in the work teams. Levels of absenteeism are low, often known about in advance and accommodated by the work team. The plant's product is value-added and almost universally bound for export. Consequently, the plant has been endorsed as meeting international quality standards for the processing and monitoring of its product. This workplace, with its 'green field' industrial arrangements, flexible work practice and 'teamness', exemplifies much of what was aimed to be achieved through workplace reforms of the late 1980s and early 1990s.

Although not always quite as glossy as just portrayed, the work practice at the plant characterises much of what is often typified in accounts of the smart workforce. As noted, the employees work in small, self-directed high-morale teams that are both independent from each other yet interdependent. Most of the teams enjoy high levels of discretion in their daily tasks. Moreover, there are few artificial demarcations that inhibit the wide use of their skills. Many workers are multi-skilled, having specific trade skills and also expertise in their particular work area. From this account it is possible to outline some common attributes required for skilled performance in this workplace. However, beyond these common attributes are variations with these common requirements that reveal complexities and complications, and which render unsatisfactory easy prescriptions, such as those just made above. For example, the control room workers do not enjoy the same level of discretion as those in the other work teams. The plant's engineering staff, who have technical supervisory roles and responsibilities, monitor the work of the control room. Some of the control room workers find this frustrating. They talk about having a 'feel for the plant'; a sense of knowing about it and how best to control the flow of product.[1] Yet, the engineering staff's directions sometimes contradict what the control room workers sense is the correct response for the particular processing situation. In addition, for these workers, the camaraderie in the work groups is inhibited by the intensity of their work and the need to monitor the plant constantly. Hence, they have to rotate through meal and rest breaks, thereby missing opportunities for discussion enjoyed by other teams. The workers in this area also require rich understanding of the plant's entire operation and an ability to interrogate the control equipment to monitor and manage the plant. In addition, they have to use the multiple levels of screens on the computer terminals to monitor, identify and respond to changes in the qualities of the ore being processed. These work requirements set them apart from other workers in the plant. There are also other ways in which the requirements for work performance are not uniform across the plant. For instance, in the laboratory, the metallurgist has a professional standing that sets her apart from her co-workers, who are essentially subordinates. Performance here focuses upon faithful adherence to, and precision with, set procedures. Hence, as well as a hierarchy in the work team, there is limited opportunity for the workers to exercise autonomy except in the execution of precision and care. Therefore, although in each area of the plant many of the qualities commonly advanced of what it means to be a smart worker are evident, there are variations in these attributes that require further clarification or detailing.

Moreover, what happens in this workplace in terms of the organisation and execution of work is far from typical of workplaces generally. In the open cut coal mines a couple of hundred kilometres to the west of this plant, adherence to demarcations, industrial agreements and historical practices associated with the constant wagering over the 'dash for the cash' are part of what it means to be an expert coal miner. In these mines there are also particular considerations, about safety and the need to use effectively, and to maintain, heavy equipment, which are quite different from those in the secondary processing plant. Consequently, uniform prescriptions of smart workforces appear inadequate because what it means to be smart will be determined by the requirements of the particular work practice(s) within particular workplaces. This is even likely to be the case when the same vocational activity is being conducted in different settings. Differences in the goals, work practice, services, division of labour and culture of practice are likely to set each workplace apart, as being in some ways unique (Billett 1996). Consequently, what is considered to be a smart workforce is influenced by the situational factors. Indeed, it is these that make each workplace and, hence, its work practice, unique.

Therefore, to understand what comprises a smart workforce requires more than identifying common characteristics (e.g. teamness, being multi-skilled) (Waterhouse 1998). It is also necessary to understand what the particular characteristics of work practice are, how their manifestations vary across different workplaces and what knowledge underpins their use in particular circumstances. Such an understanding may permit the development of educational and instructional responses best able to respond to these requirements. Consequently, the aim here is to propose a framework comprising dimensions of work practice that can be used to delineate the requirements of work practice for each workplace or work situation. This is clearly an ambitious undertaking, and claims to be wholly universally applicable are likely to be easily tested. However, such a framework may offer greater promise than seeking to identify sets of common or generic qualities of a smart workforce.

The means adopted to identify dimensions of workplace performance are through an evaluation of recent literature and, in particular, that based on empirical research. This task requires reconciling the contributions of different bodies of literature, in order to provide a basis for considering trends in contemporary work practice. The discussion commences with an overview of the recent literature on the changing nature of work practice. Next, contributions from three different perspectives about identifying work performance are discussed. These are: (i) the generic competency skills view, (ii) the cognitive perspective, and (iii) the socio-cultural perspective. Respectively, these literatures inform about the potential for some uniform and universal dimensions of capabilities; the importance of domain specificity of knowledge structures which underpin performance, and the social and cultural contributions to expert performance. Following this, a framework comprising dimensions of work practice is advanced which draws upon, and reconciles, the contributions from the literature. Initially, however, some of the characteristics required of current and emerging smart workforce are identified.

Changing bases for understanding work practice

The changing nature of work practice and what is required for performance in the workplace or work situations have been the subject of research in a number of fields. In reviewing this work it seems that these changes can be categorised under: (i) changes in the kinds of work to be undertaken; (ii) engagement with the workplace or work situation; and (iii) requirements for work performance. These three categories of changes are now discussed in overview.

Changes in work

There are changes in the kinds of work in which individuals are likely to be employed. Often, this change is seen to be that required to produce high value-added goods and a shift towards service industries, requiring levels of skill and ability to work with high technology support systems (e.g. Lipsig-Mumme 1996; Bertrand and Noyelle 1988; Zuboff 1988). There is also the claim of movement from an 'industrial society', predominantly concentrating on the manufacture of goods and products, to an 'information society', which adds value by turning information into knowledge and services. Forecasts consistently indicate a massive reduction in the demand for 'semi-skilled' and 'unskilled' work and a consequent increase in the future demand for management, professional and administrative staff (Noon and Blyton 1997; House 1995; Longworth and Davies 1996). There are also changes in the kinds of work being undertaken as governments divest themselves of functions that were previously viewed as being the sole domain of the public sector. The significance of these trends is to question earlier research (e.g. Braverman 1974) which suggested the de-skilling of workers and removal of their discretion was likely to be realised through such innovations. However, more recent work (e.g. Berryman 1993) suggests that the shift to post-industrial forms of work requires workers to be flexible, adaptable and have a depth of understanding about their work that sets them apart from their predecessors. That is, the evidence suggests that the shift is towards types of work that are more demanding, requiring higher levels of performance and, therefore, a more exacting preparation.

Engagement with work

There is increasing diversity in how individuals engage with work. Changes in the organisation of work are transforming work practice. For example, less hierarchical approaches to work practice (e.g. self-managed teams, 'green field' worksites) are held to be coming more common, as are innovations in technology and the demands of responsiveness and flexibility in the production of goods and services (Wall and Jackson 1995). Associated with this change is a shift in patterns of engagement, with part-time, home-based and contracted work becoming increasingly common (Noon and Blyton 1997). The changing nature of work is also held now to require a synergy between the interests of employers and employees. Those enterprises characterised as 'high involvement' are held to be shifting power away from management toward a focus that capitalises on workers' expertise to secure productivity and efficiency gains. In doing so, the aim is to secure the workers' enthusiasm and commitment to the enterprises' goals. Given these circumstances, Howard (1995) claims that enterprises and workers have never needed each other more. Such relationships, Carnevale (1995) states, require the removal of 'top-down' hierarchies and their replacement by approaches to work organisation which 'drive autonomy, skill resources and new flexible technologies down the line towards the point of production, service delivery and interface with the customer' (Carnevale 1995: 239). Analogous characteristics are those identified by Rowden (1995; 1997). He claims that American small to medium sized enterprises, which have endured over time and remained viable, are characterised by: (i) having a unique market niche supported by the development and maintenance of the workforce's skills, knowledge and attitude; (ii) integrating employees into the enterprises' work practice; and (iii) enhancing the quality of working life.

However, questioning these assertions, Lipsig-Mumme (1996) and Forrester *et al.* (1995) note the peripheral and precarious status of many workers, particularly in the service sector. Engagement for these workers is characterised by changing patterns of participation (e.g. part-time work, split shifts, home-based employment) and inhibiting levels of skilfulness (e.g. routine tasks). Much of the part-time work is involuntary. Certainly, for many in the workforce, what was previously accepted about career paths and permanent employment is disappearing, as are ideas about mutual trust and the rewards for hard work well done (Kempernich *et al.* 1999, in press). In addition, many public sector workplaces remain hierarchical and top-down and are unequivocally held to be responsive not to client needs but to executive government. What all this suggests is that there are likely to be complications and contradictions in the kind of trends forecasted above, as these changes are by no means uniform (Waterhouse 1998). The point here is that workers who participate fully require richer understanding to participate in this way. Those who engage peripherally (e.g. part-time workers, homeworkers), may have to work harder to remain 'in touch' and maintain their contact and currency.

Requirements for performance

The requirements for performance in workplaces are also characterised by change and difference. A number of studies (e.g. Appelbaum 1993; Barley and Batt 1995; Berryman and Bailey 1992, Berryman 1993) describe contemporary work practice as having both complex workplace organisational and work tasks dimensions. Consequently, the knowledge required for workplace performance is held to be becoming more demanding. Bailey (cited in Berryman 1993) refers to accelerated production cycles, a proliferation of products, heightened levels of uncertainty and changing work practices. The intensification of work practice as a result of greater competition also increases the demands of work practice (Noon and Blyton 1997). Consider the intensification of nurses' work. Within hospitals, patients are having shorter stays than in previous times. Consequently, most patients in a hospital ward are likely to require high levels of care. Hence, nurses' work has been made far more intense. In the banking sector, computerisation has brought about a reduction in routinised activity, thereby also making this work more intensive (Bertrand and Noyelle 1988). Hence, for nurses and bank workers, work practice has been extended to manage more intense work activities. As a consequence, higher levels of non-routine activities and accountability are required. However, intensity of work is likely to be more partial or sporadic in some situations than others. Consider the intense periods of activity in hospitality work during times of service, compared with more measured preparation time. In other workplaces, emerging demands might be associated with higher quality standards, a smaller workforce and a wider range of tasks required of multi-skilled workers. Consequently, a dimension of emerging work practice is its intensification, requiring the ability to monitor and prioritise, which demands non-routine and creative thinking rather than merely deploying standardised procedures.

Despite views to the contrary, the use of technology can also make work more, rather than less, demanding. For instance, Martin and Scribner's (1991) study of CNC lathe operators found that these workers require high levels of conceptual and symbolic knowledge. Taking the work task from the blueprint to digitally organising the lathe's work demands conceptual and symbolic knowledge. The increased use of technology in work applications may have made some knowledge opaque and consequently more difficult to learn and deploy as it is less accessible. Of course, these procedures are more demanding when workers are required to be more broadly skilled and less in number. There are also enhanced demands arising from team-based forms of work and working in flat organisational structures. Principally, the level of interpersonal skills and decision-making required to be effective in these kinds of work environments has increased (Berryman 1993). In addition, this literature suggests that the survival of enterprises and their prospects for development in a changing and competitive environment are associated with developing in employees the knowledge required for performance. Changes in work practice are indicative of these trends, which are supported by evidence of changes in patterns of employment (e.g. Barley 1996; Lipsig-Mumme 1996; Noon and Blyton 1997). However, it is premature to view these changes as being universal shifts in patterns of work and the means by which work has to be undertaken. For instance, small enterprises (particularly those managed by owners) are unlikely to fit into simple patterns of transformation found in larger enterprises (Kempenich *et al.*, in press). In other circumstances, these transformations will be patterned differently according to the requirements of the particular workplace or work situation. Taking another instance, it is likely that the armed forces and emergency services will want to maintain a 'command culture' which is 'top down' and hierarchical, rather than one that aims to be open and democratic.

From this review, it seems that factors such as the intensification of work, the opaqueness of knowledge required in work performance, an enhanced requirement for communication, decision-making and teamwork are emerging as elements of work practice for work situations. However, these elements are unlikely to be applicable uniformly. Therefore, rather than providing a universal model of emerging work practice, these changes might be seen as adding to the diversity of work practice. Consequently, it is necessary to synthesise a set of dimensions of activities and engagements that can capture the diversity of requirements of work practice. Through this synthesis, a framework that might inform about work practices in particular enterprises can be proposed. To develop some approximation of this diversity, contributions from other literatures are now discussed. In the next section, the contributions of three perspectives, concerning the knowledge required for work performance, are drawn upon to discuss a more comprehensive account of work performance.

Views about work performance

In this section, an unfolding view of understanding the requirements for performance in work practice is presented through a review of the contributions of three literatures. These are the generic skill approach, cognitive views on expertise and context-based views such as socio-cultural views of expertise. These perspectives represent current views that are largely informed by empirically based work. That is, they are well founded in evidence-based disciplines. In the discussion below it is proposed, however, that none of these perspectives alone can furnish a comprehensive view about work performance. Consequently, in the framework that follows, the discussion on these perspectives draws upon, reconciles and extends ideas from these disciplines.

Generic skills perspective

The demand for the knowledge learnt in schooling to transfer more readily to the workplace was instrumental in developing the generic competency or skill approach. The goal of this approach is to identify generic, highly transferable competencies to be learnt by students in compulsory education. The identification of these competencies is usually through employer surveys about the skills required in the workplace. In America, the Secretary of Labor's Commission on Achieving Necessary Skills (SCANS) identified skills and competencies held to be generic in so far as they are required for most jobs, yet are separable from technical knowledge likely to be vocational or workplace specific (Stasz 1997). The SCANS competencies include 'foundation skills' comprising reading, writing and arithmetic; thinking skills (reasoning, problem-solving); personal qualities (responsibility, self-esteem) and 'work competencies' (resources, interpersonal, information, systems and technology) (SCANS 1992). In Australia, the Mayer Committee (1992) identified seven key competencies (collecting, analysing and organising information; expressing ideas and information; planning and organising activities; working with others and in teams; using mathematical ideas and techniques; solving problems; and using technology). These key competencies were intended to be those, which if learnt by students, would transfer to the workplace.

Stasz (1997) evaluated key elements of the SCANS competencies (problem-solving, teamwork, communication, personal qualities) identified by employers as being necessary for work performance. In her analyses, she identified different manifestations of these generic competencies across a number of work practices (e.g. transport, traffic management, manufacturing and healthcare) (see Table 6.1). Their applications across four examples of work practice indicate that such measures are not so much 'generic' as common. However, this commonality was only apparent when disembedded from work practice. That is, these competencies require embedding in particular contexts in order to be understood and appraised. The finer-grained or more embedded competencies that Stasz (1997) identified are themselves

Table 6.1 Embedding competencies in work practice (from Stasz 1997)

Competency	Variations	Characteristics
Problem-solving	Troubleshooting	Identifying and fixing problems
	Situation assessment	Gathering and interpreting
	Quality assurance and	information
	control	Surveying for discrepancies
Teamwork	Autonomous/self-managing	Performing work within a definable social system
	Distributed knowledge	Differences in the knowledge and status of team members
	Independent work	Autonomy to operate independently in performing team activity
Dispositions	Task/organisation	Formal job characteristics
	Community of practice	Norms, values and attitudes about work
	Quality standards	Assuming responsibility and liability
Communications	Audience	Groups/individuals being communicated with
	Purpose	Appropriate communication of fact accurately
	Style	Friendliness
	Mode	Appropriateness of language

likely to vary in emphasis and meaning when applied to other work contexts. The distinction between generic and common but disembedded is important in understanding the knowledge required for performance in the workplace. Generic knowledge would be that which could be transferred and applied regardless of context; for instance, being able to work in teams or solve problems regardless of context. This view suggests that there are generalisable forms of knowledge that permit such performance in any situation. Hence, once an individual acquired the competence of teamwork or problem-solving, they would be equally effective in working in teams in all situations (e.g. traffic management, healthcare, crewing a commercial plane) or solving problems in circumstances as diverse as icing a cake as digging for coal. Among others, Perkins and Salomon (1989), and Evans (1991) have challenged the idea that generic competencies are ever likely to be robust enough to be transferable across diverse domains of knowledge. However, what is important about Stasz's work is the identification of the differing manifestations of these competencies in different types of workplace settings. The disembedded view holds that these requirements are common to a number of workplaces, but can only be understood by identifying what problem-solving or teamwork means in the particular context.

Table 6.1 depicts how the competencies vary across different work contexts. In the left-hand column are the generic competencies, in the centre column the variations in what that competency means in different work contexts. In the right-hand column, characteristics of the embedded version of the competency are presented.

The common, but differentiated, nature of key competencies has been identified elsewhere. For example, Billett (1993) examined the nature of skilled work using the Mayer Key Competencies (and two other measures). Table 6.2 depicts differences in the frequencies by which these competencies were reported being used 'most of the time' in four categories of work ('unskilled', non-trade skilled, trade, professional). Subjects from each category were able to identify aspects of their work that related to these competencies. Yet, these competencies were used with different frequencies across the categories of work. Significantly, one important commonly reported attribute was the need to be able to respond to novel situations. This ability, which requires individuals to have higher orders of knowledge, was evident across all categories of work. So while the other attributes were common across all types of work, it was the ability to use knowledge in novel ways that was most consistent. However, higher orders of procedures require context-specific knowledge to be applicable. That is, richly embedded knowledge is required for these procedures to be enacted. This table indicates that the ability to transfer (to use higher order forms of thinking) is not restricted to professionals and para-professionals. It is a requirement for all categories

Table 6.2 Mayer competencies: activities performed 'most of the time' by work category

	'Unskilled' (%)	Non-trade skilled (%)	Trade (%)	Professional (%)
Collecting, analysing and organising information	51	64	55	75
Expressing ideas and information	32	57	48	58
Planning and organising activities	34	55	52	83
Working with others and in teams	81	78	73	50
Using mathematical ideas and techniques	20	29	23	33
Solving problems	39	53	52	75
Using technology	49	42	44	58
Routine tasks	81	69	57	42
Novel situations	22	20.6	20.5	23

of workers. Consequently there are common factors across these classes of workers.

Other analyses of generic competencies in hospitality settings (Stevenson 1996) and with airline counter workers (Beven 1997) found that 'generic' aspects of work practice – such as communication, problem-solving, use of technology and numeracy – had few applications that could be described as generic. Instead, the meaning of each of these competencies was quite situational. Hence, it would be inappropriate to suggest that these key competencies are generic as their meaning can only be understood when they are embedded in a particular workplace circumstance. Even the apparently universally applicable knowledge associated with maths and language use was found to be situational.

Therefore, prescriptions for workplace performance advanced as generic competencies are likely to be most useful in describing attributes that may be common across workplaces, rather than themselves being generic. Yet, these common prescriptions are disembedded and are required to be understood within the context of a particular workplace or work situation. That is, only when they are embedded in particular situations will they have meaning.

The cognitive perspective

The cognitive literature provides useful accounts of the knowledge required for workplace performance. Indeed, much of the work within cognitive science over the last 30 years has focused on understanding what comprises expertise (smartness) in order to consider how best to develop this attribute. The efficacy of experts' responses to work tasks is partially through their ability to categorise these tasks by their means of solution. The breadth and organisation of experts' knowledge permits this categorisation (Chi *et al.* 1981; Gott 1989; Sweller 1989). Experts' rich repertoire of experiences provides the ability to view and categorise tasks by solution strategies. This permits them to engage with workplace tasks in ways quite different from novices who simply lack this knowledge (Charness 1989), and may respond only to the task's surface features (Sweller 1989). The solution-based categorisation of tasks by experts is assisted by active monitoring, involving testing and refining selected responses to a problem that are simply unavailable to novices (Alexander and Judy 1988; Eylon and Linn 1988; Owen and Sweller 1989; Voss *et al.* 1983). The rich repertoire of domain-specific experiences furnishes understandings that permit monitoring and informs experts of whether the tasks are being completed as anticipated. This monitoring is guided by a rich knowledge base, which permits the progressive evaluation of responses to problems, and promotes evaluation of alternative strategies for securing solutions (Glaser 1990). Judgements about the difficulty of the particular task, how to apportion time, assess progress and predict outcomes of the task as it progresses are enabled by monitoring and categorisation (Chi *et al*. 1982; Larkin *et al*. 1980).

Because of their rich domain-specific knowledge bases, experts are also able to apply cognitive processes seemingly instantaneously, thereby accomplishing routine tasks apparently automatically (Ericsson and Simon 1984; Sweller 1989). Previous compilation and chunking of domain-specific knowledge reduces the cognitive load, thereby freeing the working memory to concentrate on unfamiliar components of their tasks. The breadth and organisation of their domain-specific knowledge permit experts to close gaps in the available information, thus consistently producing more useful solutions than novices, and they are also more efficient with their search for solution options (Anderson 1982). Further, as a product of extensive experiences within a domain of activity, experts' knowledge has become 'de-bugged' (Ericsson and Simon 1984; Glaser 1990; Gott 1989), permitting quicker access to the knowledge required for both routine (regular) and non-routine (new) tasks in the workplace. It seems that when faced with non-routine problems, novices fare worse than experts because of experts' ability to deploy a systematic and conscious solution search (Glaser 1990).

Reference to knowledge within the cognitive literature encompasses conceptual and procedural representations of knowledge and their dispositional underpinning. It is these representations of knowledge that individuals hold in memory and are deployed in thinking and acting in the workplace. In particular, this knowledge furnishes the basis for performance within a domain of knowledge (e.g. an occupation or vocation). Comprising facts, information, assertions, concepts and propositions, *propositional knowledge* is differentiated by levels of stateable facts or concepts of increasing complexity (Evans 1991). It ranges from simple factual knowledge through to deeper or more complex levels of conceptual knowledge (such as an understanding about the workings of complex systems, law, the human body or a piece of equipment whose operating basis is hidden). Depth of understanding is premised upon the strength of relationships amongst concepts (Groen and Patel 1988; Novak 1990), thereby emphasising its interconnectedness and causal relationships. That is, deep understanding is based on linkages, associations and an appreciation of the causal links in those associations. The knowledge that enables individuals to achieve goals, such as being skilful, is *procedural knowledge* (Anderson 1982), which comprises techniques and skills. Whenever we are thinking or acting, we are deploying procedures. In reading this text you are applying a set of procedures that are associated with word and letter recognition (specific procedures) as well as procedures that are monitoring and interrogating the text. Consequently, to delineate these functions, procedural knowledge has been further classified into levels or orders to understand the different roles that procedures play. Stevenson (1991) proposes three levels of orders. First order, or specific, procedures are employed to achieve specific goals. Being specific only to routine tasks, specific procedures are not effective when non-routine or ill-defined tasks are encountered. Hence, when monitoring, evaluation and strategy selection are required, the second-order procedures are invoked. This order includes breaking the task up into a series of sub-goals so the individual can achieve the task (Greeno and Simon 1988). It is proposed that first and second orders are managed by forms of third or higher-order procedural knowledge, which act upon lower orders of knowledge by monitoring and organising activities, and by switching between orders, when necessary (Stevenson 1991).

The realisation that procedures are deployed in ways not observable has been used to dispense with earlier views that separated cognitive from psycho-motor activities. Indeed, propositional and procedural forms of knowledge are interdependent. Propositional knowledge cannot be engaged without enacting procedures (see Table 6.3). Yet, procedures are unlikely to be deployed without goals. Further enmeshing these types of knowledge are their dispositional underpinnings, comprising attitudes, values, affect, interests and identities (Prawat 1989). Perkins *et al.* (1993a, 1993b) view *dispositions* as individuals' tendencies to put their capabilities into action. That is, for example, how individuals conceptualise tasks and the values they place on the deployment of procedures. The significance of this body of literature for this chapter is that it identifies the importance of domain-specific knowledge as well as the forms of knowledge that are required for expertise within that domain.

To illustrate the application of these kinds of knowledge, Table 6.3 furnishes the responses from workers in the secondary processing plant mentioned earlier. They were asked what it meant to be acknowledged as an expert in their workplace (Billett 1994). In the left-hand column are their aggregated responses with the three columns to its right indicating approximations of their propositional, procedural and dispositional components of these measures of performance. In the Propositional column, a determination of whether the response involves factual (F) or deep understanding (D) is advanced. In the Procedural column, reference is made to whether specific (S) or higher order (HO) procedures are required. In the Dispositional column, a distinction is advanced about whether the response is indicative of organisation [workplaces] (O) or personal values (P).

The cognitive perspective identifies the breadth and organisation of experts' domain-specific knowledge required to perform non-routine (new) tasks as well as completing regular tasks almost unconsciously. The organisation of experts' knowledge around salient domain-based principles maximises the prospect for problem-solving and transfer (Groen and Patel 1988). Indeed, it is the existence and organisation of their knowledge rather than their ability to process that knowledge that sets experts apart from others (e.g. Anderson 1982; Glaser 1984; Sweller 1989; Wagner and Sternberg 1986). Therefore, this discipline holds that the ability to perform smartly is premised on having domain-specific knowledge, comprising both factual and deep knowledge, specific and higher-order procedures, underpinned by values and attitudes required for performance in the workplace. In particular, deep conceptual

Table 6.3 Cognitive structures required for performance in a secondary processing plant

Elements of performance	Propositional	Procedural	Dispositions
Knowledge of work	F – D	S – HO	O
Experienced	F	S – HO	O
Competence/ability	F – D	S – HO	O P
Minimum breakdowns	D	S – HO	O P
Planning/organisation	F – D	S – HO	O P
Control costs and budget	F – D	S – HO	O P
Effective communication/interpersonal skills	F – D	S	O P
Training others	F – D	S – HO	O P
Predicting and minimising problems	D	HO	O P
Leadership/management/supervision skills	F – D	S – HO	O P
Problem-solving	F – D	S – HO	O P
Flexibility/multi-skilled	D	HO	O
Currency of knowledge	F	S	O
Decision-making	F – D	S – HO	O P
Time management	F	S – HO	P
Liaison/co-ordination/consultation monitoring/gathering information	F – D	S – HO	O P
Common-sense	F	S – HO	O P
Meeting demands – expectations	F – D	S – HO	O P
Stress management,	F	S	P
Analytical, thinking skills, basic literacy and numeracy	F	S	P
Report writing	F	S – HO	O P
Dedication	F	S	P
Interest			P
Safety conscious	F – D	S – HO	O P
Presentation	F	S	O P
Working without supervision	F – D	S – HO	O P
Pride in work			P
Resourceful/initiative/trustworthy	F – D	S H	P
Professionalism			P
Work as part of a team	F – D	S	P
Self-esteem/identity			P
Self-evaluation	F – D	S – HO	P
Knowing when you're wrong	F – D	S – HO	P
Thoroughness/attention to detail	D	HO	P
Consistency	D	HO	P
Adaptable/ receptive to change	F – D	S – HO	P
Quality of product/ service	F – D	S – HO	O P

and higher-order procedures permit performance with new tasks and allow transfer to other circumstances. These seem key requirements of the smart workforce. Yet, these characteristics are not held to be universally applicable, as are the generic competencies. Instead, these attributes are held to reside within domains of knowledge. Two issues emerge here. First is the organisation of experts' domain-specific knowledge, which sets them apart from novices who lack both the organisation and breadth of knowledge. However, novices are not necessarily weaker at processing information and may be expert in other domains. The hallmark of expertise in this perspective is the ability to resolve non-routine (novel) problems within a particular domain of knowledge. Consequently, performance focuses on domains of knowledge such as those comprising some definable category of knowledge, for example an academic discipline or an occupation.

Secondly, the cognitive perspective also defines its potency in terms of domains of knowledge, which tend to be disembedded. It frequently refers to disciplines or occupational knowledge in a general way, rather than to its application to particular situations. In the socio-cultural perspective below, the concept of domains specifically accounts for these circumstances. As with Stasz's critique of generic competencies, the accounts from cognitive psychology fail fully to acknowledge the particular requirements of the workplace. For example, the organisational norms and values identified in Table 6.3 are likely to differ across workplaces. The goals for performance in each enterprise are also likely to differ because what passes as domain-specific knowledge in one setting may not correspond with what is required in another. This is particularly the case when the view of domains is abstracted from, rather than being embedded in, particular practice. So, for instance, an understanding about the vocation of hairdressing may not take into account what it means to be hairdresser in a particular salon. In addition, what is taken as expertise in one work setting (e.g. hairdressing salon) may not be so in another. Put plainly, this means that the knowledge required for performance in one workplace, may not be the same for another, even when the same vocational activity is enacted. The cognitive conceptualisation of expertise does not fully account for the circumstances in which knowledge is deployed. Its conception of domains is abstracted, rather than being seen as embedded, in a particular work practice. With its focus on the internal processes of the mind, cognitive psychology alone is not able to furnish a comprehensive conception of expertise, as it has social and cultural dimensions. Therefore, it is necessary to reconcile the cognitive perspective with socio-cultural theory that furnishes an understanding about situations and circumstances.

The socio-cultural perspective

As proposed in each of the two previous sections, it seems necessary to understand more fully how 'generic skills or expertise are embedded in particular practice'. Consequently, it is important to be able to account for what it means to be smart in a particular workplace or work practice. Leonteyev's (1981) definition of an *activity system* as 'the social system which shapes activity' provides a useful basis for elaborating the nature, organisation and goals of the work practice in which that activity is undertaken. Activities can be considered as the external embodiment of requirements of the workplace. As such, they determine what is required for the work practice in particular circumstances. When delineating activity systems, it is also necessary to determine how the activity is specified and constrained, and by whom (Newman *et al.* 1989). These activities can be used to identify the particular set of factors required for achieving performance in work practice. This can only be understood through a consideration of each workplace's goals, division of labour, culture of practice, etc.

In advancing a view of expertise, Scribner (1988, cited in Berryman 1993) also emphasises contextual factors and contributions. She claimed that expert performance is characterised by flexibility in modes of solutions to identical problems, creative shortcuts to simplify and economise on mental and physical effort, finely tuned to the environment, and effective use of setting specific knowledge. For example, in a study of four hairdressing salons (Billett 1995), it was shown that what it meant to be an expert differed across the salons. In a trendy inner-city salon, giving contemporary and fashionable cuts and colours, conversing about style and a holding a particular set of values was all-important. In another salon, set in a low socio-economic area, managing difficult customers who made strong demands and were prone to complain quite vociferously and forcefully was a hallmark of expertise. In a third salon, set in a provincial centre that had endured years of a rural recession and drought, expertise was in being able to maintain the clientele. This expertise included balancing the hairdressers' need to secure additional treatments from clients, with the risk of losing their clientele. In a fourth salon, being an expert required familiarity with the personal histories and backgrounds of the elderly clients who came for weekly treatments. In varying degrees and in different ways, there was a requirement for the hairdressers to be a friend, confidant and, with elderly clients, a key social contact. Moreover, there were identified differences in the activity system in each workplace, despite their sharing the same vocational practice – hairdressing.

Therefore, the domain of knowledge required for expertise has to be viewed as situational, being related to the circumstances of the deployment of knowledge. Expertise is fashioned within particular domains of activities (social practice) thus embedding it in social circumstances. Lave and Wenger (1991) refer to full participation in a community of practice, rather than expertise. Their concept of *full participation* is that all practitioners are peripheral because the work practice itself is evolving. They refer to becoming an expert as a pathway to full participation in the community. Hence, access to, and participation in, the community's (workplaces) activities are sources of understanding. Full participation implies being capable of new activities, performing new tasks and comprehending new understandings, which is analogous to, and reconcilable with, the cognitive view. This suggests that an embedded view of domain-specific knowledge is required to understand the performance requirements of particular work-places. This view then responds to the need for expertise to be adaptable and transferable. So, in advancing a view of expertise that accommodates situational requirements, its relational, embedded, competent, reciprocal and pertinent characteristics are identified. This view of expertise subsumes that within the cognitive view.

Therefore, what constitutes expertise can only be understood in the enactment of skills and judgements in terms of their utility within particular circumstances. The workplace's range of variables mean that they will have unique qualities that will determine what constitutes expert responses to particular problems (Billett 1995). Even the most apparently standardised work activities will have unique variables. For instance, the clientele and composition of staff in the particular fast food chain or bank branch will render the task of working in, and managing, that work practice in some way unique. Expertise is embedded, being the product of extensive social practice, with meaning about practice derived by becoming a full participant, over time, and with understanding shaped by participation in the activities and norms of that practice. Developing an understanding of the variables, goals and mechanism for success is likely to result from extended participation in the workplace. Expertise comprises competence in the community's discourse, in the routine and non-routine activities, mastery of new understanding and the ability to perform and adapt existing skills. Again, and analogous to the cognitive perspective, understanding the particular mores of the workplace, knowing what is and was is not appropriate behaviour or outcomes, is a premise for performance in problem-solving. Expertise requires pertinence in the appropriateness of problem solutions – knowing what behaviours are acceptable, and in what circumstances, in problem-solving is also a quality of expertise. This quality reflects the values a community of practice (a workplace) assigns to problems and the appropriate amount of effort and understanding of what knowledge is privileged. In sum, this view emphasises the rich association between setting and expertise – what is required to be smart.

Together and when reconciled, the three perspectives outlined above provide a basis for understanding further the requirements for a skilled workforce. What has been advanced is that there are likely to be attributes that are common across all types of work (e.g. problem-solving, communicating). However, what comprises performance with these attributes can only be understood when the attributes are embedded in the requirements of particular work practice. Therefore, rather than being generic, there are common attributes that are embedded in particular ways in work practice. Furthermore, the account of expertise provided by the cognitive literature can, again, only be understood when domain-specificity is linked to a particular and embedded set of activities. The socio-cultural literature yields ways of accounting for the situational factors that make sense of both common attributes and domains of knowledge. By acknowledging the circumstantial factors involved in particular workplaces, this literature provides a basis for reconciling the three perspectives to advance a set of dimensions of work practice, which can be used to determine the requirements of a particular work practice.

Planes and dimensions of work practice and performance

In this section, a tentative framework for understanding what constitutes a smart workforce is advanced. This framework has three planes. Firstly, it depicts dimensions of work practice and work performance. This is achieved by synthesising contributions from the earlier sections that outlined the requirements for contemporary and emerging work practices and the generic knowledge perspective. Secondly, these dimensions of work practice are linked to particular types of knowledge required to be enacted (see Table 6.4). The framework presses for consideration of the different means by which work is undertaken (engagement) and the knowledge requirements for tasks identified in the cognitive literature. Thirdly, these dimensions of work practice and performance, and the knowledge required for their performance, are embedded in a particular work practice. That is, these dimensions and knowledge types can only be understood through reference to the tasks, values, relationships and division of labour that comprise the activity system of a workplace. Moreover, in the same workplace, there may be a number of communities of workplace practice. For instance, in the secondary processing plant referred to earlier, there are different work areas that have their own norms, goals and values. As illustrated earlier, there are differences in the goals and discretion across the plant and some instances of those differences were evident in the comparison between the control room and laboratory. To take another example, the quality, use and means of communication is quite different in the administration area than elsewhere. Those differences include the means of communication, the formality involved and the characteristics of language. Quite different behaviour is observable in this setting than in other areas of the plant. Consequently, the third plane is the embedding of the two former planes of the framework in a particular community of practice.

Having proposed that work practice can only be understood when embedded in a particular community of work practice, the focus of the next section is on these dimensions and the knowledge types required for these aspects of performance. The dimensions identified in Table 6.4 are ninefold. They are: (i) routineness; (ii) discretion; (iii) intensity; (iv) complexity; (v) opaqueness; (vi) communication; (vii) teamness; (viii) homogeneity; and (ix) engagement. In the centre column of this table are dimensions of work practice synthesised from the earlier discussions. Each of these dimensions comprises a common attribute, and an attempt to capture the range of the dimension is then made. These accents are based on common attributes with further characterisations such as the variables provided by the literature. It is proposed that these common attributes are deployed in various ways and degrees in different workplaces. An overarching framework of activities and engagement is evident in this analysis, yet some of the dimensions are not wholly definable within just one part of this framework. The outside columns acknowledge the dispositional (D), procedural (P) and conceptual (C) bases of each of these dimensions. These columns do not detail the kinds of knowledge required in each dimension as this will only be identifiable when these attributes are understood in a particular context.

Routineness

The degree that work practice demands workers engage in non-routine activities will determine the requirement for the possession of higher-order procedures, and deep conceptual knowledge in the domain of work activity in order to transfer to new tasks and situations. Take, for example, motor mechanics. In some workshops their work will involve routine maintenance checks on the same kind of vehicle. In other workshops, the mechanic will be faced with a range of different kinds of vehicles and types of mechanical tasks, from maintenance work through to repairs that will require fabricating components and engineering tasks. Hence, the greater the demand of non-routine activity, the higher the demand for domain-specific procedures and concepts as well as the deployment of higher-order procedures to maximise transfer. In addition, there are the dispositions required to engage in the kinds of transfer required for non-routine activities. The greater the demands of routine performance, the greater likelihood that specific, but potentially highly accountable, work activity has to be undertaken. In sum, there are likely to be variations in the routineness of activities in workplaces that make different kinds of demands on the orders of knowledge that workers require. As illustrated in Table 6.3, it seems mistaken to believe that only particular categories of workers engage in activities that require higher orders of knowledge. Rather, the activities in the particular workplace will determine the degree by which tasks are routine or non-routine.

Discretion

The discretion that a worker is permitted to engage in is determined by the culture of the particular workplace and, in particular, its division of labour. If permitted only limited discretion, workers are unlikely to be required to deploy a broad range of attributes associated with non-routine decision-making. In addition, the way workers engage in work practice influences their discretionary activities. For instance, workers who are isolated or sole specialists may be required to exercise high levels of discretion. High-discretion workers are more likely to be engaged in making decisions that

Table 6.4 Dimensions of work practice

D	P	C				C	P	D

Routineness
The degree that the work practice demands the workers engage in non-routine activities.
Non-routine activities → *Routine activities*

Discretion
Degree by which an employee is permitted to use his or her discretion.
High discretion activities → *Low-discretion activities*

Intensity of activities
Degree by which the task can become highly intense.
High intensity activities → *Low-intensity activities*

Complexity
Number of variables compounding task completion.
Tasks with multiple variables → *Tasks with discernible variables*

Opaqueness of knowledge
Degree by which the understanding of work tasks remains difficult because the knowledge is remote or opaque thereby being hard to learn, hard to reach and hard to make accessible.
Task components hidden → *Task components accessible*

Communication
Qualities of communication
High communication demands (what about qualities) → *Low communication demands*

Teamness
Qualities of working as a team
High interaction with team members (interdependence) → *Low interaction with team members (independence)*

Homogeneity of tasks
The degree to which the workplace tasks are the same or different from each other
Nature of homogeneity → *Nature of heterodoxy*

Engagement with the workplace
Dimensions of engagement – full time- part-time, isolated-team member, physically or geographically separated
Part-time, shift, physically located, geographically situated → *Full-time, day hours, physically isolated, geographically isolated*

require deeper and higher forms of knowledge than when they are subject to close supervision. For example, a high-discretion worker may set his or her own goals, periods of work and means of achieving those goals. Hence, they are enmeshed in a greater diversity of decision-making and problem-solving than those not permitted wide discretion. For instance, at the second-ary processing plant, those in the fusion areas had very wide discretion in their work, which included the timing of setting furnaces to access less expensive night-time electricity and changing of the costly electrodes that were imported for the plant. The workers in the control room, however, felt frustrated and disempowered by the removal of some of their discretion. Moreover, in the hairdressing salons, discretion was quite varied. For instance, in two salons the owner/managers refused even highly experienced and long-serving staff discretion with accessing and ordering stores. Yet, in another, this was the task of the apprentice. Consequently, the division of labour deter-mined the array of discretionary tasks and decision-making. In sum, the breadth of work tasks will determine not only the knowledge required for the broader range of tasks but also the dispositions that underpin their use.

Intensity

The intensity of activities represents another dimension of emerging and con-temporary work practice. Although there have always been intense periods in work activities (e.g. the hotel kitchen and restaurant during service periods), it is suggested that work in many situations is becoming more intense, for as workforce size is reduced, workloads increase. To work intensely may require an ability to plan ahead and prepare in order to manage the workload. It is likely also to require the ability to prioritise and to deploy strategies that best manage the workload at a particular point in time, and to delegate or stage activities in order to balance the intensity of the workload. Hence, in the restaurant and kitchen, preparatory work is done ahead of the service period, thus avoiding the need to do this work at the busy time. Judgements have to be made of what kinds and quantity of preparation are required. The hairdresser may attempt to avoid booking treatments that will take time and space during a busy period. During those periods they will monitor their time and even deploy waiting strategies (e.g. sit clients at the washbasin) to best manage the workload. Again, the demands of intensity are likely to vary and, again, to manage intense workloads requires higher and specific orders of procedures and dispositions that comprise both personal and organisational values.

Complexity

Determining what comprises complexity of a work task is slippery. It is not useful to consider complexity in terms of difficulty, because what is difficult for one individual may not be so for another. The notion of routineness gets around this problem. However, it does seem that some tasks require a resolution of a greater number of compounding variables in some situations than in others. Consequently, the number of variables that have to be balanced in task completion forms another dimension of work practice. For instance, planning for an evening's service in a restaurant may have more or less variables depending on the range of dishes offered in the menu. The task of dressing the hair of a wedding party, where the same style is required, regardless of suitability for all members of the party, and to a particular deadline, presses the hairdresser to consider a range of variables. The design and construction of a piece of equipment, item of clothing or building requires the individual to consider a range of variables in producing either the plan or the manufactured article. Equally, the application of technology to a service previously conducted manually may require consideration of a range of variables. Again, the need to balance a range of compounding variables demands higher orders of procedures and deep conceptual understanding within a domain of vocational practice.

Opaqueness

Arising from the increased use of technology is a concern about the opaqueness of knowledge to be learnt (e.g. Martin and Scribner 1991). That is, some knowledge is not readily accessible through observation because it is hidden. It requires being transformed to a symbolic medium to be understood. Hence, this knowledge is not easy to learn about, develop or deploy. Moreover, the symbolic representations being abstracted from something not visible or tangible are likely to be constructed by individuals in a more idiosyncratic way. However, beyond technology there are other circumstances where hidden knowledge makes work practice demanding. For instance, the hairdressers' understanding of the structure of the hair that they want to shape through chemical or heat treatment requires conceptual or symbolic rather than an observable basis for decision-making. The factors of forces and stress that engineers use are also hidden, as is the stitch formation of a sewing machine, the thickening of the chef's sauce and the accumulation of bacteria in a food preparation environment. At the secondary processing plant, many of the processes are unobservable, being hidden within kilns, pipes and furnaces. Consequently, like the electrician, these workers have to develop symbolic representations to assist them in conducting their work tasks. Therefore, the degree by which the work task has elements that are hidden or opaque will also determine the requirement for developing rich understandings. Deep conceptual knowledge is likely to be associated with robust symbolic knowledge.

Communication

The requirement for communication in work tasks varies as do the scope and kinds of communication required. So, whereas in hierarchically organised work environments, communication might be oral and directive, in other situations it might be in a variety of forms and achieved through negotiation. In particular, the means of communication will be shaped by the norms of the workplace culture in which the communication occurs: its discourse. This will vary from the 'command culture' of defence and police forces to the negotiations of a self-managed team or work-based decision-making process. Other variables (referred to in 'Engagement' in work practice, below) are the differences in the ways in which individuals engage in work and the communication demands of these circumstances. Hence, the maintenance of work teams is now required to be associated with interpersonal skills as well as technical skills.

Teamness

The requirements for, and qualities of, teamwork are mentioned in accounts of emerging work practice. Such considerations are associated with the division of labour in workplaces and, in particular, the shift to work teams (Carnevale 1995; Davis 1995; Howard 1995; Wall and Jackson 1995). Consequently, the teamness required in a particular workplace setting will determine the need to interact with others, negotiate and communicate. However, teamness will have quite different meanings in particular situations. For instance, the workers who are producing manufactured goods may well be focused on uniformity of product and its adherence to quality or performance standards. In the underground mine, teamness extends to a reliance and dependency on team members in times of danger. In a marketing team, discordance and difference are likely to be valued in achieving a novel product. So these different manifestations of teams may demand quite different combinations of adherence to set standards, common associations or divergence. Each of these examples of work performance will require particular combinations of knowledge.

Homogeneity of activities

The degree to which tasks are homogeneous in a workplace is another dimension of work practice. For example, if all the activities are the same, the speciality is shared and support and guidance to conduct the activity is likely to be accessible. However, if all the activities are distinct, then each task, and its relationship to others, is likely to be more demanding. Contrast, for instance, the role of a technical teacher working in a large metropolitan college with 20 colleagues who teach related content, with that of the teacher in a small provincial college who is the lone specialist in the field. In the latter, the demands of teaching across courses and administrative tasks sets the work apart from that in the metropolitan college. Local government provides another exemplar of organisations that have very diverse responsibilities with individuals often comprising the sole expertise. Compare these circumstances with the workplace where large numbers of individuals are undertaking essentially the same task, some of whom have particular expertise. The store of knowledge and its availability is contrasted with the earlier examples. The homogeneous workplace may provide more support and have less discretionary demands than the workplace where the tasks are not uniform.

Engagement

As noted earlier, the ways individuals engage with the workplace are being transformed. As workers' engagement moves to being more remote, through part-time, shift or home-based work or is physically or geographically isolated, then the demands to interact and understand the changing pattern of work practice, for example, make the work task more confounding. Issues associated with communication, teamness and discretion all emerge as a result of these transformations. The remote worker has the task of staying in contact and remaining current in ways that are likely to be quite different from those of some of his or her colleagues. Hence, the transformations in workers' engagement in work activities are placing new demands on what is required for work practice.

Summary

In summary, it has been proposed that to delineate the qualities of what constitutes a smart workforce, it is necessary to understand that the requirements of work practice are quite situational. Hence, common attributes and cognitive views about expertise need to be mediated and understood in terms of the requirements of the particular workplace or work situation. Three planes have been proposed and have guided the development of a framework that has presented nine interrelated dimensions of work performance which may be applicable to particular work situations to understand what constitutes performance. The number of dimensions could be greater or less. Factors associated with work activities and engagement emerge as the key overriding concerns and some of the dimensions are identifiable as being associated with either or both these factors. However, what has been proposed here reconciles three bodies of literature about human performance as well as that which furnishes understanding about the shifts in the kinds of employment, the nature of individuals' engagement with work and the requirements for work practice. Together, these literatures provide a basis to build a framework that can be applied to workplaces in order to understand the particular requirements of smart work practice. The framework has gone beyond employer surveys and draws upon empirical work from a number of disciplines. Perhaps only through such an understanding will it be possible to consider how the knowledge required for performance in particular workplaces can best be acquired.

Note

1 These workers stated how they developed a feel for the plant and could sense how best it should work. They also spoke about returning from holiday to find the plant different from when they left it and having to adjust their feel for the plant. These observations should not be lightly dismissed. In a study of skilled workers (Billett 1997), a midwife and painter both reported similar senses of knowing about their work.

References

Alexander, P. A. and Judy, J. E. (1988) 'The interaction of domain specific and strategic knowledge in academic performance', *Review of Educational Research* 58(4): 375–404.

Anderson, J. R. (1982) 'Acquisition of cognitive skill', *Psychological Review* 89(4): 369–406.

Appelbaum, E. (1993) *High Performance Work Systems: American Models of Workplace Transformation*, Washington, DC: Economic Policy Institute.

Barley, S. (1996) 'Technicians in the workplace: ethnographic evidence for bringing work into organisational studies', *Administrative Science Quarterly* 41: 404–441.

Barley, S. and Batt, R. (1995) *The New Crafts: The Rise of the Technical Labour Force and Its Implication for the Organisation of Work*. University of Philadelphia: National Center on the Education Quality of the Workforce.

Berryman, S. (1993) 'Learning for the workplace,' *Review of Research in Education* 343–401.

Berryman, T. and Bailey, T. (1992) *The Double Helix of Education and the Economy, Executive Summary*, Teachers College, Columbia University, New York: Institute of Education and the Economy.

Bertrand, O. and Noyelle, T. (1988) 'Human resources and corporate strategy: technological change in banks and insurance companies in five OECD countries', Paris: Organisation for Economic Cooperation and Development

Beven, F. (ed.) (1997) 'Learning in the workplace: airline customer service', Griffith University, Brisbane: Centre for Learning and Work Research.

Billett, S. (1993) 'Authenticity and a culture of workpractice', *Australian and New Zealand Journal of Vocational Education Research,* 2(1): 1–29.

Billett, S. (1994) 'Situated learning – a workplace experience', *Australian Journal of Adult and Community Education* 34(2): 112–130.

Billett, S. (1995) 'Structuring knowledge through authentic activities', Unpublished PhD dissertation, Griffith University, Australia.

Billett, S. (1996) 'Towards a model of workplace learning: the learning curriculum', *Studies in Continuing Education*, 18(1): 43–58.

Billett, S. (1997) 'Experts' ways of knowing', *5th Annual International Conference on Post-compulsory Education and Training, Learning and Work: The Challenges*, Surfers' Paradise Travelodge, Gold Coast, Queensland, Australia, 26–28 November.

Braverman, H. (1974) *Labour and Monopoly Capital: the Degradation of Work in the Twentieth Century*, New York: Monthly Review Press.

Carnevale, A. P. (1995) 'Enhancing skills in the new economy,' in A. Howard (ed.) *The Changing Nature of Work,* San Francisco: Jossey-Bass.

Charness, N. (1989) 'Expertise in chess and bridge', in D. Klahr and K. Kotowsky (eds) *Complex Information Processing: The Impact of Herbert A. Simon*, Hillsdale, NJ: Erlbaum, 183–204.

Chi, M. T. H., Glaser, R. and Rees, E. (1982) 'Problem-solving ability', in R. J. Sternberg (ed.) *Advances in the Psychology of Human Intelligence, Vol. 1*, Hillsdale NJ: Erlbaum, 7–76.

Chi, M. T. H., Feltovich, P. J. and Glaser, R. (1981) 'Categorisation and representation of physics problems by experts and novices', *Cognitive Science* 5: 121–152.

Davis, D. D. (1995) 'Form, function and strategy in boundaryless organisations', in A. Howard (ed.) *The Changing Nature of Work*, San Francisco: Jossey-Bass.

Ericsson, K. A. and Simon, H. A. (1984) *Protocol Analysis – Verbal Reports as Data*, Cambridge, MA: MIT Press.

Evans, G. (1991) 'Lesson cognitive demands and student processing in upper secondary mathematics', in G. Evans (ed.) *Learning and Teaching Cognitive Skills*, Melbourne, Australia: ACER.

Eylon, B. and Linn, M. C. (1988) 'Learning and instruction: an examination of four research perspectives in science education', *Review of Educational Research* 58: 251–301.

Forrester, K., Payne, J. and Ward, K. (1995) 'Lifelong education and the workplace: a critical analysis', *International Journal of Lifelong Education* 14(4): 292–305.

Glaser, R. (1984) 'Education and thinking – the role of knowledge', *American Psychologist* 39(2): 93–104.

Glaser, R. (1990) 'Re-emergence of learning theory within instructional research', *American Psychologist* 45(1): 29–39.

Gott, S. (1989) 'Apprenticeship instruction for real-world tasks: the co-ordination of procedures, mental models, and strategies', *Review of Research in Education*, 15: 97–169.

Greeno, J. G. and Simon, H. A. (1908) 'Problem solving and reasoning', in R. C. Aitkinson, R. J. Hormiston, G. Findeyez and R. D. Yulle (eds) *Steven's Handbook of Experimental Psychology and Education*, vol 2, New York: Wiley.

Groen, G. J. and Patel, P. (1988) 'The relationship between comprehension and reasoning in medical expertise', in M. T. H. Chi, R. Glaser and R. Farr, *The Nature of Expertise*, New York: Erlbaum.

House, R. J. (1995) 'Leadership in the twenty-first century: a speculative inquiry', in A. Howard (ed.) *The Changing Nature of Work*, San Francisco: Jossey-Bass.

Howard, A. (ed.) (1995) *The Changing Nature of Work*, San Francisco: Jossey-Bass.

Kempernich, B., Butler, E. and Billett, S. (1999) *Irreconcilable Differences? Women and Small Business*, Adelaide: National Centre for Vocational Education Research.

Larkin, J., McDermott, J., Simon, D. P. and Simon, H. A. (1980) 'Expert and novice performance in solving physics problems', *Science* 208: 1335–1342.

Lave, J. and Wenger, E. (1991) *Situated Learning – Legitimate Peripheral Participation'*, Cambridge, UK: Cambridge University Press.

Leonteyev, A. N. (1981) *Problems of the Development of the Mind*, Moscow: Progress Publishers.

Lipsig-Mumme, C. (1996) 'Bridging the solitudes: Canadian perspectives on research partnerships in the New Work Order', Keynote Address. *ANTARAC Annual Conference*, Melbourne, 31 October–1 November.

Longworth, N. and Davies, W. K. (1996) *Lifelong Learning*. London: Kogan Page.

Martin, L. M. W. and Scribner, S. (1991) 'Laboratory for cognitive studies of work: A case study of the intellectual implications of a new technology', *Teachers College Record* 92(4): 582–602.

Mayer, E. (Chair) (1992) 'Employment-related key competencies for post-compulsory education and training', A discussion paper. The Mayer Committee. Available from the Mayer Committee, Ministry of Education and Training, PO Box 4367, Melbourne, Australia.

Newman, D., Griffin, P. and Cole, M. (1989) *The Construction Zone: Working for Cognitive Change in Schools*, Cambridge, UK: Cambridge University Press.

Noon M. and Blyton P. (1997) *The Realities of Work*, Basingstoke, Hampshire.

Novak, J. D. (1990) 'Concept maps and Vee diagrams: two metacognitive tools to facilitate meaningful learning', *Instructional Science* 19: 29–52.

Owen, E. and Sweller, J. (1989) 'Should problem-solving be used as a learning device in mathematics?' *Journal of Research in Mathematics Education* 20(3): 321–328.

Perkins, D., Jay, E. and Tishman, S. (1993a) 'Beyond abilities: a dispositional theory of thinking', *Merrill-Palmer Quarterly* 39(1): 1–21.

Perkins, D., Jay, E. and Tishman, S. (1993b) 'New conceptions of thinking: from ontology to education', *Educational Psychologist* 28(1): 67–85.

Perkins, D. N. and Salomon, G. (1989) 'Are cognitive skills context bound?' *Educational Researcher* 18(1): 16–25.

Prawat, R. S. (1989) 'Promoting access to knowledge, strategy, and dispositions in students: a research synthesis', *Review of Educational Research* 59(1): 1–41.

Raizen, S. (1994) *Learning and Work: The Research Base. Vocational Education and Training for Youth: Towards Coherent Policy and Practice*, Paris: Organisation for Economic Co-operation and Development.

Rowden, R. (1995) 'The role of human resources development in successful small to mid-sized manufacturing businesses: a comparative case study', *Human Resource Development Quarterly* 6(4): 335–373.

Rowden, R. (1997) 'How attention to employee satisfaction through training and development helps small business maintain a competitive edge: a comparative case study', *Australian Vocational Education Review* 4(2).

Secretary's Commission for Achieving Necessary Skills (SCANS) (1992) Washington DC: Department of Labour.

Stasz, C. (1997) 'Do employers need the skills they want? Evidence from technical work', *Journal of Education and Work* 10(3): 205–233.

Stevenson, J. C. (1991) 'Cognitive structures for the teaching of adaptability in vocational education', in G. Evans (ed.) *Learning and Teaching Cognitive Skills*. Victoria, Australia: ACER, 144–163.

Stevenson, J. C. (1996) *Learning in the Workplace, Tourism and Hospitality*, Centre for Skill Formation Research and Development, Griffith University, Brisbane.

Sweller, J. (1989) 'Should problem solving be used as a learning device in mathematics?' *Journal of Research into Mathematics Education* 20(3): 321–328.

Voss, J. F., Tyler, S. and Yengo, L. (1983) 'Individual differences in the solving of solving of social science problems', in R. Dillion and R. Schmeck (eds), *Individual Differences in Problem-Solving*, San Diego, CA: Academic Press.

Wall, T.D. and Jackson, P.R. (1995) 'New manufacturing initiatives and shopfloor job design', in A. Howard (ed.) *The Changing Nature of Work*, San Francisco: Jossey-Bass.

Wagner, R. K. and Sternberg, R. J. (1986) 'Tacit knowledge and intelligence in the everyday world', in R. J. Sternberg, and R. K. Wagner (eds) *Practical Intelligence – Nature and Origins of Competence in the Everyday World*, Cambridge, UK: Cambridge University Press. 51–83.

Waterhouse, P. (1998) 'The changing nature and patterns of work and implications for VET', *Conference of the National Centre for Vocational Education Research (NCVER)*, Charles Sturt University, Wagga Wagga, July 1998.

Zuboff, S. (1988) *In the Age of the Smart Machine: the Future of Work and Power*, New York: Basic Books.

7 Workers' texts, identities and learning possibilities in the smart workforce

Peter O'Connor

Introduction

During the 1980s and 1990s many industrialised countries undertook extensive programmes of workplace restructuring and training reform as strategies to address the massive changes occurring worldwide in the organisation and conduct of post-industrial work. In Australia, following a tripartite accord between the trade union movement, employers and government, an array of measures designed to restructure workplaces and training procedures was enacted. As in other countries, strong emphasis was placed on 'workplace communications' and the communications 'needs' of workers. One consequence of this was the emergence of workplace literacy and numeracy programmes, together with attempts to generate measures and scales of literacy and numeracy 'competence'. A great deal of activity ensued, with professional associations, colleges of technical and further education (TAFEs), universities, private providers and consultants, jockeying for opportunities to provide workplace programmes and 'packages' out of the considerable funding 'pot' provided under the national training reform agenda.

Not surprisingly, opinions as to what constituted good quality provision and how best to determine and ensure such provision varied. So did the quality of provision and packages. Nonetheless, a sizeable skills development 'industry' emerged and has been maintained throughout the 1990s, albeit under different details of provision, tendering, accountability, and so on. Moreover, the belief that enhanced communication competence on the part of workers is a major contribution to a 'smarter' and 'more competitive' workforce remains intact. This belief is continually reinforced by the notion that if our efforts to date have not been entirely successful, the answer is to redouble those same efforts: that is, literacy skills development must, ultimately, be better.

This chapter has grown out of the author's participation in a workplace literacy initiative conducted in 1996, which was funded from the skills development 'pot' mentioned above, and builds on his experience over more than a decade in adult literacy and basic skills activity: activity that has, throughout, placed heavy emphasis on theoretical, conceptual and research dimensions as well as on the practical dimension. The particular workplace programme in question became part of the company's larger 'best practice' and 'quality accreditation' strategy which was conceived very much in terms of 'smartening' the company's operation. At the time the literacy programme was enacted, the company was deep into the process of wider workplace reforms intended to improve efficiencies.

The argument that follows proposes and describes an approach to workplace communications: to addressing issues of workplace communications, to identifying workplace communications 'needs' and to developing effective ways of meeting these. It outlines a distinctive set of assumptions and theoretical underpinnings, and an approach to workplace research that emphasises active participant 'presence' in shaping, implementing, evaluating and refining workplace education interventions. It shows how such an approach covers what is too easily missed in more conventional and typical approaches. Furthermore, by demonstrating how this approach uncovered tensions and inefficiencies, and their sources, within the reform agenda of the company in question, it makes the case for such an approach actually contributing to 'smart' agendas being pursued in smarter ways.

Background

This chapter is based on an empirical study that was designed as part of the second stage of a project conducted under the auspices of an 'Australian National Literacy Program'. The project focused on assessing the communicative practices and requirements in the Australian food processing industry.

The first stage of the larger project had two key objectives. The primary objective was to investigate existing language and literacy assessment methods and practices, and their relationship to assisting effective training programmes and participatory workplace practices. A second objective was to develop principles and guidelines for the development of literacy, English language and numeracy assessments in the food processing industry.

The main objectives of the second stage were to develop and trial a number of assessment options and approaches to serve as models for activity in a particular area in the food processing industry. A key specific objective involved trialling multifaceted and collective approaches to identifying and addressing needs in particular workplaces.

The present study drew mainly on research findings from the larger project to develop conceptual and implementation frameworks for assessing and analysing workplace communicative practices. These were applied to the settings and the participants within a major Australian dairy processing company. In addition, research conducted simultaneously with other companies, together with earlier work undertaken by the author, was used to inform the present study.

Specifically, the study was concerned with an analysis of language, literacy and other communicative practices, contexts and cultures in, and otherwise related to, workplaces. It sought to challenge and complicate many traditional conventions and practices in this area that typically provide only 'thin' or superficial descriptions of workplace events, practices and learning needs of participating workers and organisations. The present study aimed to contribute to a 'deeper', more substantive understanding of these practices and contexts and to help with implementing learning initiatives grounded in collective, collaborative and socio-cultural approaches.

The theory of language and literacy employed was one that approaches workplace settings as being multidimensional and consisting of complex contexts and practices in different and shifting configurations. The research methods used attempted to monitor and examine these configurations and to emphasise factors operating on specific contexts and their practices, as well as to identify the purposes of the communicative practices and how they relate to the actual performance of work, and to identify and examine the broader social and conceptual activities which give particular contexts and practices their meanings. The idea that language, literacy and numeracy requirements (the behaviours, practices, uses, interactions, values and meanings attributed to these, and the relationships between them) are context-specific, underpinned the inquiry. This is the idea that language, literacy and numeracy requirements are shaped and influenced (although not *determined*) by the setting and its distinctive demands/structures/ cultures and characteristics, and the ways language and literacy are used, modified and valued within and between them (cf. Gee 1990, 1992, 1994; Gee *et al.* 1996).

My work was shaped by my strong belief that existing policy directions, policy priorities and educational interventions concerned with workers' literacies and learning perpetuate a limited and limiting approach to skills development and wider learning opportunities and developments. This simultaneously relates to, and is informed by, widespread practices in the sector. These are practices that have changed some of their labelling, but where the 'product' retains a low-grade quality of second-rate education. Such workplace education practices maintain a situation where blocks of colourless and insipid, yet rigid, classroom teaching activities continue to be passed off as an acceptable and adequate learning diet for sustaining vocational education and training growth and development.

The research design employed a multimethod approach, which combined quantitative and qualitative techniques and drew on ethnographic traditions and practices. This approach allowed for work that was 'scientific' yet not detached, and for validating data and findings in ways that did not exclude participants and their perspectives and experienced realities. The work and its underlying premises were motivated by a sense of urgent need to critically review practices and expectations in this area, and to begin a reconstruction process that might provide a basis for more exciting and useful workplace literacy practices.

The study shared with much ethnographic work a commitment to understanding the 'symbolic world' in which people live. It tried to gain such understanding through close examination of patterns of behaviour, customs, discourses and meanings that people in the particular workplace attributed to their own experiences; meanings which were somehow distinctive by comparison to other settings and cultures in the 'outside' world. This 'symbolic' interaction often involves knowing the 'language' of the setting, including dialects, jargon, technical terms or idiosyncratic usage of words and behaviours.

The study used a 'developmental ethnography' approach in a way that located the research as part of the processes and phenomena being investigated, as a catalyst or 'facilitator' of change brought about or generated from the research activity. The research design 'developed' and shifted its emphasis with the research as it moved towards a deeper understanding of the phenomena. Furthermore, the research approach was developmental in the sense of constituting an integral part of a process concerned with identifying and facilitating options and strategies for change. Specific research methods included an on-site advisory or planning group; briefings and familiarisations; preliminary data collection; focus groups; individual participant interviews; workplace questionnaires; critical incident activities; and workplace observations.

The following two sections have been extracted from the original research report. They illustrate the approach and underlying theoretical and conceptual framework of the study and provide a back-drop to the findings and conclusions drawn from the study.

Workers' identities, cultures and learning requirements

There can be no simple relationship or correlation between communicative practices, learning and power; between the getting of education and the acquisition of social goods. If we explore the complexities of workers' daily realities, discursive practices and relations, and interrogate the workings of workplace borderlands, our conclusions cannot be as simple as colonisers and colonised. Our explorations must more carefully examine our own limited notions of learning as well as the social roles of 'work' (paid or unpaid; formal or informal sectors) as social events or social activity. We need to investigate more carefully the values attached to these activities, as well as come to understand something of the identities of the participants in the work processes and events. If we are researching workers, workplaces, work performance, workplace communicative practices, we must constantly reflect on how limiting or expansive our own definitions, theories and methodologies are in practice.

Consider, for example, the hypothetical case of an Aboriginal elder who is employed as a cleaner in a factory in the town near where he, his family and clan live. To what extent can he ever be accurately described or understood simply as *a cleaner*? Who determines this description or classification? For instance:

- when he has a night on the drink – is he then a drunk?
- when he attends Christian church services for worship – is he a Christian?
- at home with his spouse, children and other kin – is he a father/husband/ lover/uncle/son/ grandfather/son-in-law?
- when he provides counsel to his community – is he a community counsellor/welfare worker?
- when he provides oral histories, folklore and traditions from the Dreamtime, through storytelling and participation in rituals – is he a historian/ story-teller/dancer/mystic?
- when he creates art and music as representations and records of his history and culture – is he a musician/artist/archivist?
- when he sits on regional lands councils, or lobbies governments on indigenous issues – is he then a politician/advocate/adviser/lobbyist?
- when he speaks haltingly and without confidence in English, but converses confidently and fluently across many indigenous languages – is he illiterate/a linguist/translator?

We could continue to explore our hypothetical elder's daily realities and possible range of identities, building or compiling an increasingly complex image of the person and his world. One thing we can say at just about any stage of the enquiry is that our Aboriginal elder is seldom, if at all, merely perceived or referred to as a 'cleaner', except perhaps by his immediate supervisors in the workplace, or by co-workers who, due to their discourse position, place no value on the discourses of the elder. However, even this rejection or devaluation is a tacit acknowledgement that he is more than a factory cleaner.

What have these multiple identities got to do with his paid employment, his workplace communicative practices or job performance? How do some of these identities wash over, or are brought into, the workplace? If a hierarchy of value exists between these various identities, where is that of 'cleaner' located? By whom/for what purposes? How do our education interventions acknowledge these identities, skills, experiences and relationships?

At work, is this person ever really the 'cleaner' as we originally labelled him, or does he still carry some or all of the influence, identity, meanings, understandings, status, and so on, of the tribal elder into the workplace? How does he view/describe himself? How do others, including educationists, view, perceive or respond to this person?

What are we prepared to understand of the multiple identities of our Aboriginal elder? How do we assess or analyse his workplace communicative practices? To what extent do we incorporate or screen them from our education strategies? How is our understanding reflected in our research, in our teaching programmes, in the development of optional and alternative approaches to learning, and in our own professional development efforts?

Something we can be sure of is that this person and his learning requirements cannot be understood by reference to an employee number, a job description or an occupation classification.

Another thing we can be sure of is that the recognition of the multiple identities of the Aboriginal elder, which he brings to the workplace, the ways and configurations in which they are brought and realised, and how these shape and influence his work, are only one line of enquiry in our examination of the communicative practices, and provide only one part of the story. A second line of enquiry in our ethnographic studies must interrogate the identities of co-workers, identities as collective members, as well as the specific context layers, peculiarities and idiosyncrasies of practices and meaning-making within and between those context layers and the workers and others who inhabit them, or operate within and across them.

Thus, our ethnographies become a search for discourses within workplace settings. They become a story of collisions and harmonies between the various discourses, and how meaning is generated, developed and modified through these collisions and harmonies.

Workplace and borderland discourses

Discourses, in the sense intended here, are the 'stuff' of cultural practice, social being, and personal and collective identity. It is within and through discourses that we produce and engage in everyday life. Discourses can be seen as being made up of

> people, of objects (like books), and of characteristic ways of talking, acting, interacting, thinking, believing and valuing, and sometimes characteristic ways of writing, reading, and/or interpreting (offering translations of oral and/or written texts sensitive to the cues those texts present for interpretation to these practices) . . . Discourses integrate words, acts, values, beliefs, attitudes, social identities, as well as gestures, glances, body position and clothes.
>
> (Gee 1992: 20, 107)

Who and what we are reflect the discourses we participate in. In other words, discourses 'create, produce and reproduce opportunities for people to be and recognize certain "kinds of people"'. Hence, 'we are all capable of being different kinds of people in different Discourses' (Gee *et al.* 1996: 10, emphasis in original). The myriad of discourses found within a society are 'owned' and 'operated' by socio-culturally defined groups or networks of people, and within particular social settings. People within these groups are accepted into 'membership' of the Discourse and play various 'roles' and give various 'performances' within the Discourse and its sites of operation. Through rewarding and sanctioning particular communicative practices as 'right' or 'wrong', 'appropriate' or 'inappropriate', 'normal' or 'deviant', the Discourse incorporates a normative or ideal set of actions, theories, meanings and associations, towards which its members more or less converge. Thus, Discourses 'apprentice' their members to ways of behaving and thinking as group members, and establish folk theories and associations common to the group and allow it to continue. As Gee (1992: 108) observes, 'these norms, discoverable by ethnographic study, are, in fact, where the meanings of the acts, beliefs, values, and words of the group reside'.

In adopting an ethnographic approach to understanding the play of discourses within workplace settings, James Gee's distinctions between 'primary', 'secondary' and 'borderlands' discourses are especially fruitful.

Primary discourses are those that people are apprenticed to or acquire early in life, during their primary socialisation as members of particular families or kinship networks within specific socio-cultural settings. That is, they are our 'home-based', cultural identity discourses, and the base from which we confront, navigate, acquire or resist later discourses. As we enter the 'public' world and come into contact with a range of secondary discourses, complex and multiple relations develop among discourses and individuals and their communicative practices. However, it is the primary discourse that establishes a range of identity norms, and allows identification and valuing of 'people like us' in our private and informal lives. To a large extent norms provide a unity and identity to our multiple social selves.

Secondary discourses are those that people become apprenticed to 'out in the world', as part of their socialisation within various local, state and national groups and institutions, outside early home and peer-group socialisation. These can include churches, street gangs, schools, workplaces, unions and political parties or associations. As we enter these public domains beyond the primary socialisation unit, people take on new identities as members of various secondary discourses. 'Each secondary Discourse is a tradition passed down through time – ways people who "belong" to the Discourse tend to behave now and have behaved in the past in certain settings' (Gee 1992: 109). Thus, secondary discourses constitute public identities, and that is recognisable and meaningful of our more 'public' or 'formal' acts.

It is obvious that there are, even from this brief description, areas of overlap and influence, as well as conflict and tension between primary and secondary discourses, which in turn shape and re-shape them and the relationships of individuals and actions within them. Practices, behaviours and 'norms' drift across or filter through discourse boundaries and become incorporated within other discourses. Thus, the lines we draw around discourses should be viewed not so much as solid boundaries, but more as permeable membranes that allow various elements to pass through them while filtering out others.

Thus, it is argued that people inherit – through apprenticeship in the discourse of their community, home, kin networks, schools, workplaces – ways of making sense of experiences, which in many instances have long and rich histories, but are also constantly evolving and being redefined and reconstructed. This enculturation/apprenticeship gives people within those groups or networks certain forms of language, ranging from devices at the word and clause level through to detailed and complicated texts, that are intimately connected to 'forms of life' (see Lave and Wenger 1991).

While people as speakers or writers might structure their speech or writing in ways that may appear universally consistent, say in lines and stanzas, as part of their language process, people from different socio-cultural groups pattern language in lines and stanzas in different ways and with different meanings. Thus, it is never sufficient simply to identify the superficial or formal grammatical structure of the text or language usage.

Therefore, a caution for workplace educational activity is the need to be conscious of comparing and understanding the meanings of like texts, rather than comparing with forms of text from other remote and dissimilar contexts, such as classroom or college-based texts. To generalise or compare, say, a workplace narrative text with a school, college or university essay, would be as absurd and meaningless as comparing a work-team production report with a report in a scientific journal. The danger is in comparing 'apples' with 'oranges', and trying to determine the deficiencies or how learning might be able to reshape the orange to resemble more closely the apple.

There is often an awkward attempt to assess and analyse workers' abilities and requirements, relying on overly generalised categories, or the references provided by other specific contexts that are entirely dissimilar in terms of structures, power relations, socio-cultural context and content, and the meanings that reside within these. This type of approach has served workers and industry very poorly, as it draws on and is limited by what the educator knows of the subject matter and context, and what understandings, methods, resources the educator has available, rather than those within the contexts and participants being studied or evaluated. That is, the assessor is relying on the referents and understandings within his or her own discourses, often at the expense or exclusion of those being reviewed.

Of particular significance to this discussion is the notion of 'borderland' discourses. In studying and analysing the texts of students from a low socio-economic, poor, mostly segregated neighbourhood (and particularly the account of one student of her initiation and later years in high school), Gee (1992) identifies a set of discourses that are located somewhere between the primary discourse and the secondary discourse (in this case, school), an area he refers to as a 'borderland discourse' which effectively straddles the primary and secondary discourses.

The 'borderland' is characterised by points at which the secondary 'official' workplace discourses conflict with, and are opposed to, the workers' primary discourse. There is an uncomfortable or poor fit, and at times irreconcilable differences, between the two. In these situations, workers develop a discourse that allows continued 'membership' of the work group, and at least the appearance of acceptance and adherence to the normative values, as well as making sense of, and maintaining, some loyalty and allegiance to the primary discourse. Thus, the tension is around resisting aspects of the workplace that either contradict, or are offensive to, the 'primary' (and other outside of work) discourse, or are even opposed to the ways that workers know work can and should be performed.

The student in Gee's illustration confronts, and is initiated into, the new, foreign and intimidating discourse of the school and the classroom, by relying not only on her primary discourse as a poor fitting guide, but also on the assistance of her friends from her own community, whose discourse is in conflict with the school. Thus, a peer-based borderland is created to assist apprenticeship into the school practices, as well as providing a means of resisting some of those practices. The communicative practices of someone in this situation, then, have to be understood not only in terms of the primary and secondary discourse and their relationship, but also by the borderland discourses designed by people to cope with these. The membership of the borderland discourse is defined in relationship to, and partly in opposition to, the discourse of the school and, similarly, the workplace (see Casey 1995, for a discussion of some of the tensions between the new work cultures and reshaping workers identities).

We can take the notion of borderland discourses a little further to assist our understanding of workplace communicative practices. We can argue that the borderland is characterised not only by its points of conflict, tension and resistance between primary and secondary discourses, but also by conflicts and tensions between and amongst competing primary and secondary discourses within the workplace. Thus, it provides a space and a means for workers to make sense of the various discourses which operate within the workplace, whether they be tensions between the primary and 'official' organisational discourse, between worker and management, between sections of different workplace contexts or operations, or between groups of co-workers.

At any point in time, then, there will be a number and variety of borderlands operating in a workplace. They may not be restricted, as the name suggests, to the margins or fringe of significant activity but, rather, may in fact occupy central and vital positions in particular workplaces.

The borderlands may be found around all types of groupings, such as those generally or specifically identified through membership of primary discourses (national, cultural, ethnic or language groupings); other external or public secondary discourses (religious or political affiliations, union membership, occupation, age, gender, neighbourhood or community groupings, such as street gangs, sporting clubs, and so on); or those more 'organic' to the particular workplace setting (general mixed groupings of co-workers, work teams, sections or departments, work operations, job or occupational classifications, geographic location in the workplace). As with other discourses, an individual may simultaneously belong to, and move within and between, a number of borderlands.

The borderland discourse accurately describes the situation and reality experienced by many workers, both as they enter new work contexts and as they 'colonise' and become familiar with workplace settings over time.

In most workplaces, workers quietly resist many official edicts and directives, as their own experiences tell them they will not work, or will not work as well as they can perform the task. Thus, workers employ 'unofficial' or 'theories in use' (or their specialised 'local knowledge') rather than the 'official' or espoused theories of the organisation. In a sense, this is a manifestation of the operation of 'borderland discourses'. The operation of the 'borderland' provides a terrain that is characterised by constant tension and working 'against each other'.

Borderland discourses operate in opposition and exclusion (in part or whole) to other workplace discourses, including other 'borderlands' perceived to be offensive, threatening, in opposition or conflict. New identities, pertinent to, constructed and generated in, the workplace, but incorporating composite elements of other public and private, formal and informal, identities, are shaped, developed and sustained in the borderlands. These new identities and relationships, while having their genesis in the workplace, are not restricted to this domain; they are taken 'into the world' in the form of friendships, organisational affiliations, and a range of social activities and relationships.

Through investigating how the borderlands are formed and re-formed, operate, sustain and defend themselves, it is possible to provide a fascinating introduction crucial to tapping the layers of workplace communicative practices. It is the workplace borderlands (not always visible or accessible to the observer or researcher) which potentially provide the richest research material and data in this area.

Workers are often well aware that workplace discourses are not likely to value many of the practices of their community or cultural groups and, in many instances, are in direct opposition to them. Due to these conflicts and the power relations of the workplace, it is equally likely that these community values and social practices will not gain full or equitable access to the dominant discourses or the social goods that go with them. Thus, as Gee states, the 'borderland Discourse is a form of self-defence against colonization, which like all organized resistance to power is not always successful but does not always fail' (Gee 1992: 150).

Until the values and practices of private, social and work activity are more closely aligned and integrated; until a trust exists across these domains; and until such time as workers are genuinely included in shaping the workplace 'discourse', there is unlikely to be the harmony or close cooperation that many seek, and which, indeed, will increasingly be imperative for economic survival. The challenge is to diminish the area of ground occupied by the borderland discourse in many workplaces. This may be achieved by establishing approaches that share common values and objectives, collaborative 'partnerships', and establish ownership and control of ideas, planning and learning strategies as part of the dialogue and practices of the workplace.

Thus, the question for most developing workplaces will be how to attempt to reduce or bridge the area of the 'borderland', through practices that address the tensions and conflicts between the 'official' and 'unofficial'. Ideally, work-places will seek a close alignment between the primary discourses of its workers and the secondary discourses of the workplace, whereby conflict and resistance is minimised. It is unlikely that this will ever be effectively achieved through 'conquest', but rather through a genuine convergence of the two.

The point at which workers abandon the defensive aspects of the 'border-lands' will be when they see, and are part of, changes which they value and trust, and which values and trusts them and their abilities, views and so on. This level of collaborative 'give and take' will add profound definitions to the substance of 'teamwork'. Until such time, many workers will continue to take refuge in the borderland and continue to perform work in ways they know, whether such work is officially endorsed or not. The full potential of learning along with developments that accelerate change in the workplace, for workers or the company, are unlikely to be significantly progressed until some of the major issues of the 'borderland' are addressed and reconciled.

Reading work and the workplace

One particular area of regular discussion, afforded considerable weight by participants in the study, was an area of communicative skills not raised in questionnaire or interview questions. As the focus groups explored the various communicative practices and related issues, it became clear to participants that this was only one level or layer of what actually occurred in the work-place. It was argued that, in order adequately to understand what communi-cative practices and skills were engaged in job performance, it was not sufficient simply to identify the obvious reading and writing, and so on, that took place in the company, but rather to understand 'how the work was performed by experienced operators, whose real talents and skill is in their "feel" for the work'.

As the discussion evolved, claims were made that this area was an impor-tant key to both understanding the communicative skills used and required in the workplace, and provided clues as to what skills-development inter-ventions were necessary to tap these areas. Participants claimed that experi-enced operators 'have an intuitive feel for their work and the work environment, they not only read signs and notices, they "read" their machines and the things going on around them in the context of the whole work event and processes.'

This '*feel*' for the work and '*reading*' the work environment were likened to other skilled, familiar activities, such as driving a car, where drivers 'feel' the accelerator or clutch, listen to the sounds of the engine, and accurately esti-mate speeds and distances under a range of driving conditions. The analogy drew comparisons between an operator in particular work areas and the tech-nical and spatial skills employed while driving. Operators were said to be able to focus on information and occurrences that were significant at any given moment, such as an abnormal reading on a printout, the sounds of machines, and characteristics of the product. The process involves taking in most information in the surrounding work area, and moderating and interacting with it by screening out irrelevant data or events and concentrating on the 'main messages derived from experience of the work, the surroundings and the particular equipment'. That a major communication in the workplace was between workers and the events, equipment and machinery and environment and conditions prevailing in the work area.

One participant discussed this perceived 'know-how' in some detail in an individual interview, and was adamant that it was the level of communicative skills that experienced workers develop in their work that should be the goal of skills development in this area.

> In many ways this is a more intimate way of communicating, where you use all your senses. You have to be able to listen, smell, sense and antici-pate what is happening, which often involves simultaneously taking in a whole lot of information from many sources and making sense of it. Experienced workers know when to run a machine to capacity, and when to ease off, before any warning signals go off, they can read the situation well enough to avoid emergencies and breakdowns. They com-municate more closely with their gear and the work environment than they do with most of their co-workers.

All participants agreed that to ignore the expertise and 'know-how' utilised by experienced operators would result in a focus that isolated separate skills from the context and combinations in which they are used in the performance of work. It was felt that this was the limitation of the operating manuals and many of the training efforts, in that they attempted to address specific skills requirements in isolation, ignoring their 'real' place and function in the work carried out in the workplace.

Study findings and discussion

The study identified a range of literate and communicative behaviours not traditionally considered in discussions of workplace language and literacy skills or requirements. These include, for example, the kinds of intuitive 'readings' mentioned above, the existence and maintenance of borderland dis-courses, and the unspoken protocols and passive resistances to the 'official' discourses. Participants provided examples of how new workers were inducted into the workplace through a mentoring and appraisal of the operating manuals and procedures. It was described how, as part of the new work culture, the operating manuals were rewritten by people in the workplace as a valued 'collaboration'. However, much of the content was not validated, gaps were not identified, bad habits were often immortalised in the manuals, and those workers who were given the task of documenting the work functions were not assisted in research or writing requirements. People employed as production workers, through the 'valued collaboration' of the new workplace culture, were expected to make an instant transition to becoming technical authors and trainers. The manuals soon came to be viewed by most workers as 'more dead resources' of little or no use to their actual job performance. None the less, they were accepted as the 'official' operating references, as part of the collaborative process; but they were simply not used as operating resources in practice.

Participants described the reconciliation between the 'official' and 'unofficial' occurring as follows. As new employees were recruited, the experienced workers responsible for inducting them would take the recruits through the official process, precisely as instructed. New recruits were taught the workplace and job performance procedures in accordance with the operating manuals. However, as soon as the new employee commenced on the job they would be provided with the unofficial induction by the same experienced workers, who would explain that the information in the manuals is inaccurate and should largely be disregarded, and would then proceed to demonstrate how things were actually done. At this point, then, new employees – having received the official training and preparation – began to be inducted into the actual job performance discourses and were introduced to the borderland discourses that allowed the official and unoffical to coexist reasonably comfortably.

The study also reinforced the premise that many of these behaviours or skills are not transparent. They are not readily visible or accessible to researchers or other 'outsiders.' Uncovering them requires some depth of study for instance, going well beyond the usual scope of needs analyses and observations of the kinds of readily apparent texts on display in the work setting. It is necessary to frame questions, observations, prompts, etc, and to elicit responses that consciously recognise that the communicative practices of workplaces extend well beyond the '3 Rs' and the more obvious print-based or oral literacies and texts usually identified. (Some recent South African and US examples of research, which reinforce the diverse and subtle practices across a number of workplaces, are provided by Prinsloo and Breier 1996; Hull *et al*. 1996).

The kind of approach taken in the study requires us to consider the 'know-how', 'intuitions' and 'experiences' of workers in ways that redefine traditional views of reading, writing, numeracy and other communicative practices. Many important areas and forms of reading and writing work in the workplace only became visibly apparent as the study evolved, trusts developed, and participants felt at ease in reflecting upon the issues being addressed. These were not evident from preliminary data collection, workplace tours, or from answers to the workplace questionnaire.

While the intended focus of this study was on identifying and understanding communicative practices, the consultative and participative approach that was adopted over the six-month period of investigation allowed participants to engage in and reflect on a wide range of work-related issues and, in so doing, modelled some of the possible processes that could be implemented to bring about change in the communicative cultures and practices of the company.

To date, very few close and theoretically informed investigations have been undertaken on the actual reading and other communicative requirements of workers and workplaces, and of what types of reading and communications actually take place within workplaces in performing work and related social activities of workplaces. The study found clear evidence of diverse and complex communicative practices taking place, and of communicative requirements being placed on workers at all levels of the company in performing their work and in other daily events within the workplace. Through the ethnographic approach used, it confirmed that more traditional characterisations of workplace 'language', 'literacy', 'communicative' or 'basic' skills often barely touch the surface of the actual discursive practices, behaviours, cultures, identities and relationships that influence or constitute the communicative realities of workplaces. Many of these accounts remain 'thin descriptions' (Darrah 1992) of what is actually happening in particular workplace settings.

In discussing their findings from a study of 'traditional' and 'high performance' workplaces, Hull *et al.* (1996: 202) argue that:

> Little attention is usually paid by those in charge of workplace innovation to who workers are – their backgrounds, their biases, their goals in their current job, their plans for the future.

This attention to the identities and cultures of workers needs to be extended beyond the workplace boundaries, as well as deeply into its more invisible recesses. As participants in the present study insisted, it is equally necessary to acknowledge and understand the range of communicative practices in a workplace – from basic form-filling to the 'feel' for the job – which constitute and are integral to the work and cultural events that occur in the workplace. Hull *et al.* (1996: 204) make the point powerfully as follows:

> Contrary to popular opinion, workers don't just need the 'basics', whether those basics are cast in a traditional mold of readin' writin' and 'rithmetic or re-cast as 'higher order thinking skills' or other decontextualised competencies listed on various skill lists. We have observed workers using literacy for purposes that run the gamut of our categories. Indeed, our argument is that a literate identity means being able to do precisely that – being able, that is, to dip appropriately and as needed into a wide and deep repertoire of situated ways of using written language and other forms of representation in order to carry out a work-related activity.

Those education texts and resources that have addressed some of these issues have tended to provide taxonomies of print-based texts found in workplaces, but have generally failed to identify the layers and complexity of *'reading the world of work'* that is carried out by workers in making meaning of the work events and processes in which they are centrally engaged. Similarly, they are limited in the types of 'texts' that are identified – seldom do we include in the lists of workers' reading items such as machinery, production lines, consoles or operator terminals, environment or atmosphere, physical, historical or political locations. We tend not to include in our taxonomies the discursive or material practices or relationships, the histories, mythologies, images or constructions of corporate or individual identity which constitute the air the workers breathe. Nor do we incorporate the cognitive, emotive and sensory skills that are used in the reading of these texts.

To take the illustrative example provided by focus group participants in the study, we may consider here the subtle nuances of operating a motor car. Most people would be familiar and comfortable with the notion that all senses are engaged in the activity. Obviously, a driver looks ahead, and in rear and side mirrors, to view the road conditions, direction of movement and other traffic. As drivers, we estimate speed, distance, and space, and so on, but we also listen to the engine, wheels, chassis, in order to detect any malfunctions or warning signals, and we can smell engine oil or fuel spills or burning, hydraulic or brake fluid leaks, overheating brakes, or engine overheating. When we accelerate, brake or steer the car, we 'feel' our way around these, rather than employ a standard measure, and we seldom use a slide rule to perform reverse parking. These are some of the areas of learning that we would attempt to impart to a new or inexperienced driver, in order for them to develop the necessary expertise to drive a car competently under a range of conditions.

When it comes to determining educational and learning interventions and strategies in most workplaces, however, we tend to ignore the more subtle texts and their readings in particular contexts, even though the complexity of these activities is often considerably greater than that of driving a car. We fail to acknowledge and respond to the full range of 'texts' that workers engage with in the course of performing their work. When we look for 'authentic' workplace texts to incorporate in learning activities, we tend only to gather superficial samples, and usually do not include the machinery, tools, processes and expert 'senses' for these as texts. Under these circumstances, the texts or workplace materials we gather soon become decontextualised, stripped of their authenticity, and meaningless as aids to learning. It is argued that if education, training or learning interventions continue to focus on the superficial texts of memos, notices, safety signs and the like, then the learning options developed will continue to be poorly matched to the deeper requirements and realities of workers' job performance and work events.

To locate deeper understandings of these texts, and how they are used, manipulated, generated, reshaped, and given meaning, we need to incorporate more than just the technical ability to read print-based texts. We need also to take account of the range of non-print-based texts found and 'read' in workplaces. This understanding needs to include cognition and meta-cognition, tactile and sensory perceptions and interactions, imagination, memory, a range of pooled and shared experience, cultural and contextual values, understandings, practices and meanings of the participants, which are generated, sustained and modified in the range of discourses that exist in any given workplace.

A number of significant discourses operated within the workplace, and part of the communicative practice required workers to be aware of these, and how to engage, ignore or resist them as appropriate. It was also evident that the bases for some of the discourses were, to a large extent, shaped by occupational or work area commonalities, while others were clearly aligned to primary discourses (Gee 1991, 1996) operating and originating externally to the workplace (e.g. in homes, local communities, clubs, churches, sites of leisure and entertainment, etc), while others appeared to be formed and sustained around sub-groupings that cut across these other discourses. To operate effectively in the workplace, workers often had to navigate the various discourses operating in any particular context, and to be able to move and adjust between the identities required of the various discourses.

The study also provided considerable evidence of tensions between the 'official' discourses of the company and the 'unofficial' discourses of the workers and work groups, in the ways in which work was performed, and the roles that communicative practices played in them. It reflected a paradoxical situation where, on one hand, the company could be seen to be pursuing a range of workplace reforms to improve efficiencies. Consultants had been engaged to facilitate 'best practice' and international quality accreditation, resulting in a range of training, new work systems, 'downsizing' of the workforce, and the introduction of formal operating manuals and directives. These changes carried with them significant demands in terms of communicative skills and practices. On the other hand, however, the company failed to engage or consult the workforce in most of these changes. Furthermore, the changes were intended to operate more or less within existing structures, with little support or infrastructure put in place to allow or encourage workers to navigate the transition to the new systems and their requirements.

Daily realities and practices of workers and their work settings were not accommodated in the proposed and attempted changes. The cultural and communicative activities, identities and skills abilities and needs were not a significant consideration in the new reforms. Thus, while attempting to overcome some of the traditional inefficiencies seen to result from poor operational systems, communications breakdowns, and the gap between the perceptions, expectations and practices between senior management and the shopfloor, the reforms in fact reinforced and entrenched many of these problem areas.

The gap between the 'official' and 'unofficial' discourses remained wide, and may actually have been widened, by the work reforms and systems changes being implemented. The study found that, as a means of surviving and resisting many of the changes, workers had created a range of 'borderland' discourses. These 'borderlands' could be seen to provide both a safe haven – a 'shelter from the storm' – and a lively and active source of making meaning and strategies of the tensions and conflicting demands and requirements of the workplace. They also provided workers with the means to continue to communicate, interact, and perform their work, often in spite of tensions surrounding these activities.

The approach and methods used in the study facilitated a process that allowed and encouraged participants to view communicative practices as part of a 'bigger picture', as an organisational issue, rather than an individualised or isolatable skills 'problem'. Responses and contributions from participants, therefore, included a range of training and non-training strategies, as well as structural and systemic issues and adjustments. Thus, while the process did not preclude the consideration of individual skills needs, it located them within the perspectives of the broader context and requirements of the organisation as a whole.

Along with the identification and discussion of communicative practices, issues and future requirements addressed by participants in the study, came no shortage of suggestions, options and strategies. As was discussed in the research findings chapter of the thesis, participants' formalised some of these ideas into a detailed options paper presented to the company management. Many participants were left feeling despondent at the conclusion of this phase, due largely to the discussions around the options paper lapsing into a traditional 'negotiation' rather than a consultation. The options 'negotiation' was limited by historical suspicions (both by workers and management) around the 'who', 'why' and 'how much' which lay behind the proposals. The suspicions and their limitations are reflected in the willingness of management only to consider those components that were considered 'uncontroversial' and 'cost-effective'.

The frustration of this process was summarised by one participant in the following terms:

What's the point of us sitting around talking about improving communications, improving work performance, offering suggestions about things we know, if they won't listen?' This is not new, we've always been prepared to talk openly about changes that can be made. This so-called 'new management' style is just as deaf as the old ones. That's still the biggest communication problem we've got here.

Participants in the study implicitly and explicitly expressed frustration at what was perceived as a devaluing of the collective expertise and experiences of long-term employees. Examples were repeatedly reported of unilateral decisions and change, resulting in less effective communication and job performance, and often giving rise to new problems. The frustration seemed to be heightened by the constant rhetoric of 'participation', 'consultation' and 'flexibility'. The described and observed experiences, however, reflected a dual system in operation, where there was tentative (and at times bold) experimentation with new approaches, which were simultaneously constrained by the coexistence of the older systems, structures and hierarchies. It was a widely held view of participants that many of the problems could have been avoided or minimised if the rhetoric and promises of the 'new' were allowed to prevail over the more 'traditional' culture lurking in the background.

The tensions and paradoxes of some of the attempts at new organisational cultures attempting to exist alongside only partially dismantled older cultures and structures is captured in the following passage from Casey (1995: 137).

> The logic of industrialism struggles to survive the postmodern impulses challenging its dominance. What is happening now is a nostalgic restoration of industrial solidarities, and pre-industrial mythical memories of family and belonging, to hold together the social sphere and to ensure production for the time being. It is an effort to shore up the corporation against the effects of wider cultural changes that are now upon us. The new corporate culture and its manufactured post-occupational solidarities, as currently manifested, do not herald truly new forms of social life beyond industrialism.

Some implications from the study: towards taking a smart approach to developing a smart workplace

The effectiveness and equity of any workplace programme will be determined by the extent of:

- our understanding of, and respect for, the settings in which it occurs;
- our understanding of, and respect for, the workers and other participants in the programme;
- our understanding of, and respect for, workers and others with an interest in the programme.

In setting our objectives we need to avoid the temptation to be drawn into the popular discourse of individual workers' deficits as the source of economic problems, workplace inefficiencies or low productivity. We need also to avoid false promises that rest on workplace literacy programmes solving these and myriad other problems (perceived or real). Moreover, we have a responsibility to assert and articulate the existence of workplace and worker literacies as the basis for any planned education intervention. As Glynda Hull (1993: 44) argues:

> We need . . . , to seek out the personal stories of workers . . . , and to learn what it is like to take part in a vocational program or a literacy class and what effect such an experience has, really, on work and living. We need to look with a critical eye at how work gets accomplished and to examine what roles literacy has within work and what relationships exist between skills at work and the rights of workers.

The overwhelming tendency of much contemporary education and vocational reform is to simplify, standardise and render predictable all kinds of phenomena. This tendency can be seen as an 'administrative' approach to education and work. In contrast, using the ethnographic approach outlined here, which creates problems rather than simplifies, allows us more adequately to address complexities, promote creative and collaborative problem identification and resolution, and begin to map out new directions and strategies for learning in the workplace.

Aronowitz and Giroux (1991: 51) maintain that:

> to argue for a recognition of the dialectical quality of literacy – that is, its power either to limit or enhance human capabilities as well as the multiple forms of expression it takes – is a deeply political issue. It means recognizing that there are different voices, languages, histories, and ways of viewing and experiencing the world, and that the recognition and affirmation of these differences is a necessary and important precondition for extending the possibilities of democratic life.

As the present work and that of other studies (e.g. Hull 1992, 1994; Hull *et al.* 1996; Gowen 1994) demonstrate, developments in workers' education do provide professional and political challenges and positive opportunities for change consistent with the development of a more democratic and just society. Our work needs to both reflect and respect those opportunities, as well as taking full responsibility for our contributions. We must ultimately take responsibility for our own expertise, biases, political stance, theories and the practice we bring to workers' education, and for the quality standards and outcomes of our interventions in workplace language and literacy education.

James Gee (1990: 42) puts the point this way:

> A text, whether written on paper, or on the soul (Plato), or on the world (Freire), is a loaded weapon. The person, the educator, who hands over the gun, hands over the bullets (the perspective), must own up to the

consequences. There is no way out of having an opinion, an ideology, and a strong one, as did Plato, as does Freire. Literacy education is not for the timid.

To invoke Carole Edelsky's (1991) words: through their practice, critical educationists must enact 'resistance to educationally sponsored means of oppressing and interrogation of taken-for-granted assumptions about language, text, knowledge and learning.' Edelsky cites Ira Shor's (1990: 2) belief that 'if we do not teach in opposition to the existing inequality of races, classes, and sexes, then we are teaching to support it.' Hence, while the notion may be uncomfortable for many educationists, the realities and demands of many workplaces force a choice.

If understanding workplace education extends to the specific and broader ideological interests and power relations of particular employers and their corporate and political associates, particular unions and their histories, internal and external politics, and extends to a critical awareness of the political interests of the institutions educationists work for, and to geographic, demographic and cultural considerations, it must also and equally extend to acknowledging that the various relationships are riddled with numerous tensions, paradoxes and inconsistencies within and between the groups of players and their connections. In this context the intervention of educationists may be necessarily complex and prone to manipulation and abuse by any single or combined set of interests.

The terms and conditions negotiated for educational interventions, methodologies, content, curricula, evaluation and assessment tools are not neutral. The choices educationists make; how thoroughly they research, analyse and prepare their work; how forcefully and convincingly they negotiate aspects of their intervention; whether they are ever prepared to withdraw their services, expertise or involvement if genuinely held 'principles' will be compromised: all these things will determine what and whose interests they ultimately serve. Educationists must somehow come to terms with the often contradictory roles, goals and impact of their research or instruction interventions and those of the workers to avoid or minimise the possibility of their models monopolising the workplace education debate.

Much of the work occurring in this area is driven by commercial interests of educational institutions servicing the express interests of employers. Educationists will often discount their own expertise by developing programmes based on an employer's perception of workers' literacy needs and in response to their perceived solutions to addressing these needs. An alternative is to develop our own skills, strategies and methodologies to enable workers increasingly to determine and control their own learning activities, resources and structures, rather than continuing to perpetuate and sustain approaches that merely use workers' learning as a means of satisfying other interests that often have nothing to do with learning, or individual or collective workers' needs.

This study has attempted to contribute, in some small measure, to these goals and ends. The study demonstrates that ethnographic approaches to workplace communicative practice are capable of drawing on and developing rich sources of information. Through these approaches, we may be able to develop deeper understandings and more innovative responses to our workplace interventions.

The future of workplace education and learning initiatives cannot be viewed in terms of educational market opportunities or as a continuation of the attempts to scrub a messy reality clean of its past, its contradictions, its conflict and its injustices. The workplace as a site of formal and informal learning, as with all other such sites, contains a plurality of voices and narratives, and conflict and disunity, which must be incorporated into our understanding of the grounds on which human action is construed. Our theory and practice must develop to express and articulate the diversity and differences, as tools for extending learning opportunities to workers previously excluded or marginalised by education systems and processes.

To work in the interest of contributing to the potential empowerment of workers through intervening and shaping some of their formal learning is manifestly more difficult and demanding than simply delivering predetermined 'education' programmes. It carries with it the burden of viewing skills acquisition as a holistic, complex set of related processes, as multidimensional rather than narrow and one-dimensional neatly organised along a vertically linear progression. It forces the critical educationist to challenge the prevailing vocationalism dominating formal worker education, and to contribute through debate, theory and practice in the training room, at negotiating tables, on the shop floor or in policy forums, to viable alternatives. It requires a close collaboration with workers in everything we do with or for them, and a willingness and propensity to learn from workers as to how their interests and learning requirements may be best respected, safeguarded and extended.

Opportunities exist to use and engage these sites in innovative political projects of resistance and opposition to traditional boundaries and barriers. The opportunities exist for educators to cross new borders with confidence, to redefine the purposes of those border crossings, and to be welcomed into workers' settings and realities as allies rather than uncomfortable curiosities. The intervention of educationists can assist workers in redefining the relationship between power, culture and learning at work, representation and domination, into a more equitable and just set of social relations. Workplaces are 'awash with literate activity' (Hull *et al.* 1996) and a complex range and combination of communicative requirements – the challenge remains for educationists to become sufficiently immersed in, touched and informed by, these discursive practices.

Paradoxically, perhaps, we are likely to find that adopting such an approach will prove a smarter option in the interests of enhancing the development of smart work, smart workers, smart workplaces and smart citizens at large, than options that are more formulaic, mechanistic or 'administrative', and/or that simply acquiesce to the perceptions, prejudices or interests of a single interest group.

Some abiding issues for the smart agenda: clues from the workplace literacy study

The pace of change under post-industrialism has been rapid and unrelenting. Adaptations and responses must often be made 'on the fly'. There is often insufficient time to give issues the in-depth and reflective treatment they need. Moreover, the pressures exerted by rapidly changing agendas on individuals at all levels within organisations often generate conditions that can impede growth and development in new directions. Drawing on some of the tendencies observed in the workplace literacy studies, it is possible to identify some issues for future agendas in organisations undertaking restructuring and training reform in search of a smarter operation. This chapter concludes by considering two key issues.

Skills development and cultural change

Talk of developing smart workers and workplaces is a subset of the much wider context of talk about the massive changes in the world of work in terms of cultural change, and the need to change workplace cultures. Such talk has become ubiquitous and, often, more or less unthinking. Yet notions like culture are complex and demanding, and efforts to enhance workplace culture will be repaid by giving such key informing concepts the attention they deserve.

Michele Barrett (1999: 1) reminds us that 'beyond the irreducible traces of the distinction between the arts and popular or mass culture, and connotations of elitism, privilege, of cultural capital, of the canon' there are several distinct uses of the word 'culture' in play that are relevant to our topic, and these should be identified at an early stage in any discussion of cultural change. In particular:

> There is culture in the classic anthropological sense of a way of life, the fabric and texture of a people's distinctive manner of going about things. Of course, in the contemporary world, where migration and diasporization have produced more complex 'hybrid' cultural identities, these generic descriptions of culture as a 'way of life' have become far more complex. This points to issues of 'cultural difference' and the question of whether and how we could, or should 'translate' experience.
>
> (Michele Barrett 1999: 1)

In this sense of 'culture,' cultures run deep; they are not surface level phenomena, and they are not amenable to quick fixes.

As of mid 1999, it seems reasonable to claim that much of the workplace and training reform agenda in Australia has stalled, as far as deep-rooted cultural change is concerned. It has gone into a holding pattern around skills development and nominal organisational structures. Yet, skills development is a poor substitute for cultural change, as is relabelling work groups as teams, or supervisors as coaches or team coordinators. On the other hand, 'skills development' (including literacy work and enhancing workplace 'communications') can be seen as providing a useful distraction and holding bay for any genuine cultural change that might unsettle some interests. Much current reform has become obsessive around skills development, as is evident in seemingly endless attempts to fashion and refashion descriptions of competence and ideas about how to deliver competencies to the workforce.

It is arguable that we have lost sight of the roles skills development may have in broader and deeper reforms – namely, *cultural* change – and, instead, have come to treat skills as ends in themselves. Many workplaces simply do as much skills development as possible, believing that such activity must ultimately yield productive outcomes. Workplace reformers and educators rarely study exemplars in detail, or investigate how collectives actually combine to become effective teams. A crude sporting analogy is widely assumed without understanding that beyond certain skill levels most 'top shelf' teams win or lose as a consequence of other cultural variables. Skills development is, in fact, the minimum criterion in establishing the team. Beyond that point, skills development is never the determining factor in the effective life of the team. Moreover, workplace change is often pursued with little understanding of the psychology of collective behaviour and motivation, and forgetful of the fact that, whereas many of our team analogies are based on participants voluntarily partaking in the activity, the team environment in most workplaces is coercive. Likewise, paradigm cases of top performance teams seek out and develop skills based on the requirements and objectives of the team: that is, they have very clearly defined skills requirements and strategies for achieving them that are 'internal' to the team's existence, composition and *raison d'être*. In contrast, in the world of workplace change, skills requirements and strategies are often generic, pre-packaged, and elaborated from 'outside' the team.

Preoccupation with skills development has its own spiralling dynamic, built on the assumption that more must be better. This assumption becomes self-reinforcing. Workplace educators benefit because they are needed to deliver programmes or bundles of skills; unions have something to hook job classifications and wage rates to; managers have something else to manage and, in any event, are often convinced by management texts that this degree of activity and 'smartening' must ultimately be good for business.

Cultural change and survival of the unfittest: a lesson from prehistory

In spite of these conceptual and theoretical developments in understanding culture and cultural change, there is a strong tendency for key players in workplace change agendas to conceive workplace cultures and cultural change in very limiting ways, and without taking time to consider, apply and adapt available insights and theories in this area.

One paradoxical outcome of this, as far as the quest to develop a smart workforce is concerned, is how amenable and sustainable the 'new' workforce landscape remains for the easy survival of various species of 'dinosaur'. At the level of management, the 'Tyrantasaurus Rex' can still thrive in the midst of workplace change, despite remaining largely the same itself. Those who promote, and otherwise have stewardship over, workplace cultural change are often the last to embrace the changes in their own practices, as well as being amongst the least capable of embracing them. Middle managers are very often preoccupied with their own survival in the organisation and, furthermore, concerned that even if they do survive they may be leapfrogged over for promotion. These considerations encourage them to resist any cultural changes that may work against their interests. In such cases, not only do management philosophies fail to fit: they may actually be counterproductive in facilitating or permitting change.

The author's own involvement in facilitating and implementing consultative work practices within the rail industry provides a constant reminder of the uncomfortable and limited applications of the new culture. Many managers continue to control, operate and manipulate the processes along very traditional and rigid protocols and visions, yet use the new 'collective caring and sharing' ethos as a mechanism for achieving improvements. Similarly, many workplaces have not reinvented their management structures or philosophies, and many managers simply cannot articulate a management philosophy. To a large extent we still find managers who are not actually managers by profession, but professionals (in the rail industry, notably engineers) who have been promoted to management positions without any serious induction into management discourses. While they may have been high-quality engineers, they make inadequate managers.

Other species managing to survive in the world of workplace change landscape include Industrial (Brutasaurus Rex) and Education (Opportunasaurus Rex) species. Many unionists have embraced the new workplaces from a perceived sense of necessity and as a means of short-term survival. They too are often characterised by a distinct lack of vision, and motivated by short-term gain based on a culture of opposition and trench warfare. Patches of territory and ill-defined snatches of terrain sustain lengthy battles, often for meagre long-term results, and rarely form part of a broader vision or battle plan incorporating work and working conditions in the future workplace.

In the context of diminishing support from traditional fiscal sources, the education dinosaurs have strong requirements to be, and to be recognised as, integral to the new landscape. Their survival strategies, however, typically do not extend to providing new theories or practices but, rather, are largely confined to a *modus operandi* of providing more of the same in larger quantities (cf. Lankshear and O'Connor 1999). They proliferate instruction-based skills development programmes in various shapes and forms. There is also very often an 'anti-theory' call from this quarter, in the name of pragmatics, of getting in there and getting the job of education done.

These different species tend to follow each other around, mimicking each other's behaviours and noises, but without offering clear leadership or vision to each other. In the landscape of workplace cultural change, their habits present major impediments to change progressing in ways that might reasonably be described as 'smart.'

References

Aronowitz, S. and Giroux, H. (1991) *Postmodern Education: Politics, Culture and Social Criticism*, Minneapolis: University of Minnesota Press.

Barrett, M. (1999) *Imagination in Theory, Essays on Writing and Culture*, Cambridge, UK: Polity Press.

Casey, C. (1995) *Work, Self and Society: After Industrialism*, London: Routledge.

Darrah, C. N. (1992) 'The rhetoric of skill requirements', Paper presented at the *American Educational Research Association Annual Meeting*, San Francisco, April 1992.

Edelsky, C. (1991) *With Literacy and Justice for All: Rethinking the Social in Language and Education*, London: Falmer Press.

Gee, J. P. (1990) *Social Linguistics and Literacies: Ideology in Discourses*, London: Falmer Press.

Gee, J. P. (1991) 'What is literacy?', in C. Mitchell and K. Weiler (eds) *Rewriting Literacy: Culture and the Discourse of the Other*, New York: Bergin and Garvey.

Gee, J. P. (1992) *The Social Mind: Language, Ideology and Social Practice*, New York: Bergin and Garvey.

Gee, J. P. (1994) *Quality, Science, and the Lifeworld: The Alignment of Business and Education*, Focus: Occasional Papers in Adult Basic Education, No 4, Adult Literacy and Basic Skills Action Coalition (ALBSAC), Sydney, Australia.

Gee, J. P., Lankshear, C. and Hull, G. (1996) *The New Work Order: Behind the Language of the New Capitalism*, Sydney, Australia: Allen & Unwin.

Gowen, S. (1994) '"I'm no fool": reconsidering American workers and their literacies', in P. O'Connor (ed) *Thinking Work, Volume 1: Theoretical Perspectives on Workers' Literacies*, Sydney, Australia: ALBSAC.

Hull, G. (1992) *'Their Chances? Slim and None': An Ethnographic Account of the Experiences of Low-Income People of Color in a Vocational Program and at Work*, National Center for Research in Vocational Education, University of California at Berkeley, USA.

Hull, G. (1994) 'Controlling literacy: the place of skills in "high performance" work', in P. O'Connor (ed) *Thinking Work, Volume 1: Theoretical Perspectives on Workers' Literacies*, Sydney, Australia: ALBSAC.

Hull, G., Jury, M. Ziv, O. and Katz, M. (1996) *Changing Work, Changing Literacy?: A Study of Skill Requirements and Development in a Traditional and Restructured Workplace*, Final Report, University of California, Berkeley, USA.

Lave, J. and Wenger, E. (1991) *Situated Learning: Legitimate Peripheral Participation*, Cambridge, UK: Cambridge University Press.

Lankshear, C. and O'Connor, P. (1999) 'Response to "Adult Literacy: The Next Generation"', *Educational Researcher* 28(1).

Prinsloo, M. and Breier, M. (eds) (1996) *The Social Uses of Literacy: Theory and Practice in Contemporary South Africa*, Bertsham, South Africa: Sached Books and John Benjamins Publishing.

Shor, I. (1990) 'Liberation education: in interview with Ira Shor', *Language Arts* 67, pp. 253–342.

8 Transfer of learning to strengthen workplace training

Rod Gerber and Charles Oaklief

Introduction

When something is learned during the practice of working in a company or an organisation, is that the end to the process or is the process of learning something that permeates the workplace well beyond the specific learning event or experience? The arguments advanced in previous chapters demonstrate that the process of learning in workplaces is not restricted to single learning events or experiences but, rather, that learning is a complex process that extends far beyond the individuals or the work team who have done the learning. What is important is for all people in companies or organisations to recognise this complexity and its duration as it permeates through the company or organisation, or across companies and organisations. These understandings demonstrate how transfer of learning can strengthen workplace learning and, by so doing, lead to smarter results.

Consider the following situations. A person learns a specialised set of skills to make a particular kind of optical instrument in one company. At a time of high competition among rival optical companies, this person is poached by a rival company that is making other, but similar, instruments. The expectation is that the acquired employee, who is an expert in one company, will be able to transfer her skills immediately to the manufacture of the similar instrument in the second company. However, the transition is not a smooth one and the newly acquired expert takes some time to adjust to the alternative manufacturing process.

A second team of workers employed in a large plant manufacturing portable homes and other buildings for remote mining sites has been engaged in the construction of portable human accommodation projects for several years. A change occurs in the industry and their management decides to focus on the construction of beds for the hospitality industry. The work team had a set of finely honed skills in place prior to this decision. They were then asked to adjust to a different manufacturing situation. Are they able simply to use the same skills in the construction of these beds? Do they interact in the same manner in the construction process? Are there new skills to be learned? Are there old skills that will be lost? Do some of the skills have to be adapted to the new situation?

A third group of workers comprises the management and labour force of a local hospital. This is a recently established workplace in a rapidly expanding suburban area. Both the management and the general workforce have been hired from many urban and regional areas. They bring with them the skills that they have learned in their pre-service and in-service experiences. The challenge for the manager of the hospital is to maximise this plethora of skills to develop an efficient hospital and a distinctive organisational culture. How can this be achieved in the smartest way to enhance the hospital's stature in the local community?

What these examples do is to promote the idea that workers may possess different skill sets and they may interact variously in the conduct of their daily work activities. However, if they are going to be successful as individual workers and as groups or work teams, then they are likely to have to adjust their behaviours and previous knowledge to the new situation if they are going to be most effective and the company or organisation is to realise its potential and/or profitability. There is most likely going to be some transfer of learning of knowledge skills and values, if smart practices are to be utilised in their work.

Current thinking about transfer of training in workplaces

For decades educational psychologists have defined 'transfer of learning'. In an early example, Klausmeier and Goodwin (1966: 463) defined transfer of learning as 'when whatever is learned in one situation is used in a new and different situation.' Such transfer may be lateral – that is, the new task is performed at about the same level as it was learned – or it may be vertical that is, performed at a higher level of complexity than that at which it was learned. While such a definition is useful in learning terms, it is but a starting point for use in workplace training, especially where the concept of smart workers is concerned. This concept of transfer can initially be refined by: considering the concept of commonality of workforce skills and competencies; understanding how learning can be transformative; appreciating the nature of shared workplaces; understanding the importance of teamwork in workplace learning; valuing the importance of the concept of situated workplace learning; understanding the concept of apprenticeship in workplace learning; and adopting a cognitive approach to human action.

According to Mansfield and Mitchell (1996: 236–237), the issue of *commonality* of workplace skills and competencies is related to transferability in two ways: first, the common description of workplace activities that are functionally similar enables workers and their managers to understand the common skills that underpin apparently different activities; and second, 'if common skills can be included within common functional units these can be applied in different sectors, thus providing clear links between different occupations' (Mansfield and Mitchell 1996: 237). They further suggest (Mansfield and Mitchell 1996: 238) that there is additional pressure to include common processes such as negotiating, advising and informing, and also to use these across different sectors of employment. Such an approach to linking commonality with transferability, while academically useful, is less useful when discussing how transferability of learning is valuable for promoting smart workforces because it results in an overgeneralised, decontextualised approach to workplace learning that does not prize the relationships that develop amongst work teams and shows little regard for the precise nature of the work in a particular company or organisation. This reinforces the demand for situated, relational and collective approaches to work practices that are found in Chapter 3 in this book. However, it is the basis for the generic workplace skills movement that is championed in a range of post-industrial countries today.

When the learning process is considered in workplaces, it may be thought of as transmissive, transactive or transformative. Learning through transmission occurs when one worker instructs another on an effective way to do a task. Here, workers simply add more knowledge to their meaning schemes. Transactional learning occurs when the instructor and the learner work their way through a task, often on a negotiated basis. The interaction in the transaction between workers is the basis of the learning process.

Transformational learning in workplaces was defined by Mezirow (1990, 1991) as learning based on reflection and on the interpretation of the experiences, ideas and assumptions obtained through prior learning, i.e. through varying life experiences. Mezirow (1997: 60) proposes that transformational learning involves three phases – critical reflections of a worker's assumptions, discourse to validate the critically reflective insight, and action that ranges from making a decision to a radical political protest. While it is possible for the transfer of learning to occur in transmissive and transactional learning, it is more likely that it will occur in transformative learning, because in addressing dilemmas that they encounter in workplaces, workers will use previously learned skills and attempt to transfer them to new situations either through talking about them via discourse or in their actions in the act of learning. While the key concepts in such learning consist of experience, critical reflection and development, there is growing concern about some aspects. These have been summarised by Merriam and Cafferella (1999: 333–338) as the extent to which the theory of transformational learning takes the workplace learning context into consideration; whether the theory relies too heavily on Western rationality; clarification of the place of social action instead of focusing on individual learning; and the educator's role in facilitating transformative learning.

An increasing focus is now being placed on workplaces as those situations in which people do not operate and behave as a group of individuals. Rather, the focus is on workplaces as *shared* areas for learning and working. In shared workplaces, such as in an aircraft cockpit (Hutchins and Klausen 1998), the operations room in an airport (Suchman 1998) or in a railway control room (Heath and Luff 1998), the shared experiences in learning often involve the transference of learning from one person to another within the workspace so that the tasks that are conducted there can be most effective. Once the shared or transferred skills or competencies have been mastered by all the workers in the area, the workers can function as though on automatic pilot or apparently by instinct, because they possess a shared understanding of the work tasks. We can therefore say that the most effective of these work groups operate as *teams* that give the appearance of being well drilled in the sense that each team member knows what his or her colleagues are doing and so acts seemingly without thinking because he/she knows how the other team members will react.

The act of transfer of learning is something that does not occur in a vacuum. The *situated nature of workplace learning* has been emphasised by Engestrom (1994) in his publication *Training for Change*. Drawing on the work of the Russian educational psychologist Davydov, Engestrom (1994: 32–33) describes an integral learning process of six steps, each of which requires specific learning actions. These steps are as follows:

1   Motivation: the worker develops a conscious, purposeful interest wanting to know about a subject, e.g. how does a machine work? This interest occurs because the worker becomes engaged in a cognitive conflict and searches for a solution.
2   Orientation: the worker develops a preliminary hypothesis on how to resolve this conflict. Here, the worker analyses the cognitive challenge as an explanatory and active model in order to see and select the essential points of interest and to link them together, e.g. in learning about the operations of a machine, the worker identifies the key components of the machine and establishes how they are interrelated.
3   Internalisation: the worker interprets and integrates new information into his/her preliminary model and then examines the properties of the model itself. Up to this time, the model has been external to the worker, i.e. he/she has observed its parts but not in a carefully understood way and so the operations of the machine have been cognitively understood as discrete parts of something bigger, but it has not been understood as a whole operational system that functions in a particular work context. Once the model has been internalised, the worker can often operate the machine automatically for he/she has come to appreciate the wholeness of machine as an operational device.
4   Externalisation: the worker is now able to take the model that has been developed, i.e. his/her understanding of the operations of the machine, and can use it as a tool for solving specific problems in the workplace. In fact, it is the step when the worker tests and evaluates the model that has been developed in specific situations in the workplace. As a result of this evaluation, the model may be revised and so re-internalised. Here, the transfer of the learning done in internalising the model occurs

as the worker searches for a solution to a specific challenge associated with the operations of this machine in another work situation, and reconstructs his/her explanatory model through the use of drawings, speech, plans and actual actions. Such applications that occur in this step serve to enrich the understanding and theory about the operations of types of machines and raises new questions to be resolved.

5   Critique: this step is important for the worker's cognitive development for it offers the chance for him/her to establish the limits of the applicability of the model in the work context. Here, the worker searches for weaknesses in his/her understanding of how types of machines operate and considers how far it can be stretched in different work contexts.

6   Control: now, the worker pauses cognitively and reflects on his/her understanding about the operation of machines and considers how robust is the cognitive model about the operations of machines. Here, the worker may engage in the transfer of some learned tasks and understandings to the refinement of the cognitive model that has been framed, critiqued and reconstituted. The worker will go as far as reflecting on his/her actual learning methods as well as what has been learned in the cognitive model.

This learning process is highly relevant for workplace education for it treats people's actions in doing their work as a series of events or activities that are meaningful within particular work environments. Besides emphasising the holistic and interrelated nature of workplace learning, it demonstrates how the transfer of learning can be explained as an integral component of the workplace learning experience. The smarter workers recognise these connections and are conscious of them in all of their work practices.

Learning in workplaces can also be understood as an *apprenticeship*. This is not to be confused with apprenticeships that operate in various industries. The concept of apprenticeship in learning has been developed by Rogoff (1990). She argues that apprenticeship in learning occurs when competent people support or facilitate less competent workers to become effective members of the work team through: providing bridges from the known to the unknown in workplace practices; structuring situations and transferring responsibility; and offering opportunities for workers to engage in learning through guided participation, i.e. making arrangements for workers' activities and revising the workers' responsibilities as they gain knowledge and skill. These arrangements and adjustments assist the workers in extending their existing knowledge to encompass new work situations. They allow workers to transfer what they have learned in one work situation to another in an organised and consistent way.

The aspects of workplace learning that have been developed here demonstrate a cognitive approach to human action. There are, however, two interpretations that can be put on such a cognitive approach. The traditional one, argues Weick (1979), treats the perceived work situations as an input in which the worker receives knowledge when the work is represented in his/her mind and then develops an internal representation of the work. Here, the relation between worker and work is external. Sandberg (1994: 37–39) offers an alternative interpretation. His interpretation rejects the idea that workers' conceptions of work are inner representations of an external work. He proposes that when workers conceive their work they are actively involved in making sense of it. Consequently, Sandberg (1994: 45–46) proposes an interpretative approach to human competence at work. Such an approach is 'to come as close as possible to the workers' own experience or sense making of their work'. He continues:

> . . . the more precisely we can identify the particular meaning structure of workers' experience of their work, the more able we will be to describe the essential aspects of workers' competence in accomplishing their work.
>
> (Sandberg 1994: 46)

The approach to the transfer of learning in workplaces that is promoted here is one that relies very heavily on the learning being situated consciously and meaningfully. However, it is one that promotes the importance of the workplace *culture* in determining whether the transfer is to be successful or not. The importance of organisational cultures has been emphasised by theorists such as Schien (1997). Succinctly, an organisational culture can be defined as:

> A pattern of shared basic assumptions that the group learned as it solved its problems of external adaptation and internal integration, that has worked well enough to be considered valid and, therefore, to be taught to new members as the correct way to perceive, think, and feel in relation to those problems.
>
> (Schien 1997: 12)

It is characterised by aspects of socialisation, behavioural regularities, shared understandings and symbols. Overall, it focuses on groups of people working and interacting with each other rather than as a group of individuals. A collective orientation typifies the behaviours and practices of workers as they engage in the different work tasks. In terms of transfer of learning, then, it is reasonable to think of learning being transferred from person to person in a work team as the whole team becomes competent in particular work practices and functions as a cohesive work unit. It may also be possible for individual workers to transfer what they have learned in one particular work setting to another one in which the learning can be used meaningfully, e.g. being able to analyse the chemical composition of paper in different work teams in a paper manufacturing mill. Whether the workers act individually or collectively in the transfer of learning, they only engage in the transfer process when they are acting consciously and intentionally, i.e. they mean to do some work task effectively.

Relevance to workplace education

The call for lifelong learning has become the rallying call for encouraging the transfer of learned skills, knowledge and values from one aspect of our lives to another. In terms of workplace learning, this call has resonated around the desire for workers to learn new knowledge and skills that they might use to improve their work practices, productivity and performance. Therefore:

> If employees are to become more adaptable to a greater variety of occupational tasks then, it is argued, they will need a secure foundation of 'core' or general knowledge and skills that will allow them to transfer flexibly to different work contexts. A skills passport is needed to recognise individuals' lifetime learning, updating and accumulation of competence, and thus the capacity to progress to more complex modes of work.
>
> (Ranson1998: 12)

The concept of a bagful of core skills that can be used in different workplaces is a very attractive one to many company managers, i.e. literacy skills once gained can be used in whatever work environment workers find themselves. These skills can be developed by workers through formal training and teaching in structured situations or they may be learned through guided participation in a variety of everyday experiences. It is likely that these skills will be acquired from a range of experiences, including those just mentioned. However, this concept of developing flexible transferable skills for the world of work is much too simplistic to be effective. Whatever skills and knowledge workers acquire must be demonstrated in situated work environments. These skills are not acquired in a vacuum. For example, it might be assumed that technological literacy can be applied equally to any work context once the associated computing skills have been developed. However, as Lankshear *et al.* (1997) have demonstrated, such skills must be applied in specific contexts for them to become meaningful to the people using them. In some cases the technological skills that have been developed have been surpassed by newer ones. This is especially relevant when the emphasis moves from an individual focus to a networked approach. Certainly, it may be possible for some basic technological skills to be transferred automatically from one work context to the next. However, what is being questioned is the extent to which the core technological skills can be transferred easily from one work situation to another. For example, using a computer for measuring the density of juice in a drink factory may involve quite different techniques from those required to conduct an ultrasound scan of an unborn baby in a hospital. Similarly, reading the code of drums of inflammable materials in a hazardous chemical factory is likely to involve different interpretive skills from those required to interpret a map as a taxi driver taking a fare from one part of a city to another.

What is being highlighted here is the reality that the transfer of knowledge and skills in workplaces generally occurs within different defined contexts. Theorists such as Offe (1996) call for a much more enriched understanding of the nature of work and wealth creation. Here, the feeling is that the nature of work cannot be separated from the social and cultural relations between generations, races and sexes, which define who works, and the social conditions of economic growth. The potential for different institutions to support their workers' learning new capacities can also affect just who will learn the new skills and who will not (Bennett *et al*. 1994). Such thinking has influenced Gee *et al*. (1996) to promote the concept of learning for 'a new work order' in which making decisions will be valued over simply following directions in a workplace. Active participation in learning in workplaces will be a prerequisite for the transfer of learning.

There is little doubt that the concept of transferability extends far beyond the world of work to incorporate the outcomes of many of the other facets of people's lives. Workers, for example, develop driving skills in their normal lives; they learn how to use computers for pleasure, often from relatively young ages; they can navigate around their local environments thanks to childhood explorations; they develop manipulative skills from operating their videorecording machine; and they learn to function in groups from the earliest days of formal education. The knowledge and skills that have been learned in these other life roles have involved the development of competencies that are used naturally in different workplace tasks. The extent to which these life skills are actually transferred into work practices depends on the astuteness of the particular worker. Some workers will draw heavily on their wider life experiences for insights as to how to perform a task. Others will not. However, the opportunity exists in all work practices for such a transfer to occur.

Enhancing workplace practices and outcomes through transfer of learning

It is quite dangerous to propose any set of workplace practices that should be implemented to guarantee smart workplace training through transfer of learning. However, it is reasonable to offer suggestions on how all workers can use transfer of learning to improve their behaviours and, hopefully, the outcomes of their work activities. Even if there were agreement amongst workplace educators and trainers that there are common generic work skills and common work processes – such as negotiating, advising and informing – this would not be sufficient grounds for promoting learning activities that developed such skills and processes. What is quite dangerous is to take such skills and processes out of the context in which they are developed, used and transferred and to believe that they are easily transferred from one work context to another, even in somewhat similar work environments.

One way to approach this challenge is to follow Mansfield and Mitchell (1996: 237–238) in identifying occupational standards and then considering how transferability impacts on each of these areas. They identify five such key areas and suggest that the implications for transferability are as follows.

- The strategic area, i.e. standards that describe the strategic decision-making processes including organisational planning, setting targets and mission statements.
- The operational and technical area, i.e. standards that operationalise the mission and strategic planning statement for the organisation.
- Operational management, i.e. standards that enable the operational statements to be distributed and delivered effectively.
- Organisational management, i.e. standards that describe the contributions of individuals to the management and effectiveness of the organisation.
- The value base, i.e. standards that represent the core values, ethics and behaviours that underpin good practice in an organisation.

They arrive at the following points about the extent to which the above-mentioned standards may be relevant to the transfer of learning in workplaces. In the strategic area, the concept of strategic outcomes is common across occupational sectors, but the extent to which they can be transferred from one sector to another has not been tested. For example, the types of outcomes that are promoted in the manufacturing industry may not be the ones that are relevant for the university education sector. In the operational and technical area, the standards are specific to a particular industry or organisation, e.g. a tiler could accept a standard entitled 'The capacity to cut and lay tiles with a defined margin of error'. Such a standard may not easily be transferred to a pastry chef for whom the relevant standard may be 'The capacity to mould and arrange pastry to make designated types of baked food'. The capacity for transfer of learning is quite modest in this area of standards.

Mansfield and Mitchell (1996: 240) agree that operational management standards may be divided into those that can be transferred, e.g. the ability to recruit and to manage a design team, and a considerable number are sector-specific, e.g. outcomes, methods and processes. Organisational management standards are generally transferable across occupational sectors. It is contended that information management, financial management, human resources management and systems management may be applied similarly across different occupational sectors. This claim can still be contested on the basis that, while on the surface, these areas appear to be transferable, at a micro level this view is less supported because the context and the culture of the specific workplace varies even within a single occupational area.

Finally, they conclude (Mansfield and Mitchell 1996: 240) that the value base incorporates the ethical, moral and value context in which the work takes place. While similar methods and processes may be identified in different occupational areas, the purposes of these activities may differ. The promotion of equity amongst workers may mean different things in different industries. For example, the promotion of equity in one industry may refer to pay equity while in another industry it may refer to paternity/maternity leave equity. As usual, the value of values is fraught with danger when any attempt is made to consider the transfer of values from one occupational area to another.

Cook and Yanow (1990) provide a very interesting example from the flute manufacturing industry (as addressed in Chapter 3 by Sandberg) of the need to be cautious when considering the transfer of learning from one flute manufacturing company to another in the same metropolitan area. The general idea that they investigated was that a skilled flute maker from one company could easily move from one company to another and remain a successful worker. This was not always the case because each company measured and valued the quality of their products, the finished flutes, in different ways. Similar characteristics were used by both companies to express their value of the flute; however, the finest flute was valued differently in terms of the sound that it produced, the nature of its exterior finish, and the way that it would be played to produce the best sounds. Associated with this were the different ways in which the work teams operated within the two companies to produce their flutes and the quality assurance processes that were used to check the final product (see Chapter 3). In effect, what is being emphasised here is that overgeneralised aspects of work behaviour and product manufacture can be considered to be transferred, but that company-specific aspects cannot because they represent different aspects of the workplace culture.

The transference of learning can still be used as an important approach in workplace education and practice when it is considered from an activity basis. As mentioned earlier, Davydov promoted the focus of transformations in people's practices in specific activities as evidence that transfer can take place. Lompscher (1999: 269) states that the reliance on superficial similarities in the transfer of learning is insufficient for the consideration of complex problem-solving that occurs in many workplace activities and for the transfer of knowledge and methods to unknown domains and subjects. He argues that what is required is for the workers actively to transform the object of their study, i.e. they should study real transformations of the object of their work and so go beyond the outward structure of the work to understand its inner structure, its essential features and relationships. Therefore, the workers should engage in the application of previously learned skills and knowledge to new situations not just for the sake of doing so. Rather, they should reflect on the links between the knowledge and skills in regard to the new work activities so as to both complete the new applications successfully and also to understand how the transformed knowledge and skills relate structurally to the new situation or activity. In some ways, this relates to Klausmeier and Goodwin's (1966) concept of vertical transfer without any reference to the context in which the transformation has occurred.

Taking Lompscher's view a little further, it is possible to advance a case for the transference or transformation of learned knowledge and skills to be considered in the context of the actual work activity, and to suggest that it be masterful and meaningful. The placement of the transference or transformation in its context gives the activity clarity in terms of the work that is actually done, instead of thinking of it as generic knowledge or skill. It is, therefore, realistic to the workers rather than being theoretical and possibly distant to them. It is masterful and meaningful when the workers think about the knowledge and/or skills that have been transferred or transformed in some systematic way. Here, they are able both to reflect on what they have done and give some structure to the outcomes of their learning in their job. The development of such a complex action structure occurs through considerable experience of workplace activities and some experience in people's wider lives. The smarter workers will, therefore, not only be able to transfer learning from one situation to another at a similar level or at an advanced one – they will be able to represent it mentally as an activity structure that generalises the process of transference and the outcomes of the experience of learning in the new situation.

For these ideas to be useful in the training of smart workers, it is worth considering an instructional strategy that can be promoted in workforces to enhance the transfer and transformation of learned activities. Such a strategy should be based on the facts that learning activities in workplaces are based on individual workers reproducing societal knowledge and skill, and that such learning occurs in situations of social interaction, as workers in work teams cooperate with each other to complete the work activities successfully and efficiently. Rogoff's concept of apprenticeship identified earlier in this chapter is very important in a proposed instructional strategy that can be applied to the transference of learning in workplaces. As Aberg-Bengtsson (1998: 202) says in relation to children learning about graphs:

> The children, by their participation both in unplanned and organised activities where they are guided and challenged by other people, are successively appropriating the conventional and culturally developed ways of using the artefacts of graphics. Certainly, the outcomes of these activities are multiple and constituted in several dimensions.

Similarly, workers who are transferring and transforming their knowledge and skills will be guided and challenged by other members of their work team or organisation to perform successful acts in doing their work in differing situations. The results of such activity-based learning in workplaces are variable depending on the extent to which each worker can internalise a structure of the learning that has occurred in the performance of the everyday work activities. As in Rogoff's processes of guided participation, the success in transferring learning in workplaces will depend on how successful the organisational managers, supervisors and individual workers are at building bridges from the known to the unknown through verbal and non-verbal communication, intersubjectivity (the sharing of focus and purpose between workers and their more skilled co-workers and managers), the extent to which learning situations in the workplace are structured, and the extent to which there is an opportunity for the transferring of responsibility to the workers once they have been able to demonstrate that transference or transformation of learning has been achieved.

An example of transfer of learning in workplaces

An example from a large mill where paper is made for newsprint will serve to demonstrate the concept of transfer of learning in workplaces. In this worksite, a variety of approaches for encouraging the transfer of learning were revealed. These examples indicate how transferring learning can assist in the improvement of work practices.

At the mill, workers are organised according to the type of work that they do as a part of the mill operations, e.g. several teams work in shifts to make newsprint on the two large papermaking machines. Other teams are engaged in manufacturing the woodchips from which the paper is ultimately made, performing chemical analyses of the newsprint, despatching the rolls of newsprint to the publishing companies, and so on. The workers are initially organised into discrete work teams, but they do interact with other workers in formal training sessions at the company's teaching centre and informally with other workers socially or during emergencies when they may substitute for an absent worker.

All mill workers have received a range of essential training during the working shifts and they learn a considerable amount of new knowledge and skill through interacting with fellow work team members. All the formal training offered to workers is in line with the mill's mission statement. Therefore, the developers of the training programmes in the mill centre have developed or purchased and repackaged basic training modules that develop initial knowledge and skills or advanced modules that consciously seek to promote transfer of existing knowledge and skills to new and sometimes more advanced situations. By engaging in these modules, the workers are encouraged to extend their knowledge to the work situations and so to become more competent and confident employees. In the formal training sessions, the workers are encouraged to use both lateral and vertical forms of transfer in their learning, i.e. in a lateral sense they learn to apply exactly what they had learned in a previous work situation to a new one: for example, learning how to operate a particular type of machine to press the moisture out of the paper. In a vertical sense, they may be learning how to use a different and more complex kind of paper machine. This involves the workers learning how to take the papermaking skills that they had learned and transform them into adequate skills so that they can operate the more advanced papermaking machine.

Often, the more powerful kind of transfer occurs when the workers are operating in their teams. Here, they can function as individuals to improve their own learning by extending their skill range and knowledge through experimentation and through watching other workers perform specific advanced tasks. Through a form of guided participation, these workers observe how another person performs the task of cleaning down a machine and then they do the job for themselves through something of a process of trial and error. More frequently, these workers will learn collectively in their work team because such work behaviours involve greater employee interaction. The importance of transfer of learning through discourse is high-lighted by an employee having difficulty doing a task, e.g. measuring the air pressure on a machine. The worker immediately seeks advice from a team member who has been chosen as a worker who should know what to do in the circumstance. This is learning by interaction with co-workers. Through such a dialogue, the experienced worker may explain what to do, s/he might demonstrate how to complete the operation successfully, and s/he might watch the novice complete the task several times to make sure the novice becomes experienced in a particular operation. If the training session is a success, the less experienced worker will transfer the learning about machines and air pressure that s/he has done in pre-service training to a new and more complex work situation. If s/he is smart, this worker will then explain how to complete to task to fellow team members and practise the technique her/himself until s/he has mastered this task. In the end, several team members have improved their understanding of air pressure and how it is read on specific machines in the immediate work place.

Another practice in the company is to transfer workers from one work team to another, especially when it involves changing shifts. Even though both work teams are engaging in working on the same papermaking machines, the challenge of transfer of learning cannot be forgotten because the culture of each work team in the company is different. Workers that make this change of shift have to use their basic communication skills to establish how to communicate effectively and efficiently with his/her new team members. Preferred ways of learning may be different in the new work team. For new members there may be limited demonstrations on how to do a task. Rather, learning experiences may emerge through discussions amongst team members and then the learning workers may be left to their own devices to complete the task, hopefully successfully. Sometimes, the new worker may share his/her knowledge and skill to the new work team, i.e. the new worker becomes the teacher and the transfer of learning occurs for the other member of the team who may not know a particular technique. If this occurs, the team members benefit in terms of transfer of learning and the particular worker learns another way to learn.

Importantly, the transfer of learning in these work teams will be promoted if the workers are all encouraged to remain active, thinking people during their work practices. They will surely transfer some of the knowledge and skills from their other life activities to their workplace behaviours because the world of work does not exist in a vacuum. It is an integral part of each worker's 'life-world'. The presence of active minds in work teams is likely to ensure that the learning and any transfer or transformation will be a collective experience that occurs in a specific context, i.e. it will be a meaningful workplace learning experience. However, it will be most effective if all members of a work team or a company develop values that match the act of transfer of learning. Central to these values are those of valuing the importance of taking risks in learning; believing in the importance of shared understanding of work practices; acting safely in the work environment; and appreciating the contributions of all members of each work team to the work outcomes. By so doing, the work teams can extend how they operate in order to reach higher levels of productivity, while at the same time enjoying what they are doing in their work practices.

Taken to its macro scale in a company such as this papermaking plant, the transfer of learning can be facilitated by the management and the workers to promote the concept of the workplace as a learning organisation. This can be achieved if both the management and the workers in the organisation realise that the concepts of learning that have been promoted at the team level can now be extended to the organisational level. The idea of transfer of learning can be extended now to teams of workers promoting the transfer of ways of operating collectively to other work teams in the organisation through demonstration, discussion groups or through mentoring sessions. The idea here is that the techniques, skills and even knowledge that one work team has developed can be shared more widely in the company to further the prospect of achieving the mission of the organisation. Such a transformation of a workforce can be achieved – as Ricardo Semler (1993) demonstrated in his Brazilian company and as Belasco and Stayer (1993) have promoted through a wide range of industrial examples. However, this normally requires an enlightened form of facilitative leadership from the company management. The benefits from such efforts by management, in concert with the majority of the workforce, can be measured in terms of the whole company understanding what the goals of the organisation are, how they can be achieved, how they are achieved, and how such achievements are both desirable and pleasurable.

Conclusion

Transfer of learning can be applied to workplaces just as it can be applied to any other part of our lives. It is a concept (which has components derived from psychology) that can be used positively in the development of smart workers. Understanding that it consists of transfer of learning at similar and advanced levels in terms of a worker's practice is essential if the concept is to be applied successfully in effective workplaces. This helps to explain why some workers only achieve lateral forms of transfer, but, smarter workers achieve both lateral and vertical forms of transfer of learning. The most effective examples occur when workers are able to act individually or collectively in order to advance their work performance and, hopefully, their company's productivity, by making leaps in their practices by engaging in vertical forms of transfer of learning. Some of these leaps in knowing and doing will result in transformations of work behaviour and practice that will benefit the whole company and not just the workers who have made the initial advance.

The consideration of such transfer of learning in terms of activity theory or within the context in which it occurs is important if workplace educators and trainers want to maximise these experiences for the benefit of the whole organisation. The merits of a holistic approach to transfer of learning are based on the need to understand that the acts of learning do not occur in a vacuum. They occur within a workplace that espouses particular values, has a declared mission, involves workers of varying levels of experience in this and related types of work and promotes the idea of a learning organisation. The leader in this situation facilitates different forms of learning and celebrates the learning that emerges from workers collaborating to improve both the outcomes of their work and the learning processes through which these outcomes are achieved.

References

Aberg-Bengtsson, L. (1998) *Entering a Graphicate Society: Young Children Learning Graphs and Charts*. Göteborg Studies in Educational Sciences 127. Gothenburg: ACTA Universitatis Gothoburgensis.

Belasco, J. and Stayer, R. (1993) *Flight of the Buffalo: Soaring to Excellence, Learning to let Employees Lead*. New York: Warner Books.

Bennett, R., Wicks, P. and McCoshan, A. (1994) *Local Empowerment and Business Services*. London: University of London Press.

Cook, S. and Yanow, D. (1990) 'What does it mean for a culture to learn? Organisational learning from a culture perspective', paper presented to the *Third National Symposium of Public Administration Theory Network*, Los Angeles, CA.

Engestrom, Y. (1994) *Training for Change: A New Approach to Instruction and Learning in Working Life*. Geneva: International Labour Organisation.

Gee, J., Hull, G. and Lankshear, C. (1996) *The New Work Order: Behind the Language of the New Captialism*, Sydney and Boulder, CO: Allen & Unwin and Westview Press.

Heath, C. and Luff, P. (1998) 'Convergent activities: line control and passenger information on the London Underground', in Y. Engestrom and D. Middleton (eds) *Cognition and Communication at Work*, Cambridge: Cambridge University Press, 96–129.

Hutchins, E. and Klausen, T. (1998) 'Distributed cognition in an airline cockpit', in Y. Engestrom and D. Middleton (eds) *Cognition and Communication at Work*, Cambridge: Cambridge University Press, 15–34.

Klausmeier, H. and Goodwin, W. (1966) *Learning and Human Abilities*, 2nd Ed, New York: Harper International.

Lankshear, C., Bigum, C., Durrant, C., Green, B., Honan, L., Morgan, W., Murray, J., Snyder, I. and Wild, M. (1997) *Digital Rhetorics: Literacies and Technologies in Education – Current Practices and Future Directions*. Canberra: Department of Employment, Education, Training and Youth Affairs.

Lompscher, J. (1999) 'Activity formation as an alternative strategy of instruction', in Y. Engestrom, R. Miettinen and R-L. Punamaki (eds) *Perspectives on Activity Theory*, Cambridge: Cambridge University Press, 264–281.

Mansfield, R. and Mitchell, L. (1996) *Towards a Competent Workforce*, Aldershot, Hampshire: Gower.

Merriam, S. and Caffarella, R. (1999) *Learning in Adulthood*, 2nd Ed, San Francisco: Jossey-Bass.

Mezirow, J. (1990) 'How critical reflection triggers transformative learning', in J. Mezirow *et al.* (eds) *Fostering Critical Reflection in Adulthood: A Guide to Transformative and Emancipatory Learning*, San Francisco: Jossey-Bass, 1–20.

Mezirow, J. (1991) *Transformative Dimensions of Adult Learning*, San Francisco: Jossey-Bass.

Mezirow, J. (1997) 'Transformative theory out of context', *Adult Education Quarterly* 48(1): 60–62.

Offe, C. (1996) *Modernity and the State*, Cambridge: Polity Press.

Ranson, S. (1998) *Inside the Learning Society*, London: Cassell.

Rogoff, B. (1990) *Apprenticeship in Thinking*, Oxford: Oxford University Press.

Sandberg, J. (1994) *Human Competence at Work*, Gothenburg: BAS.

Schien, E. (1997) *Organisational Culture and Leadership*, 2nd Ed, San Francisco: Jossey-Bass.

Semler, R. (1993) *Maverick! The Success Story Behind the World's Most Unusual Workplace*, London: Arrow.

Suchman, L. (1998) 'Constituting shared workspaces', in Y. Engestrom and D. Middleton (eds) *Cognition and Communication at Work*, Cambridge: Cambridge University Press, 35–60.

Weick, K. (1979) *The Social Psychology of Organising*, Massachusetts: Addison-Wesley.

Part 4

Directions

9 Lifelong and life-broad learning

Staffan Larsson

Lifelong learning is a key educational concept that has gained renewed topicality. The concept is old and has been discussed before.[1] In discussions of the concept of lifelong learning two dimensions have been distinguished (Rubenson 1996). One deals with learning as a process that covers an entire lifetime – from the cradle to the grave. The other dimension – life-broad learning – refers to the attitude that learning should not comprise a narrow sector of life, but rather life to its full extent. The meanings of these concepts are the theme of this chapter.

Life-broad learning

When I was growing up, a good all-round education was highly valued. One reason for this was that my home was characterised by a high appreciation of education. Beyond this, the high value ascribed to a good well-rounded education also reflected the spirit of the times. A person with such an education was the obvious ideal. To me, an all-round education meant that you should be well-oriented in all sorts of phenomena. Disputes at the dinner table could be settled by consulting reference works. Respect for knowledge and the ability for impartial argument were base values. From the standpoint of knowledge as a good, this ideal commands respect and probably still holds good today.

One part – although *only* one part – of this ideal was the view that one should know as many facts as possible. We see this in quiz shows where 'memory athletes' who know everything about Elvis or Napoleon can earn themselves a reputation. The view of knowledge, which we can imagine lies behind this development, has been criticised. This criticism includes the claim that gathering facts is a limited aim and accomplishment, and is just a part of what the real aim should be. For the aim to be complete it is assumed that the facts must be put into a context – that the part is included in the whole. Facts as such become unusable when one takes a standpoint on something – for then you need the overall view and context.

A second criticism that can be levelled at the fact-gathering ideal is that it is, one could say, bookish, and that it ignores practically acquired knowledge.

This also applies to other cultural and educational ideals. Everyday knowledge, such as growing potatoes or the art of making a sad person feel better, is not valued as highly as it was in earlier times.

A third kind of criticism is that it is not enough simply to know things – a person who has much knowledge can still be a 'one-sided' person. In contrast, being a well-rounded person also has a sensual aspect. The visual experience of variations in nature, the play of colour around us and the body's experience of the rhythm of music, are important dimensions of a well-rounded person.

The picture that is being drawn here is based on a humanistic tradition where the aim of learning and study is to foster the well-rounded person (see the recent work by Gustavsson 1996). Actually this was probably the cultural and educational ideal of my childhood and youth, although it was not so clear to me as a child. The well-rounded person thus becomes a person for whom nothing is foreign – neither the intellectual nor the sensual, neither practice nor theory. This may appear to be a superhuman requirement, but as a vision it is important as it provides a contrast to the way of talking and writing about education that is increasingly dominating the public arena. The concept of what learning is all about is exceedingly important as it forms the visions that are the basis for forming real, existing culture and education in society. Indirectly this contributes to forming people and the circumstances in which they find themselves. That the vision of the well-rounded person cannot be fully realised is entirely human.[2]

This ambitious ideal is being challenged in our times by a way of thinking in which education is seen as a means of obtaining greater financial returns from the workforce. From public discussion in the press and other media it becomes clear that a narrow economist view on the meaning of education is dominant at the beginning of the twenty-first century. This change in the view on education has occurred during the last decade.[3]

Views concerning knowledge or the meaning of study are gaining significance because they are forming the basis for decision-making at all levels, from the immediate and local to the national and international. They are also significant as they can be taken for granted in the everyday world of study – all of us have, more or less consciously, opinions on the meaning of study. It is easy to lose sight of the basic issues when education is taking place in our everyday lives and concrete details are readily assuming an important role. Being aware of these overall perspectives becomes particularly important when new forms of education are being canvassed and developed. Expressed explicitly, the perspectives we have on culture and education actually determine the society of the future – this is why the specific design of education is of great interest.

Adult study and the ways it is designed have to do with the needs adults have and with the qualities, dispositions and prior accomplishments they bring with them to adult education. Adults' learning needs are related to the present, but not only the present – studying also involves an attitude towards the future.[4] In an education policy arena the problem is the same –

the value of study does not just involve the present, but also how it is related to the future. To a large extent, education is about the future; it contributes to forming the future by leaving an impression on people both socially and in terms of knowledge. Society designs education, but education also affects the future of society. The problem with the future is that it is elusive, and speculating about it can easily become embarrassing, once we have seen what actually happened compared with what was predicted. To a large extent, prognoses about the future reflect our picture of the present. Nevertheless, everyone who participates in designing education must have some attitude towards the future.

The contradictory future

If we try to summarise the picture of the future by investigating society, the outcome seems to be contradictory. We can note two tendencies from which conclusions about the future could be drawn, and our attitude to the tension between these two different views is perhaps decisive for the tenability of adult study which is now formed through decisions at various levels.

One view focuses on work of the type we are currently familiar with. This is currently accompanied by a tendency for state authorities to steer education in certain specific directions, towards what are assumed to be useful subjects – natural science, technology, modern languages, and so on. Beneath this lies a belief that education is primarily motivated by financial reasons and that the future is largely a scenario of economic competition between various major powers.[5] A planned investment in useful areas of competence, particularly for product manufacture and technically oriented services will then be the aim. This is emphasised not least by representatives of trade and industry: education should mainly be aimed at the needs arising in information technology, electronics and the export industry. The focus is on university-level courses of education. Following this logic, we could say that producing more technology graduates appears to be the solution to the problems of the future. Some focus on current levels of unemployment and the need to reach solutions to this pressing social issue is required. Accordingly, much educational policy is also aimed at this state of affairs, and assumptions of the capacity for education to help create work and alleviate unemployment will be decisive in whether education is experienced as being meaningful. This idea is expressed directly in the tendency to prioritise courses of education that lead to work, and indirectly in so far as belief in education as a means for developing the potential of trade and industry is given a central position in educational policy discussions.

An alternative picture of the future is drawn by those who believe it will be a different society from those we have previously experienced; who talk about a late-modern or post-modern society, which has different characteristics.[6] These people emphasise variety in the form of many cultures operating side by side, and maintain that local initiatives and activities will become increasingly more important while central control will become more and more complicated; that design will be just as important as functionality in products; and that experiences and culture will fill our time and will increasingly form the basis of economic development. People's activities will be characterised more by social abilities such as (health) care, selling or teaching than by producing goods. Changes in society occur rapidly, and cultural and technical innovations influence large sectors of humanity quickly and mercilessly. Boundaries between work and leisure will be vague. A flexible or even a messy society appears where flexibility and social and cultural qualifications are in the forefront.

Extending these societal diagnoses, we see different types of education; particularly with respect to content but also with regard to the type of education. On the one hand, education involves adults getting particular qualifications – preferably in technology, natural sciences and languages – which seem to be important in a society whose future is dependent on its ability to compete technologically in a world market. By various means, students will have to be tempted to follow particular paths.

On the other hand, education involves locally anchored content, culture and aesthetics, as well as opportunities for specific cultures to develop their own traditions or, possibly, to cross-fertilise each other. Here again it is human relations that are important, both for work and daily life in society. The flexibility involved means that it is not possible to favour a particular professional group – it is the whole population that must apply itself to education.

All the problems connected with multiplicity, decentralisation and adaptation to the market have proved to be complicated and often paradoxical. The decentralisation of decision-making for compulsory school education and upper secondary school levels has, for example, been followed by a strong central control over content as, for example, in English schools. In England, it seems that the introduction of quasi-markets in these areas has led to reduced differences in form and content (Whitty 1997). In Sweden a powerful state policy in the area of adult education has led to a wide multiplicity of learning opportunities. One side of this seems to be that both adult education (in various forms) and mature students have had financial conditions imposed, which have meant that there is a limited range of activities, while, at the same time, those locally in charge have had relative freedom when it comes to content and form. Adult education has formed the most prominent example of an area where a relative autonomy *vis-à-vis* the state, despite state subsidies, has led to great variety in content and function (see Larsson 1995; Andersson *et al.* 1996).

A conclusion that can be drawn is that the specific designs and the specific material and ideological interests that guide the form of activities are significant. For this reason it is important to review the consequences of the different designs.

Any discussion of adult education in the future must consider the tension between the very different characteristics of current and future societies. This is a serious issue – where pride goes before a fall. Should a multiplicity of courses be promoted or should adult education be more focused?

It is important that the concepts of both lifelong and life-broad learning are considered when designing the future for adult learning. The concept of lifelong learning has a bearing on our problem of contradictory futures. Currently, while the concept of lifelong learning has gained renewed topicality, it is important that life-broad learning – which is, in fact, about learning to be well-rounded – is not neglected. It is particularly important to develop a discussion about life-broad education when public debate about education is phrased more and more in economic terms, with the result that wider perspectives are becoming marginalised. That education is important for economic life is not in doubt. The problem lies rather in the fact that this aspect becomes a so-called 'super-ideology' which excludes everything else. At the decision level, it is about who controls the design of studies. If courses of education are ordered to satisfy purely economic needs, it will be difficult for the life-broad perspective to assert itself (Assarsson and Norling 1995). That is, the material perspective will be completely dominant – using language from a debate within the labour movement that started more than 100 years ago: 'The filling-the-stomach issue' (i.e. the material needs) will beat the 'cultural issue' (Furuland 1996). At that time, the discussion was whether it was meaningful for workers to spend time on culture before their material needs were satisfied. The need for another such debate, is now, striking.

Lifelong learning

The other dimension one must bear in mind is that learning occurs over one's entire lifetime. This is in regard to how someone's learning over the years hangs together, or perhaps how it *should* hang together. From the perspective of organised study, it involves, not least, what you have learned from life before study, and how this is utilised in courses of education. It also involves consideration of the impact organised study has on life and on learning after studies. Discussion on the meaning of adult studies can therefore be improved by beginning with a consideration of learning as it occurs in daily life. People's knowledge does not depend purely on study, but also on knowledge that is collected, transmitted and acquired in daily life. Organised study must be seen in the light of the knowledge that adults already have. However, adult studies should not be based just on the knowledge the students already have; studies should also lead to a more developed learning in daily life. In this way we can state the meaning of adult education where the principle perspective is lifelong learning: that is, there is an interplay between organised studies and learning in daily life.[7]

Public discussion of education is also often narrow in that it neglects learning in daily life – educational policies deal exclusively with activities in schools or other formal educational institutions. Another perspective would be for the educational policy discussion also to include the conditions for learning in society generally. In such a perspective, the circumstances and content of learning in daily life would be put in focus. This means that working life, the mass media and leisure activities can all be considered as sources of learning and as activities whose design is of significance for the knowledge and skills of the population. Against this background we can then discuss the contribution of adult education to the whole, i.e. the real, all-round, education of people.

What is this learning in daily life then? To get some perspective on the question we need to theorise a little. This theorising is facilitated by the fact that the scientific discussion of both learning and the nature of knowledge has been lively. Inspiration has come from several different theoretical perspectives.[8] Learning in daily life has been a focus in these discussions.

By way of introduction, we should rid ourselves of all prejudice about learning as an organised activity. Instead we should consider daily life in its most basic meaning – that we simply are in the midst of reality. This means that we experience things around us, that we have a set of impressions. This is not so much a question of intention, but rather a necessary and inevitable part of life. Our days are also filled with memories, imagination and dreams. The given place we have in existence affects us as it provides our consciousness with its content. If learning is about change, then a change arises here in that we have new encounters and experiences.

We can take the next step in this reasoning by introducing the concept of interpretation. Our experiences do not stop at being a collection of single items, like a pile of facts, but join with, and become integrated into, our old knowledge. One might say that our impressions are given fixed meanings at the moment we experience them. When meeting somebody, our overriding impression is not of colours and shapes, but rather the complete person. Those who have tried to paint a portrait know how difficult it is to see colours and shapes, as we have such definite preconceptions of how people look: children's drawings demonstrate this clearly. We also 'know' what objects around us can be used for – despite the fact that the axe is hanging on the wall, what it is used for is part of how we experience the axe. We add meanings that are not present in the immediate situation. This constant interpreting occurs without us necessarily having such an intention, it happens automatically. It is through the interpretation that we know the world we find ourselves in. There is no other existence for us. When we see objects and people around us, we often discover that our interpretations do not fit, or that we see the object in a different way than we did initially. We can say that this has to do with learning: we have developed a new interpretation. We can define learning as changes in interpretations.

In daily life, in all possible situations, learning arises in this way, where we adjust or build on the interpretations we already have. An important part of this perspective is that we always have a so-called 'pre-understanding' when we approach a situation, text or person. This pre-understanding partly forms the result. We are not empty slates: we have with us all the experiences that have formed our interpretations, and carrying these with us we meet the world around us. As this is an ongoing process, our interpretations are built up through a combination of our pre-understanding and the experiences that happen to us.

A central part of daily life concerns all the interpretations that are presented to us through other people, TV, newspapers and books. There are often different interpretations; we no longer live in an isolated culture that is governed by one single view of the world.

A decisive issue from the perspective of learning is, then, the character of this daily life that we find ourselves in is. Our life may be of the kind that our impressions seldom change because they are never challenged. Work and leisure can be so routine that learning is very limited. This has great importance historically, geographically and socially, for the circumstances for learning, as our learning is largely dependent on the challenges to which we are exposed. However, this involves an interplay between the requirements our existence places on us, and our own decisions to search further and find knowledge. In any case, we interpret the world in different ways depending on where we happen to be in life. Where in time and space our lives are lived has, then, a decisive importance on what we experience and how we interpret the world around us – and, of course, what we learn.

Similar reasoning can be employed for our actions. In the same way, our competence to undertake action increases by our participation in new activities or just by finding new ways to do things. It may be the case that we have worked out a new idea, i.e. reflection is a means of change, but it may also be about developing a skill that becomes unconscious and routine, for example a slalom skier who cannot understand why she skis faster than before. Here, too, we learn through the previously existing skills, forming the basis for developing new ones.

All in all, it is through our consciousness and our actions that we have a relationship with the world around us. We live in an experienced, perceived world in which we act; phenomenologists call this the 'life world'.[9] Learning is about changes in this life world: we interpret something differently or perform more dextrously.

From this perspective, lifelong learning becomes a constant opportunity – it does not just take place in an organised form, but can occur anywhere. The learning of a single person cannot be described in any complete way as it is too complex and elusive, we can just reason in general terms about it. We can assume that learning in daily life is extremely important. It is important because it has such extensive consequences: some people who find themselves in beneficial circumstances learn new things practically all the time. Others, who have a different reality, can gain hardly any knowledge from their daily lives, as these lives may consist of constant repetition. Learning in daily life is also important for quantitative reasons: compared with the time we spend on adult study, daily life forms an immense amount of time.

It is, therefore, not strange that knowledge gaps between people are constantly becoming greater in daily life – if you have a job that constantly offers new challenges and if you read newspapers and books in your spare time, you soon pull away from people whose work is founded on narrow routines or who do not use their spare time for new challenges. This becomes even clearer when some people can extend their knowledge by having access to technology, not least computers, so that they actually have access to more than they have learned.

A central conclusion that can be drawn from this line of reasoning is that people's knowledge is highly dependent on 'the quality of society as far as knowledge is concerned'. If the mass media are of good quality and reach many people with this quality, then these media have a major significance for the knowledge of the population. If local communities cut back on many cultural activities, this has a major impact on all-round knowledge. If a large number of the occupations people live by provide major changes with respect to knowledge, this will have a major significance for the knowledge of the individuals. It is actually the case that the demands of work are highly decisive for basic skills such as reading comprehension (Elbro *et al.* 1991). Much of this has to do with political decisions as well as the other initiatives that affect society. Circumstances for learning in daily life should be part of educational policy.

The meaning of adult studies

The perspective that has been presented can function as a starting point for another type of reasoning. Learning in daily life cannot be viewed in isolation from organised education. In fact, the interplay between education and learning in daily life is extraordinarily strong. Those individuals who have the best circumstances for learning in daily life have almost always achieved these circumstances via a formal education. If we look at the context of working life, a higher level of education generally means that work is more varied and that it offers greater challenges, both in terms of knowledge and action. In the same way, a better education provides a basis for cultural activities and the use of the mass media. The lack of a good education often excludes people from a life that contains good conditions for learning. In the same way, a lack of higher education reduces opportunities for benefiting from the mass media as a source of knowledge. In addition, education is not just about knowledge, it also is instrumental in developing interests and taste.

There is, then, an interplay between formal education and learning in daily life. When considering the role that adult study can play, we can focus on how organised studies influence learning in daily life. We can also turn our attention to another state of affairs, namely the result of learning in daily life: the student's way of interpreting and acting are what should change if his or her education can be said to be successful. We can also draw the conclusion that adult study is most needed for those who have poor conditions for learning in daily life. We could say that this involves breaking down patterns that limit learning in daily life. The starting point for this view is a humanistic perspective, that learning concerns the needs of the person and not just the system.[10]

At a societal level, this all becomes more complicated. After all, the education system also contributes to this situation by sorting individuals into different career tracks, which lead to different material circumstances. Adult study also contributes to this gap, as those who have a higher education are overrepresented. Only by investing in those who have the least skills can adult study be an equality project. However, this will not be considered in the present study. Instead, the focus is on the importance of education as a force for breaking individuals' patterns for learning in daily life.

Organising adult education should therefore deal with breaking those patterns that are characterised by learning in daily life but which are not dynamic. What does this require?

In a different context, I have distinguished four kinds of consequences of an effective education if the perspective is lifelong and life-broad.

- First of all, an effective education involves new knowledge, i.e. different interpretations from those people have when they start studying. By studying and learning one acquires new knowledge, which makes it possible to interpret what one meets in life in a new way. Through the knowledge one has acquired, one can understand in a deeper way, for example, what is reported in the media: the same message can be interpreted in a different way to gain a fuller or different meaning. One can put the message into a larger context of theories and facts. The opportunities then open up for building on this further in daily life: the financial pages in the newspapers, for example, become a source for building better and better knowledge after studying economics, or the computer's abilities can be investigated better after studying computer science.
- Studies may also be of decisive importance because they create the grounds for different interests. The interests are basic to which choices one makes and thus for which life world one builds up. By making choices in a different way, one builds up new knowledge via the abundant possibilities for knowledge in daily life. After studying, one can choose to read other texts and do other things and thus, in daily life, build up other knowledge.

    In both these cases, the effect of studies does not just involve learning something important during those studies, but also that knowledge and new interests result in one learning more from (and in) daily life. In the best case, one has moved into a track where studies have changed one's life world so that knowledge grows out of daily life. The external reality does not necessarily need to have changed in any essential way.

- Studies, however, often lead to external changes. In the main, there are usually changes in working life where work duties require more knowledge. However, this also means that adults have the opportunity to use the talents they possess. Consequently, the circumstances for learning in daily life change as one achieves a new place in life which challenges old interpretation patterns.

- One of the best established effects of adult education is that participants report greater self-confidence. The poorer the education students had when beginning their studies, the greater the perceived effect (Höghielm 1987; Lundqvist 1989). In relation to learning, this has great general significance for obvious reasons, as in this way one opens up to participating in new contexts. An important view on learning is just that learning is, to a great extent, just 'participating in activities'. A lack of self-confidence is often expressed by avoiding new contexts, by shrinking one's life world.

Conclusion

The value of adult study must be viewed with the greater perspective of how knowledge and skills interplay with daily life. From such a perspective it is important to cultivate new interests. Adult education should be seen as a highly important step in a greater whole, where there is room for the contributions of learning in daily life. The contribution of learning in daily life will then be put in focus. To return to the introduction: we can assume that a well-rounded person lives in a society where this well-roundedness has a place – this means that people can not only perform competent work, they can also be mature citizens who can take a stand on important issues regarding life and society.[11] And this is the core of the democratic utopia. This also means that society is so rich, culturally, that the sensual aspect mentioned earlier can be encouraged. If society lacks these qualities, education will become an oasis or a formality. On the other hand: if education does not cultivate these qualities, in the long run society becomes impoverished. Lifelong learning must be both lifelong and life-broad.[12]

Notes

1 According to Borgström (1988) the concept was used as early as 1929 by Yeaxlee as the title of a book and it was chosen by UNESCO in the early 1960s to designate its view on education.

2 Compare the expression 'nothing human is alien to me'. According to Holm (1976: 216) 'from Latin: *homo sum; humani nil a me alienum puto. Terentius,*

Hauton Timorumenos I. 1, 25; actually referring to understanding for and sympathy with human weakness, originally coming from Greek (Menander)'. The quotation from Holm has been translated from Swedish here.

3 Oftedahl Thelhaug (1990) provides an early analysis of this shift in education policy rhetoric.

4 In a research project we have used the term 'education and culture project' for this. That particular study has a meaning based on history and the present, but the aim is directed at the future (Gustavsson and Larsson 1994).

5 This became clear, for example in the documents of the Swedish government at the time of launching extra funds for education for the unemployed, the predecessors of the 'raising the knowledge level' project (Prop 1992/93: 150; Andersson *et al.* 1995).

6 Hargreaves (1996) distinguishes between post-modernism as a philosophy and post-modernity as a state of society – here we use the term in the latter meaning.

7 The reasoning in the rest of this article is presented in more detail in an article in *Livslångt lärande* (*Lifelong Learning*, in Swedish) (Ellström *et al.* 1996).

8 It has involved phenomenology, hermeneutics, situated cognition, activity theory and also pragmatic and Wittgensteinian philosophy. See Larsson (1996) for a more detailed description.

9 'Life world' is a concept that is used by phenomenologists, and also by Habermas (1991) meaning a world which people experience and act in according to their own norms and conception of truth, as distinct from the 'system' which forms action independently from humans' own perceived reason.

10 From a non-humanistic perspective, human development is not an independent value but becomes important only if it leads to problems for those values that are considered superior to humans – state usefulness, economy or the fatherland. A consequence of this, for example, is that the further education of those people with a limited education will occur as it does not lead to as great a profit as the further education of already highly educated people. In a non-humanistic perspective this would be irrational. From a humanistic perspective, the starting point must be how learning promotes people's dignity and complete development.

11 Kant (1989, emphasis in original) probably distinguishes between 'role' in a professional capacity and as a private person: in the latter you have to take a standpoint; be mature: '*Enlightenment is the human's withdrawal from his self-inflicted minority. The state of minority* is the inability to use your intellect without another's guidance. The minority is *self-inflicted* if the reason for it does not lie in a lack of intellect, but in a lack of resolve and courage to use it without anyone else's guidance. *Sapere aude!* Have the courage to use *your own* intellect! is the motto of enlightenment.'

12 In the anthology *Livslångt lärande* (*Lifelong Learning*) the theme is developed in more detail, but also on a broader scope by discussing which qualities adult education should focus on for it to fulfil its role as an education that has consequences for learning in daily life outside and after studies (Larsson 1996).

References

Andersson, E., Laginder, A-M., Larsson, S. and Sundgren, G. (1996), Cirkelsam-hället. Studiecirklars betydelser för individ och lokalsamhälle (in Swedish). SoU, 47, Utbildningsdepartementet.

Andersson, P., Larsson, S., Olsson, L-E., Thång, P.-O. and Wass, K. (1995) *Utbildning av arbetslösa i Komvux*. En studie av lokalt beslutsfattande (in Swedish). Report no. 1995: 12, Inst. för ped. Gothenburg University.

Assarsson, L. and Norling, C. (1995) 'Hur formas egentligen personalutbildning?' (in Swedish). Rapport från Linköpings universitet: LiU-PEK-R-185, Linköping.

Bergstedt, B. and Larsson, P. (eds) (1995) *Om folkbildningens innebörder* (in Swedish), Linköping: MIMER.

Borgström, L. (1988): *Vuxnas kunskapssökande – en studie i självstyrt lärande* (in Swedish). Stockholm: Brevskolan.

Elbro, C., Möller, S. and Munk Nielsen, E. (1991) *Danskernes læsefærdigheter. En undersögelse af 18 – 67-åriges laesning af dagligdags tekster* (in Danish), Köbenhavn: Projekt Laesning og Undervisningsministeriet.

Ellström, P-E, Gustavsson, B. and Larsson, S. (eds) (1996) *Livslångt lärande* (in Swedish), Lund: Studentlitteratur.

Furuland, L. (1996) 'Magfrågan' och 'kulturfrågan' i svensk arbetarrörelse (in Swedish). Manuscript.

Gustavsson, B. and Larsson, S. (1994) 'Möten mellan bildningsprojekt i folkbild-ningens vardag' (in Swedish), Application to HSFR.

Habermas, J. (1991) *The Theory of Communicative Action. Volume 1: Reason and the Rationalization of Society. Volume 2: Lifeworld and System: A Critique of Functionalist Reason*, Cambridge: Polity Press.

Hargreaves, A. (1996) *Laererarbeid og skolekultur. Laereryrkets forandring i en post-moderne tidsalder* (in Norwegian), Oslo: Ad Notam Gyldendal.

Holm, P. (1976) *Bevingade ord och andra talesätt* (in Swedish), 14th edn, Stockholm: Bonniers.

Höghielm, R. (1987) 'Studerande i komvux. En uppföljning 1980–85' (in Swedish), *Högskolan för lärarutbildning i Stockholm, Inst.för pedagogik. rapport 1987: 10.*

Kant, I. (1989) 'Svar på frågan: Vad är upplysning?' (in Swedish), in B. Östling (ed) *Vad är upplysning?* Stockholm/Stehag: Symposion Bokförlag.

Larsson, S. (1995) 'Folkbildningen och vuxenpedagogiken' (in Swedish), in B. Berg-stedt and P. Larsson (eds) *Om folkbildningens innebörder*, Linköping: MIMER, 35–57.

Larsson, S. (1996) 'Vardagslärande och vuxenstudier' (in Swedish), in P-E. Ellström, B. Gustavsson and P. Larsson (eds) *Livslångt lärande*, Lund: Studentlitteratur.

Lundqvist, O. F. (1989) *Studiestöd för vuxna. Utveckling, utnyttjande, utfall* (in Swedish), Gothenburg: Acta Universitatis Gothoburgensis.

Oftedal Telhaug (1990) *Den nye utdanningspolitiske retorikken* (in Norwegian), Oslo: Universitetsforlaget.

Prop 1992/93: 150 med förslag till reglering av statsbudgeten för budgetåret 1993/ 94 m m (in Swedish). Reviderad finansplan m m.

Rubenson, K. (1996) 'Livslångt lärande: Mellan utopi och ekonomi', in P-E. Ellström, B. Gustavsson and S. Larsson (eds) *Livslångt lärande* (in Swedish), Lund: Student-litteratur.

Whitty, G. (1997) 'Quasi-markets in education', in M. W. Apple (ed) *Review of Research in Education*, no. 22, Washington: AERA.

Index